# The Encyclopedia of Bible Crafts

# Important information

## Photocopy permission

The right to photocopy material in *The Encyclopedia of Bible Crafts* is granted for the pages that contain the photocopying clause, 'Reproduced with permission from *The Encyclopedia of Bible Crafts* published by BRF 2010 (978 1 84101 590 3)', so long as reproduction is for use in a teaching situation by the original purchaser. The right to photocopy material is not granted for anyone other than the original purchaser without written permission from BRF.

Permission to photocopy from *The Encyclopedia of Bible Crafts* granted for local church use. Copyright © Group Publishing, Inc., P.O. Box 481, Loveland, CO 80539. www.grouppublishing.com

## The Copyright Licensing Agency (CLA)

If you are resident in the UK and you have a photocopying licence with the Copyright Licensing Agency (CLA), please check the terms of your licence. If your photocopying request falls within the terms of your licence, you may proceed without seeking further permission. If your request exceeds the terms of your CLA licence, please contact the CLA direct with your request. Copyright Licensing Agency, 90 Tottenham Court Road, London W1T 4LP. Telephone 020 7631 5555; fax 020 7631 5500; email cla@cla.co.uk; website www.cla.co.uk. The CLA will provide photocopying authorization and royalty fee information on behalf of BRF.

BRF is a Registered Charity (No. 233280)

# The
# Encyclopedia
## of
# Bible Crafts

187 fun-filled, easy-to-do
craft activities for children

## Edited by
## Laurie Castañeda

Text copyright © BRF 2010
Contributing Authors: Patty Atkins, Teryl Cartwright, Ruthie Daniels, Enelle G. Eder, Rebecca Erickson, Abby
Flesch-Conners, Sheila Halasz, Laure Herlinger, Regina Miller, Julie Savage, Larry Shallenberger, Bonnie
Temple, and Courtney Wright

Illustrations copyright © Sharon Holm 2010

**Published by**
**The Bible Reading Fellowship**
15 The Chambers, Vineyard
Abingdon OX14 3FE
United Kingdom
Tel: +44 (0)1865 319700
Email: enquiries@brf.org.uk
Website: www.brf.org.uk

**ISBN 978 1 84101 590 3**

Originally published in the USA
by Group Publishing, Inc. under the title
*The Encyclopedia of Bible Crafts for Children*
Copyright © 2002 by **Group Publishing, Inc.**

UK edition published 2010
10 9 8 7 6 5 4 3 2 1 0
All rights reserved

**Acknowledgments**
Unless otherwise stated, scripture quotations are taken from the Contemporary English Version published
by HarperCollins Publishers, copyright © 1991, 1992, 1995 American Bible Society.

Scripture quotations taken from the Holy Bible, New International Version, copyright © 1973, 1978, 1984,
1995 by International Bible Society. Used by permission of Hodder & Stoughton Publishers, a member of the
Hachette Livre UK Group. All rights reserved. 'NIV' is a registered trademark of International Bible Society.
UK trademark number 1448790.

A catalogue record for this book is available from the British Library

Printed in Singapore by Craft Print International Ltd

# Contents

# Introduction

In the beginning of class, John created his world. Oh, it didn't turn out looking like the magnificent perfect world that God originally created. But it was John's world just the same, cut from various colours of craft foam and glued together seemingly at random on to a misshapen circle. Five-year-old John was the beaming creator as he ran to show his dad at the end of class. 'Look, Dad, God made the world, and so did I! Will you hang it from my ceiling when we get home?'

Many early learners are just like John—perhaps at first saying, 'I can't do that' and then experiencing the thrill of accomplishment. *The Encyclopedia of Bible Crafts* provides you with 187 proven crafts for key Bible stories from Genesis to Revelation. You'll find age-level icons to help you choose crafts that children will feel successful creating, indexes that help enhance your Bible teaching sessions, step-by-step instructions and a teaching point that will help the child understand the Bible point and make a connection between the Bible and everyday life.

*The Encyclopedia of Bible Crafts* is an essential tool for all children's workers interested in helping children explore and understand the Bible. You can use this book in Sunday school, children's church, midweek group, after-school clubs, or any other place where children are gathered together. So get ready for unique, motivating crafts that will inspire your children to learn about the Bible in no time at all!

# Genesis

## God creates the world

Bible story
Genesis 1:14–19

Bible point
**God made the sun for us.**

## Activity

### Sunrise surprise

Make a hanging sunrise to remind us to appreciate the beauty of one of God's creations.

### ● You will need

4cm polystyrene balls, yellow poster paint, coffee filters, watercolours, small cups of water, orange pipe cleaners, white glue, paintbrushes, scissors, paper towels, 30cm pieces of string

### ● Preparation

Paint the polystyrene balls yellow at least a day ahead.

### ● Handy hint

Paint your suns with little mess by pressing a craft stick into each ball to hold it easily. Press the other end of the stick into an upside-down egg carton to dry. Before class, pull out the stick and keep the hole at the back of the sun.

### ● Step-by-step

1. Lay the coffee filter flat on a paper towel. Starting in the middle and going in circles, paint the filter red, yellow and orange.
2. Paint a thin layer of glue on one side of the filter, then set it aside to dry.
3. Cut four 2.5cm and five 5cm pieces of orange pipe cleaner. Bend one of the longer pieces into a U-shape and stick the two ends into the polystyrene ball to make a loop. Stick the other wires in the ball

to look like sun rays, alternating the long and short pieces.
4. Pour some glue into the centre of the coffee filter and then place the sun on it.
5. Tie a piece of string through the loop to hang your sun.

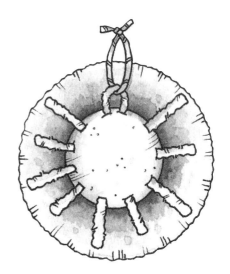

## Teaching point

When the children have finished, read the story of how God created the sun, moon and stars. Then ask:

- Why did God make the sun for us?
- If we didn't have the sun, what would happen?

Explain that when God created the world, he knew that we would need the sun to live. The sun gives us warmth and light and helps animals, plants and people to grow and be healthy. God made the sun for us because he gives us everything we need to live. Lead the children in a prayer to thank God for providing what we need, especially the sun.

# God creates the world

> Bible story
> Genesis 1:20–31; 2:15
>
> Bible point
> **God wants us to care for his creations.**

## Activity

Make a bird feeder.

### ● You will need

One-litre fruit juice or milk cartons, white spray paint, stapler, coloured tissue paper, coloured card, glue, paintbrushes, scissors, knitting yarn, sheets of clear sticky-backed plastic, craft sticks, felt-tipped pens, newspapers, aprons

### ● Preparation

Staple the tops of the cartons shut and paint them with white spray paint. When the cartons are dry, cut an arched semicircle on two sides, no lower than 2.5cm from the bottom. Cut one sheet of clear sticky-backed plastic to fit around each carton but do not place on the carton at this stage.

### ● Handy hint

To increase the children's interest in this project, research which birds live in your area. Bring in pictures, if you can, and share some interesting facts. Extend the Bible point further by giving each child some bird food (such as seeds, bread or dry cereal) in a resealable plastic bag to take home with the bird feeder.

### ● Step-by-step

1. Before beginning, give each child an apron to wear. Then colour two craft sticks with felt-tipped pens. Glue one stick to the other to make a cross.
2. Cut two 5cm by 10cm rectangles from coloured card and round off one short side on each to look like church windows. Cut one 5cm circle from the same paper.
3. Spread glue on one of the shapes. While the glue is still wet, cut tiny pieces of the coloured tissue paper and sprinkle over the glue. Repeat with the other two shapes, then trim the tissue paper from the edges.

4. Glue the long windows on the two uncut sides of the carton. Glue the circle above one of the holes on a third side to make the front.
5. Cover the entire bird feeder with clear sticky-backed plastic to waterproof it.
6. Poke holes in the top of the carton. Cut a piece of knitting yarn about the length of your forearm, from your elbow to your fingers, and thread it through the holes to hang. Glue the cross to the front, above the circle 'window', to complete your church bird feeder.

## Teaching point

Read Genesis 1:20–31 and 2:15. Then ask:

- How does a bird feeder help us to care for God's creations?
- Why did God put people in charge of everything living on earth?
- How have we done a good job? How have we done a bad job?
- What can we do to correct our mistakes and take care of all living things, as God wants us to?

Explain that God created so many amazing plants and animals here on earth. Taking care of them was not just Adam and Eve's job; that responsibility has been passed on to us. Every fish, flower and bird is here for a reason. Let's do our best to take care of them. Pray together, thanking God for all these wonderful living things.

# Noah builds the ark

Age guide: 6–10s

Bible story
Genesis 6:9–22

Bible point
**God blesses our obedience.**

## Activity

Build an ark light-switch plate.

### ● You will need

Coloured craft foam, pens, scissors, tape, glue, fishing line or clear craft string, felt-tipped pens, glitter pens, double-sided tape or fun tack, and pre-made foam animals

### ● Preparation

Copy and cut out several sets of the ark shapes found on page 11 for the children to trace.

### ● Handy hint

Add more dimension to the ark with extra craft items, such as sequins for the fish, sticks for the hull and clear glue for water drops (make sure the ark isn't too heavy to hang!). Create a switch plate cover yourself, and place it on a switch in the classroom to remind children of this lesson throughout the year.

### ● Step-by-step

1. Trace around the shapes of the roof, cabin, hull, waves, fish, bird and leaf from different-coloured craft foam. Then cut out all of these shapes.
2. Decorate the pieces using the felt-tipped pens and glitter glue pens. Glue the boat pieces together and add the pre-made animals, except the fish, to create an ark.
3. Cut one 9cm and one 10cm piece of fishing line. Tape the end of one piece to the back of one of the fish. Tape the other end to the back of the ark. Repeat with the other fish and line.
4. Stick two strips of double-sided tape to the back of your ark. When you get home, peel off the tape covering and stick your ark on a light-switch plate.

## Teaching point

Bring the children together and review the story of Noah and the ark. Emphasise the obedience of Noah and his family even though they were facing an overwhelming task. Because of their obedience, they were saved. Then ask:

- How might Noah have felt when God told him to build an ark in the middle of the desert?
- Can we think of times when it was difficult to do what we knew was right? What happened?
- What happens when we obey God?
- What will our light-switch plates remind us of each time we use them?

Explain that it's not always easy to do what God wants us to do. We can all imagine how Noah probably felt when he built the ark. Still, Noah obeyed God because he loved the Lord. And because he did, Noah, his family and the animals were saved. When we obey God, he is pleased with us, too!

# Ark template

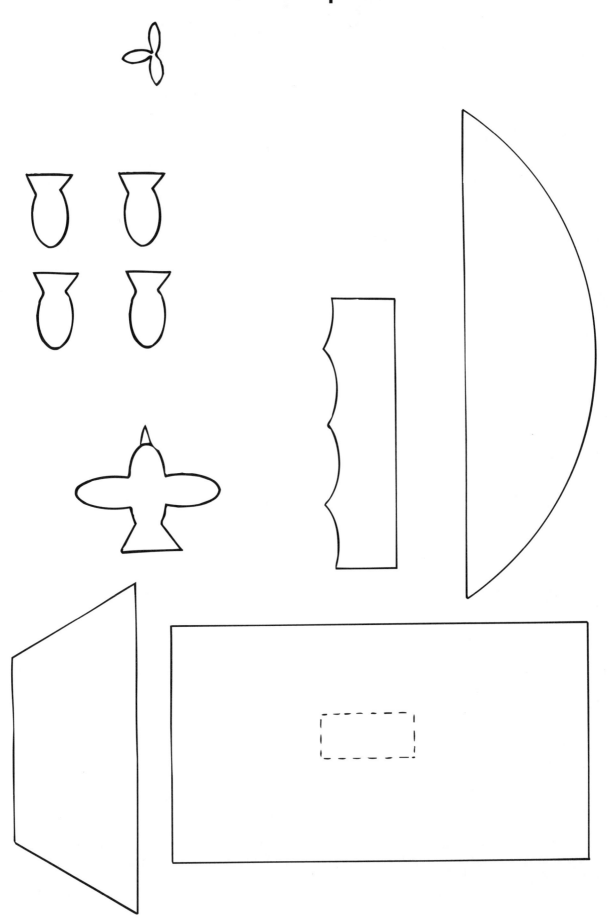

# People build a tower at Babel

Age guide: 7–11s

---

> ## Bible story
> ### Genesis 11:1–9
>
> ## Bible point
> **We need God on our side.**

## Activity

### Wie geht's ('vee gates'): What's up?

Create and play a game to understand the importance of God's support.

### ● You will need

Cardboard tubes from rolls of wrapping paper or paper towels, medium-weight card, rulers, scissors, felt-tipped pens, copies of the game cards, and an egg timer or stopwatch

### ● Preparation

Make several copies of the game card sheets (see page 13) and glue them on to medium-weight card. Practise saying the words on the cards so that you can teach the children correctly.

### ● Handy hint

Let the children practise saying the words in the different languages with the English translations before beginning their game.

### ● Step-by-step

1. Choose a partner to help you make and play the game. Work together for the first ten minutes to make the game and learn the rules.
2. Have one partner cut the cardboard tubes into different lengths, from 5cm to 10cm. (The more pieces you have, the bigger your tower will be!) Separate the tubes into two piles.
3. The second partner can cut out the game cards and mix them up.
4. Work together and use felt-tipped pens to draw windows and bricks on the tubes. As you work, practise saying the different words in German, Spanish and French.

5. Take turns with your partner being the Reader and the Builder and try to build the highest tower using only the cards for directions.
6. To play the game, the Reader chooses a card from the pack and reads the word to the Builder in a different language (without saying what it means in English). If the Builder guesses the correct move, he or she follows the directions by adding tubes 'up' or deleting tubes 'down' and then continues with another card. If the Builder guesses incorrectly, the Reader becomes the Builder and the game begins again.

## Teaching point

Play the game for as long as you have time. Gather the children together and read the story of the tower of Babel. Point out the vanity—and folly—of the people to think they didn't need God. Then ask:

- Was it easy to take directions from your partners? Why or why not?
- How did it feel when you could understand your partner and build your tower?
- What happened to the people of Babel who decided they didn't need God?
- What happens when God is your partner?

Explain that the people of Babel became proud and sinful. They wanted to build something bigger and better than anything God had made. They thought they didn't need God. God changed all their prideful plans simply by mixing up the languages that they spoke. When God is on our side, we can do anything!

| **English** | **German** | **French** | **Spanish** |
|---|---|---|---|
| one up | eins hoch | un en haut | uno arriba |
| | (eye-ns haw) | (uh on oh) | (oo-no a-ree-ba) |
| | English: one up | English: one up | English: one up |
| **English** | **German** | **French** | **Spanish** |
| two left | zwei links | deux gauche | dos izquierdo |
| | (svy links) | (deh go-sh) | (doe-s iz-scare-do) |
| | English: two left | English: two left | English: two left |
| **English** | **German** | **French** | **Spanish** |
| none down | keins runter | ne pa en bas | nada abajo |
| | (kye-ns roon-ta) | (neh paw on ba) | (na-da a-ba-hoe) |
| | English: none down | English: none down | English: none down |
| **English** | **German** | **French** | **Spanish** |
| four up | vier hoch | quatre en haut | cautro arriba |
| | (fear haw) | (cat-ra on oh) | (cwa-troe a-ree-ba) |
| | English: four up | English: four up | English: four up |
| **English** | **German** | **French** | **Spanish** |
| three left | drei links | troi gauche | tres isquierdo |
| | (dry links) | (twa go-sh) | (trays iz-scare-do) |
| | English: three left | English: three left | English: three left |
| **English** | **German** | **French** | **Spanish** |
| two up | zwei hoch | deux en haut | dos arriba |
| | (svy haw) | (dehz on oh) | (doe-s a-ree-ba) |
| | English: two up | English: two up | English: two up |
| **English** | **German** | **French** | **Spanish** |
| three down | drei runter | trois en bas | tres abajo |
| | (dry roon-ta) | (twa on ba) | (trays a-ba-hoe) |
| | English: three down | English: three down | English: three down |

Reproduced with permission from *The Encyclopedia of Bible Crafts* published by BRF 2010 (978 1 84101 590 3) www.barnabasinschools.org.uk

# God makes a covenant with Abram

Age guide: 6–10s

## Activity

### Inheriting a galaxy

Make a jar of stars.

### ● You will need

Baby food jars with lids, narrow masking tape, aluminium foil, star hole punch, silver glitter, golden syrup, water, blue food colouring, blue foil star stickers, glue, silver ribbon

### ● Preparation

Have two separate work areas—one for filling the jars and another for decorating the outsides. Have warm soapy water and towels handy to rinse off the golden syrup.

### ● Handy hint

Give children even more choices for their galaxy with small sequin stars and moons, which you can purchase in large quantities at craft shops. Also, you can use glitter pens to decorate your foil lid.

### ● Step-by-step

1. Fill a small glass jar a little more than half-full with golden syrup. Add one drop of blue food colouring and water, leaving about 1.5cm of air at the top.
2. Punch 10–15 stars out of the aluminium foil and drop them into the jar. Sprinkle in silver glitter, screw the lid on tightly, and shake to mix well.
3. Seal the lid with masking tape. Cut out an 8cm circle of foil, shape it to cover the lid, trim the edges and glue it on.
4. Place the blue foil stickers on the top of the lid and tie a 40cm piece of silver ribbon into a bow around the neck of the jar, covering any masking tape.
5. Shake to enjoy your family of countless stars.

## Teaching point

When finished, gather the children together and read Genesis 15:5–6. Explain why God made this promise to Abram and how he kept his word. Then ask:

- What promise did God give to Abram?
- What did Abram do to earn such a great blessing from God?
- What promises can you believe God for?
- How will your miniature galaxy remind you to believe God's promises?

Explain that God planned great things for Abram, but Abram needed to obey and trust God. When we believe what God promises us, even though we don't understand, we learn that God always keeps his word. We can't count how many stars are in the sky, but we can always count on God. We can believe God's promises to us.

# Isaac marries Rebekah

Age guide: 6–10s

Bible story
Genesis 24:1–4, 10–27

Bible point
**Serve others gladly.**

## Activity

### A well of kindness

Make a well.

#### ● You will need
Empty soup cans, light brown coloured card, clear tape, scissors, pencils, black felt-tipped pens, brown pipe cleaners, unsharpened pencils, egg cartons, hole punch, 30cm pieces of knitting wool

#### ● Preparation
For each child, cut out one cup from an empty egg carton. Cut pieces of light brown card about 20cm by 20cm.

#### ● Handy hint
If you use waterproof glue instead of clear tape, and small plastic cups instead of the egg carton cups, children can really draw water from their wells!

#### ● Step-by-step
1. Measure and cut the card to cover your soup can, leaving a little extra card at the top. Use a black felt-tipped pen to draw stones on one side and then tape the paper to the can. Carefully tuck the extra card inside the can to cover any sharp edges and tape it down.
2. Twist two pipe cleaners together, leaving the ends sticking out to form a Y shape. Repeat with two more pipe cleaners. Tape them opposite each other inside the can.
3. Place the unsharpened pencil in the groove of the Ys and twist the ends together to close in the pencil. Bend a third pipe cleaner on one end of the pencil to make a handle.
4. Punch two holes opposite each other in the egg carton cup. Thread one end of the wool through both holes and tie it to itself 5cm above the cup.
5. Tie the other end of the wool to the middle of the pencil and wind up.

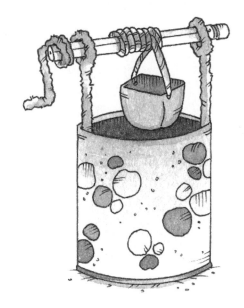

## Teaching point

Ask the children to bring their completed wells with them and pretend to draw water as you tell the story of how Rebekah willingly served Abraham's servant. Then ask:

- Why did Rebekah give water to the servant and his camels?
- What happened when Rebekah showed kindness?
- How do you feel when you are kind to a person or animal?

Explain that it's not always easy to do something nice for someone. Sometimes, we're tired after a long day or we might be busy. Still, Rebekah drew water from the well for Abraham's servant and all his camels, and she was asked to become Isaac's wife. Even if we don't hear a 'thank you', God sees what we do. When we are kind to others, it makes three people glad: the person we helped, ourselves and God! Let's remember to serve others gladly.

# Jacob's dream at Bethel

Age guide:
6–10s

Bible story
Genesis 28:10–22

Bible point
**God is always with us.**

## Activity

### A stone pillar

Make a memorial stone paperweight.

● **You will need**

Clean flat stones found outside, pieces of coloured felt, wood glue, scissors, pens, thin felt-tipped pens, scrap paper

● **Preparation**

Collect four or five small flat stones per child, or ask the children to bring in their own.

● **Handy hint**

Glues work differently depending on many factors, including the temperature in your room and the porosity of the stones. Experiment to find what works best for you, and remember that all glues must be allowed to set before there is a permanent bond.

● **Step-by-step**

1. Invite the children to spend a few minutes thinking of a time when they knew that God was with them. Ask them to remember this as they make their pillar of stones.
2. Trace around the bottom stone on a piece of felt. Cut out the felt shape and glue it to the bottom of the stone.
3. Begin the pillar by gluing two flat stones together. Wait a minute for the glue to set and then repeat to add two more stones.
4. Using the thin felt-tipped pens, write 'I am with you', one word on each stone.

## Teaching point

While the glue dries on the pillars, gather the children together and read Genesis 28:10–22. Explain that the stones are not something to be worshipped, but are to be used as reminders of God's presence in our lives. Then ask:

- What does your stone pillar mean to you?
- Why was the stone in the story special?
- How is your stone pillar like Jacob's?

Explain that many people in the Bible marked a special place with a pillar of stones: Abraham, Isaac, Jacob, Moses and Joshua are just a few. These pillars reminded people that God was always there to help and protect them. The stone pillar paperweights we made today can remind us of the same thing: God is always with us, watching over us and guiding us to make the right choices. Isn't it great to know that he's there?

# Joseph has disturbing dreams

Age guide: 5–7s

## Activity

### Joseph's troublesome coat

Make magnets of Joseph and his colourful coat.

#### ● You will need

People-shaped biscuit cutter, craft foam, narrow coloured fabric ribbon in different colours, black wool, wiggly eyes, white glue, thin black felt-tipped pens, sticky-backed magnets, scissors

#### ● Preparation

Use the cutter to trace and cut out one person from craft foam for each child in your class.

#### ● Step-by-step

1. Choose a foam person to be Joseph. Cut strips of coloured ribbon to design Joseph's coat. Put glue on to Joseph's body and place the ribbons down on to the glue.
2. Cut and glue short pieces of black wool on Joseph's head and use the marker to make his face.
3. Place a sticky-backed magnet on the back of Joseph's coat. Write the child's name on the back and set the magnet aside to dry.

## Teaching point

Gather the children together and let them show each other their magnets. Briefly tell about the coat that led Joseph's brothers to sell him into slavery, how Joseph prospered in Egypt and how, ironically, he saved them years later. Then ask:

- Why were Joseph's brothers jealous of him?
- How did they treat him?
- How did Joseph pay them back?
- Why does God want us to forgive each other?

Ask the children how it might have felt to have been Joseph's brothers. They were so angry when their father gave Joseph the beautiful coat that they sold him into slavery, but Joseph forgave them and saved his family from starving many years later. Even though Joseph was a slave, he was free in his heart from bad feelings like hatred and anger. That's because he forgave his brothers. God will always turn that into something good! God wants us to forgive others and be free.

# Exodus

## God protects Moses

> **Bible story**
> Exodus 2:1–10
>
> **Bible point**
> **God protects us all.**

## Activity

### Moses in the bulrushes

Build a baby Moses and a basket that really floats.

### ● You will need

White polystyrene bowls, white pipe cleaners, felt or fabric scraps, black wool, small wobbly eyes, 2.5cm wooden craft balls, cotton wool balls, glue, felt-tipped pens, scissors, a hole punch, a bowl of water

### ● Preparation

Set up the supplies in a designated area. Place the bowl of water in a separate area.

### ● Handy hint

As less expensive alternatives to the wooden craft balls, you can use felt circles or polystyrene balls painted with beige craft paint ahead of time (push a small cocktail stick into the balls for easy handling and remove later). Also, polystyrene food containers work well for this craft.

### ● Step-by-step

1. Cut the black wool into a handful of small pieces. Glue the pieces of wool on to a craft ball for hair, then add two wobbly eyes. Set the head aside to dry.
2. Using a black or brown felt-tipped pen, draw lines on the outside of the bowls to look like weaving.
3. Punch two holes about 8cm apart along the lip of one polystyrene bowl. Place this bowl upside-down on top of a second bowl, mark corresponding holes along the lip of the second bowl, then punch out those holes. Put the first bowl back on top of the second.
4. To make hinges, cut two 8cm pieces of pipe cleaner, lace them through the holes and twist the ends together to make loose loops.
5. Squeeze some glue inside the bottom bowl, add a small pile of cotton wool, and then glue down a scrap of material to cover the cotton wool as a blanket. Glue the baby head at one end of the blanket. Then gently place the basket in the bowl of water to see it float.

## Teaching point

Gather the children together and read the story of how God saved Moses' life with some help from Moses' sister and mother. Then ask:

- How do you think Miriam felt as she watched her little brother float down the river?
- How would you protect your little brother or sister if you were Miriam?
- How do you think God has protected you today?

Explain that when our baskets floated on the water, the baby Moses we made stayed safe and dry. Each one of us is just as special to God as Moses was, and we can be sure that God will protect us, too!

# Moses meets God at the burning bush

Age guide: 6–10s

Bible story
Exodus 3:1–10

Bible point
We are all chosen by God.

## Activity

### Your own burning bush

Make burning bush badges.

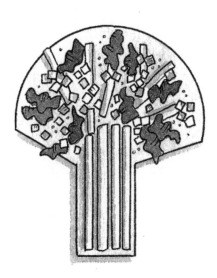

### ● You will need

Raw spaghetti, ruler, glue, green craft foam, green glitter, masking tape, safety pins, scissors, tissue paper in red, yellow and orange

### ● Preparation

Cut one 10cm x 10cm square of green craft foam for each child.

### ● Handy hint

Remind the children to make sure the glue is dry before they wear their badges.

### ● Step-by-step

1. To make the trunk of the burning bush, break raw spaghetti into four pieces—each one about as long as the child's thumb. Squeeze some glue on to the green craft foam square and lay the spaghetti pieces on the glue side by side.
2. Break more spaghetti into smaller, different-sized pieces and lay them at the top of the trunk for branches.
3. Drip glue on the branches and sprinkle with green glitter to create leaves. Cut the red, orange and yellow tissue paper into tiny pieces. Drip on more glue and sprinkle the paper on top of the branches and leaves to look like fire.
4. Trim the craft foam around the trunk and branches in the shape of a bush.
5. Tape the safety pin to the back of the bush.

## Teaching point

While waiting for the bushes to dry, gather the children together and take turns reading Exodus 3:1–10. Explain what it means to be 'chosen' by God, explaining that he has a plan for each one of us to do something special with our lives. Then ask:

- Why do you think God talked to Moses in a burning bush?
- What special work did God have for Moses to do?
- What special work do you think God might have for you to do for him?
- What can you do for God this week?

Explain that God has chosen each of us to do a special work for him, just like he chose Moses to lead the Israelites out of slavery in Egypt.

# The Israelites cross the Red Sea

Age guide: 5-7s

Bible story
Exodus 14:21–31

Bible point
**God can do miracles.**

## Activity

### Parting the Red Sea

Make models of the Red Sea that open and close.

### ● You will need

Heavy-weight blue card, sandpaper, coloured paper, small craft shells, glue, blue plastic wrap or blue tissue paper, scissors, pencils, felt-tipped pens, sticky-backed Velcro™

### ● Preparation

For each child, cut a 50cm x 15cm rectangle of card. Make a fold 12cm from each end, in towards the centre. Then make an outward fold, 1.5cm from each end. Cut a 20cm x 3cm piece of sandpaper for each child. Set up the supplies for the children.

### ● Handy hint

As you come to the Teaching point, use visual reminders of everyday miracles, such as a picture of a sunset, real flowers, a picture of a bird, and even a child in the class.

### ● Step-by-step

1. Open the card with the folded ends lying upwards at right angles and glue the sandpaper in the centre to make the sandy path.
2. Then cut simple shell, starfish or fish shapes out of the coloured paper and glue them and the craft shells on the sandy bottom.
3. Tear off two pieces of plastic wrap, a little longer than the card sea. Place a smooth layer of glue on the outside of one of the 'walls' and lay one of the pieces of plastic wrap down, letting it wrinkle to make it look like waves. Repeat the process for the

other wall. (If wished, cut more small fish to glue inside the waves.)
4. Attach the Velcro™ pieces to the flaps at the top of the walls, then invite everyone to show the person next to them how God parted the Red Sea for the Israelites.

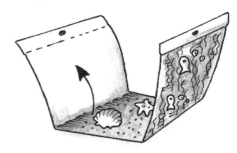

## Teaching point

Ask the children to bring their models with them to open and close their Red Seas at the appropriate times as you tell the Bible story. Emphasise the greatness of this miracle, then point out that there are wondrous things happening around us every day. Ask:

- Why did God part the Red Sea?
- Can God save us today like he saved the Israelites? Why or why not?
- What kind of miracles do we hear about today?

Explain that in this Bible story, we learn about an amazing miracle: God parted the Red Sea so that his people could escape, then he closed it back up again. But not all miracles are so big. Some are very small and happen every day: babies are born, birds fly, flowers grow, the sun rises and sets. Yes, God can do miracles! We need to stop, look at the miracles around us and remember to say 'thank you' to God.

# The song of Miriam

Age guide: 5–7s

> Bible story
> Exodus 15:19–21
>
> Bible point
> **We can praise God with music.**

## Activity

### Joyful noise tambourines

Make tambourines and create a joyful noise.

#### ● You will need

Aluminium food trays, hole punch, black bag ties, colourful ribbons, stickers, scissors, and anything that jingles such as small craft bells, old keys, paperclips and buttons

#### ● Preparation

Punch holes about 25mm apart along the edge of one 20cm food tray.

#### ● Handy hint

For a more elaborate tambourine, staple one food tray upside-down on top of another. Before sealing it completely, put some beans or rice inside to make it extra noisy. Add noise makers, ribbons and decorations as described below.

#### ● Step-by-step

1. Thread the bag ties and long pieces of ribbon through most of the holes in the food tray. Tie anything to them that makes a noise.
2. Decorate both sides of the tray with stickers.
3. String colourful ribbons through the other holes and get ready to sing a song of joy like Miriam and the Israelites.

## Teaching point

Gather the children together and read Exodus 15:19–21. Explain that there are many ways to praise God, such as praying silently, singing, dancing, painting, writing and speaking to others. Then ask:

- What are some ways we can make a joyful noise to God?
- How can we praise God with music?
- How does God feel when we play our new tambourines?
- What are some other ways we can say 'thank you' to God or tell him that we love him?

Explain that Miriam and the other Israelites were so happy to escape from Egypt that they sang and danced. The Bible says, 'Sing a new song to the Lord!' (Psalm 98:1). Praying quietly by ourselves is important, but God also likes it when we are noisy and show everyone how much we love him. When we feel like singing, we can praise God with music. Sing or play music that the children can accompany with their tambourines.

# God sends quail and manna

> Bible story
> Exodus 16:11–21, 31, 35
>
> Bible point
> **God always provides for us.**

## Activity

### Food from heaven

Weave a basket.

### ● You will need

Small plastic containers such as butter tubs, spray paint, scissors, rulers, pencils, several skeins of coloured wool, plastic or wooden beads

### ● Preparation

Ask the children to bring containers to class a week or two earlier. Spray-paint them a day before class.

### ● Handy hint

Use beige or brown spray paint, replace the wool with string and use natural-coloured beads to make a more realistic basket. Give the children some mini crackers to put in their baskets to represent the manna that the Israelites gathered.

### ● Step-by-step

1. Use the ruler, pencil and scissors to cut 25mm strips down around the container. Start each cut at the top and go to the bottom edge, leaving the flat bottom uncut.
2. Cut a piece of wool one metre long. Tie one end on to a strip of the container and slide it to the bottom. Weave the wool in and out through the strips. Tie on new pieces of the same colour wool to continue weaving, or change wool colours by tying the new wool to the end of the first piece. String beads on, making sure they are on the outside of the basket.
3. Cut the wool when finished and tie the end inside the basket.

4. Make two plaits. For each plait, cut three 25cm pieces of wool. Plait the three pieces of wool together, taping the ends so that they don't come apart. Repeat this for the second plait. Tie the plaits on opposite sides of the basket to make handles.

## Teaching point

Gather the children together and read them Exodus 16:11–21, 31 and 35. Then ask:

- How many baskets of manna do you think the Israelites gathered for each meal?
- Why do you think God fed the Israelites, even though they complained and disobeyed him?
- How does the Lord provide for you?

Explain that God made a promise to Abraham thousands and thousands of years ago. God promised to make Abraham's descendants God's holy people. God would bless them, protect them and provide for them always. Even when the Israelites were disobedient and complaining, God took care of them. When they obeyed him, like when they gathered the manna in their baskets, God blessed them even more. Our baskets can remind us that God provides for us, too. All we have to do is gather up the blessings!

22

# God gives the Ten Commandments

Age guide: 6–10s

Bible story
Exodus 19:3–6a; 20:1–17

Bible point
Love God and others.

## Activity

### Tablets of love

Make bookmarks.

### ● You will need

Bibles, paper, pencils, craft foam, fine-tipped felt pens, scissors, coloured card or ribbon, clear sticky tape, glue, tablet patterns

### ● Preparation

Create a few tablet patterns for children to trace. Set up one area for creating the craft.

### ● Handy hint

Use real ribbon instead of coloured card. (You will not need to use the sticky tape with real ribbon.) Use your bookmark to mark your favourite Bible verse or story about loving God or others.

### ● Step-by-step

1. Ask the children to read the Ten Commandments from Exodus 20:1–17 with a partner. Help them think of ways in which we can love God or love others better.
2. Cut a 8cm x 25cm rectangle out of card. Cut a point into the bottom of the rectangle so it looks like the end of a ribbon. Leaving the top 25mm blank, use a thin marker to write how we can love God or others better.
3. Trace a tablet shape out of craft foam, and cut it out. Use a thin marker to draw a line down the middle of the tablet and write 1, 2, 3, 4, and 5 on the left of the tablet and 6, 7, 8, 9 and 10 on the right.
4. Glue the tablet to the top of the card on the blank area. Cut a piece of sticky tape the length of the card and lay it down, sticky side up. Place the card face down on the sticky tape. Cut another piece of tape the same size as the first and lay it over the top. Press down and remove all air bubbles. Trim the edges of the tape to make them even.

## Teaching point

Ask the children to bring their bookmarks with them as you gather together. Read Exodus 19:3–6a and 20:1–17. Then ask:

- Why do we need to know about the Ten Commandments?
- How will our bookmarks remind us of God's laws?
- How can we love God and others better?

Explain that God told the Israelite people that if they obeyed his ten commands, he would make them his special holy people. When we obey God's laws and welcome him into our hearts, we are his special people, too. God promised unimagined blessings for those who obey him. God wants us to follow his laws and guidelines so we can learn to love him and love others better each day.

# The sacred chest

> Bible story
> Exodus 25:10–22
>
> Bible point
> **God deserves our best.**

## Activity

### Building a sacred chest

Make replicas of the sacred chest that housed the Ten Commandments.

● **You will need**

Small boxes with lids (shoeboxes work well), heavy-weight gold card, gold spray paint, rulers, pencils, scissors, scrap paper, packing tape, gold cord, glue, gold pipe cleaners, copies of the ark instructions and empty tubes from paper towels, or wrapping paper

● **Preparation**

Collect small boxes with lids and paper tubes ahead of time. Spray-paint these items and the card with the gold paint. Make copies of the sacred chest instructions to hand out.

● **Handy hint**

To give the children a true understanding of the sacred chest that housed the Ten Commandments, make an actual-sized model from a large box. Spray-paint the box, then decorate the outside with the two angels and place a paper replica of the Ten Commandments inside the box. Use dowel sticks for the carrying rods. Remember that a cubit is approximately 45cm.

● **Step-by-step**

1. Ask the children to find a partner to work with on this craft and read the following instructions together carefully. Remind them throughout the craft that we should do our very best for God.
2. Glue the gold cord to the four sides of the box for moulding. If needed, use tape to hold the cord in place while the glue dries, then remove it later.
3. Draw two angels on scrap paper, trace them on to the gold card, cut them out and tape them to the lid.
4. Poke two holes in each of the four corners of the box. Thread pipe cleaners through the holes in each corner, form circles large enough to fit the paper tubes through, and secure the pipe cleaners tightly to form the four carrying rings. Use two paper tubes for the carrying poles. Slide the poles through the rings and tighten the pipe cleaners.
5. Draw and cut out a picture of the two tablets with the Ten Commandments written on them, and place them inside the ark.

## Teaching point

Invite the children to display their craft work. Read or review the Bible story from Exodus 25:10–22. Then ask:

• Why did God ask Moses build something so beautiful and elaborate?
• Why does God expect our very best?
• What are some ways we can give our best to God?

Explain that the Israelites used their most skilled craftsmen to build the sacred chest exactly as God wanted, and God was pleased. Let's all try to give God our very best every day. It's not always easy, but God will be pleased that we're trying!

# Leviticus

# God sets the priests apart to serve him

Bible story
**Leviticus 8:7–13**

Bible point
**God chose us to work for him.**

## Activity

### Dressed to bless

Dress up a figure of a Levite priest.

● **You will need**

Medium-weight card in a variety of colours that suggest different skin tones, sharp scissors, white felt, ribbon, several small buttons, craft glue, people-shaped paper template

● **Preparation**

Trace a person shape on to the card for each child. Cut out one square, one rectangle, and one semi-circle for each child from the white felt, to fit the person figure.

● **Handy hint**

For extra fun, make a bulletin board with the heading, 'God chose us to work for him'. Staple each of the children's priests to the bulletin board. Ask parents for permission for the children to bring in a current photograph of themselves. Cut a hole in the priest's face and tape the picture behind the hole so that the child's face is shown.

● **Step-by-step**

1. Ask the children to choose a person-shaped figure as the priest. Glue the white felt semi-circle to the top of the head, the square to the priest's chest and the rectangle on the lower part of the body to complete the robe.
2. Decorate the priest's robe by gluing a few buttons on the chest plate and gluing the ribbon on as a belt.

## Teaching point

Summarise the passage to the children. Explain that many people wear special uniforms when they go to work. Police officers, football players, nurses, firefighters and shop workers all wear uniforms. In our Bible story, God asks his special helpers, called priests, to wear uniforms as they do special things for God. Ask:

- Who does God choose today to work for him?
- Does God expect us to wear special clothes as the priests did in the Bible?
- What kinds of things can we do for God?

Explain that God chose the Levites as special people to minister and work for him. God chooses us today to work for him and bless others with God's love.

# The scapegoat

Age guide: 6–10s

Bible story
Leviticus 16:6–18

Bible point
**God carries our sins away.**

## Activity

### The goat is the hero

Make goat puppets.

#### ● You will need
Buttonhole thread, large embroidery needles, empty small cardboard tubes (such as those used for snack-size crisps, or cocoa powder), card, craft sticks, glue gun, 5cm foam balls, felt-tipped pens, glue sticks

#### ● Preparation
For younger children, make the holes in the card tubes beforehand and give closely supervised assistance with the needle and glue.

#### ● Handy hint
String can be used instead of buttonhole thread. The card tubes can be painted or covered with cotton wool or pieces of scrunched-up tissue to finish.

#### ● Step-by-step
1. Turn the card tube sideways and use an embroidery needle to poke four holes in the bottom of the tube. Place the holes where the goat's legs will attach to the body. Then place four more holes directly above the leg holes.
2. Cut four 25cm pieces of thread. Slip one piece of thread through the eye of an embroidery needle. Push the needle through two foam balls, through one of the leg holes on the tube and out of the hole on the corresponding top side of the tube. Glue one end of the string to the bottom foam ball and the other to a craft stick. Repeat for each of the remaining legs.
3. Glue a foam ball on the front of the goat as a head. When the glue sets, use felt-tipped pens to add eyes and a mouth.

## Teaching point

Review Leviticus 16:6–18 with the children. Explain that the Bible teaches that when we disobey God, it hurts our friendship with God. One of the worst things about disobedience is that the sin 'sticks' to us and we can't get rid of it. God loves us and planned a way to get rid of our sins. Before Jesus came, God had the priest lay his hands on a goat to symbolise all of the people's sins being laid on the goat. They called this special goat the scapegoat.

Invite the children to think about things they have done wrong—maybe telling lies, or being unkind. Give them a moment to think. Older children could write these things on to post-it notes. Explain that when the priest placed all of the people's sins on the goat, the goat and all of the sins were driven out of the camp. Then God forgave the people and treated them as if they had never sinned. Have the children place their hands (or post-it notes) on to their goat puppets. Ask them to walk their puppets to a far corner of the room and then return to the teaching area. Ask:

- What do we think about the practice of giving the people's sins to a goat?
- Was God being fair to forgive the people's sins in this way?
- How is Jesus like the scapegoat?
- When Jesus took our sins, was what happened to him fair? Why or why not?
- How have our sins been taken away?

Explain that Jesus is like the scapegoat. The Bible says that, through Jesus, God carried away our sins.

The children can take their scapegoat puppets home as a reminder of God's ongoing forgiveness to us.

# Numbers

## Moses sends spies into the promised land

---

**Bible story**
Numbers 13:1–3a and 17–33

**Bible point**
God gives his children good gifts.

---

## Activity

### Grape escape!

Make gigantic grape clusters like the spies found in Canaan.

### ● You will need

Purple or blue balloons, brown crêpe paper, clear sticky tape, masking tape, green card, pencils, scissors, green pipe cleaners

### ● Preparation

Cut one 2m length and four 20cm lengths of paper for each group of children. Create groups of about four to five children to cooperate in creating a grape cluster.

### ● Handy hint

If you have children who have difficulty inflating or tying a balloon, pair them up with another child who can do it. One can inflate while the other ties. You can also divide the class into leaf makers and grape makers if you have limited time.

### ● Step-by-step

1. Twist the lengths of crêpe paper to look like vines. Wrap the pipe cleaners around the ends of the vine, about every 15 to 30cm. This will secure the ends and prevent them from untwisting.
2. Join the smaller branches to the larger branch using masking tape.

3. Show the children how to make a leaf by placing their hands on a piece of green card and tracing an oval shape around it. Make several and then cut them out.
4. Inflate the balloons, tie them off and attach them to the branches. As a finishing touch, attach the leaves above the grapes at the stem.

## Teaching point

Read the story from Numbers 13 to the children. If time permits, let the groups act out the story using their grapes as props. Ask:

- How would we feel if we saw such good food in the land that God wanted to give us?
- Would it be worth fighting giants to live in a land that had so much plentiful food? Why or why not?
- What good gifts has God given us?
- How do we feel about the good gifts God gives us?

Explain that God gives his children good gifts. Sometimes challenges (like the giants in the Bible story) come with the gift. But when God gives us a challenge, he also gives us the gifts of wisdom and courage so that we can fight the giants in our life.

# Moses sends spies into the promised land

Age guide: 5–7s

## Activity

### Just a little grasshopper

Make grasshoppers to remind the children how small the spies felt.

### ● You will need

Sprung wooden clothes pegs, green pipe cleaners, a medium-sized mixing bowl, water, green food colouring, vinegar, paper towel, wiggly eyes, glue

### ● Preparation

Fill the bowl with water and add five drops of green food colouring and a tablespoon of vinegar. Soak the clothes pegs in the dye for half an hour. Drain the bowl and air-dry the clothes pegs on paper towels. Cut two 1.5cm by 2.5cm pieces of green tissue paper for each child. Cut the pipe cleaners into 15cm lengths, enough for each child to have three pieces.

### ● Handy hint

When you have a room full of similar-looking crafts, be sure to write the child's initials or name in a discreet place on the craft. You will avoid a lot of confusion and heartache when it's time to take the work home.

### ● Step-by-step

1. Help the children to glue the centre of the pipe cleaners along the top of the clothes pegs to make legs. Let the glue set for a few moment.
2. Turn the clothes pegs so that the legs are on the bottom. Bend the grasshopper legs into shape.
3. Glue eyes on at the end of the clothes pegs near the spring coils. Then glue two green tissue paper

rectangles to each clothes peg behind the eyes as wings. Set the grasshopper aside to dry for several minutes.

## Teaching point

Review the Bible story of the spies reporting back after they returned from their mission. Emphasise verse 33 and how they felt like little grasshoppers. Point out that God gave the people a big job to do. They had to take the land away from the giants. They felt like tiny little grasshoppers when they looked at the giants. The people didn't think that they could do the job God gave them to do, but the Bible shows us later that God proved his promise through their sons and daughters. Ask the following questions:

- When might we feel as small as a grasshopper?
- What jobs have we had that we didn't think we could do?
- How does God help us do hard things?

Finish by saying that sometimes we feel like tiny grasshoppers. Sometimes we don't think we can do the things that God tells us to do. That makes us feel small. But God helps us do everything he tells us to do. That's great to know!

# God gives a reminder

Age guide: 6–10s

Bible story
**Numbers 15:37–41**

Bible point
**Remember and obey God's word.**

## Activity

### The no-hassle memory tassel!

Make tassels to remind the children to obey God's word.

● **You will need**

Assorted colours of knitting yarn (including purple), scissors, pipe cleaners, rulers

● **Preparation**

Gather and set out all the materials.

● **Step-by-step**

1. Ask the children to choose the colour or colours of yarn they would like to use to make their tassels. Cut twelve 20cm lengths of yarn. Tie a small knot at both ends of each piece of yarn.
2. Lay all twelve pieces of yarn next to each other. Place a piece of pipe cleaner across all the pieces. Fold the pieces of yarn in half across the pipe cleaner. Bend the ends of the pipe cleaner together and twist so that it tightly grips the yarn.
3. Cut a 10cm length of purple yarn. Wrap it around the tassel about 1.5cm below the pipe cleaner and make a tight knot. Let the children attach the tassel to one of their shoes by tying the pipe cleaner around a shoelace. Make a second tassel for the other shoe.

## Teaching point

Read Numbers 15:37–41 to the children. Explain that God wants his people never, ever to forget his word. He told people to tie special tassels to the bottom edge of their clothes. As their tassels swished and swirled as they walked, the people would have a constant reminder that they needed to remember and obey God's word. With tassels on their shoes, let the children walk in a large circle around the room. Ask:

- If we wore these tassels every day, would we get used to them and forget the reminder? Why or why not?
- Why did God think it was important to remind the people to remember and obey his word?
- What can we do to remember God's word?

Finish by saying that God wants us to know and obey his word so that we can live lives that please him. God knows that we forget things—that's why he gave his people an easy way never to forget God's word. We need to remember his word, too.

# Moses and the bronze snake

> Bible story
> **Numbers 21:4–9**
>
> Bible point
> **God provides us with the way to find forgiveness.**

## Activity

### The snake of forgiveness

Build a model of the bronze snake.

### ● You will need

Cardboard paper tubes, knitting yarn, craft supplies such as glitter glue, felt-tipped pens or crayons, a broomstick, hole punches, Christmas tree stand, newspaper or some old towels

### ● Preparation

Cut two 15cm pieces of yarn per child. Cut the cardboard tubes down to about 12cm in length.

### ● Step-by-step

1. Give each child a cardboard tube and show them how to punch two holes, one on each side of the tube at both ends (four holes in total).
2. Let the children use the craft supplies to decorate their own section of the snake.
3. Work together to connect each individual section of the snake to everyone else's using the yarn. Loop a piece of yarn through two end holes of their own and two end holes of someone else's snake section, and knot the ends together. Repeat until all the sections are connected.
4. Mount a broomstick upright using a Christmas tree stand. Wrap newspaper or towels around the bottom of the broomstick to make the bottom of the pole wide enough for the screws of the tree stand to grip. Then let a volunteer hang the snake from the top of the broomstick.

## Teaching point

Briefly review the story in Numbers 21:4–9 with the children. Explain that God provided a way for the Israelites to be forgiven by having them look at the snake. Then ask:

- How might the people have felt when the snakes were biting and killing everyone?
- How might they have felt when Moses told them how to be healed from the snakes?
- How has God provided forgiveness for us now when we sin?

Finish by saying that Jesus took our sins and died on the cross to take away all the wrong things we do, think or say. When we look to Jesus and ask him for forgiveness, he forgives us and saves us from our sins, just like the bronze snake healed the people when they looked at it.

# Balaam's donkey speaks

Age guide: 5–7s

Bible story
**Numbers 22:22–35**

Bible point
**Pay attention to God.**

## Activity

### The reluctant donkey

Make donkeys that stubbornly sit.

### ● You will need
One copy for each child of the 'sitting donkey' template (see page 32) photocopied on to card or traced on to craft foam, scissors, felt, white glue, brass paper fasteners

### ● Preparation
Consider cutting the donkey out in advance for the youngest children. Set the supplies out in your art area.

### ● Handy hint
For extra fun, retell the story and let the children make their donkey sit whenever the donkey tries to avoid crossing the angel in the story.

### ● Step-by-step
1. Cut out the two pieces of the donkey's body. Then connect the two halves of the donkey's body with a paper fastener.
2. Apply glue and attach felt on the areas that make up the mane and tail.

## Teaching point

Briefly review the story in Numbers 22:22–35 with the children by explaining that Balaam set out to visit Balak even when he knew God didn't want him to go and place a curse on God's people. God was angry with Balaam because Balaam chose to disobey and go anyway. When Balaam's donkey saw God's angel, he tried to stop, even when Balaam beat him. Have the children bend their donkeys at the joint so that they sit down. Ask:

- Why was Balaam willing to disobey God when he knew it was wrong?
- When have we been tempted to do something that we knew would make God unhappy?
- When we are tempted, do we act more like the donkey or Balaam? Why?
- What can we do when we don't want to obey?

Explain that Balaam was tempted to obey Balak instead of God. He knew that Balak would give him a large reward for placing a curse on God's people. However, Balaam's donkey saw the angel and stopped. We need to obey God in the same way when he tells us what to do—stop, listen, and obey.

# Sitting donkey

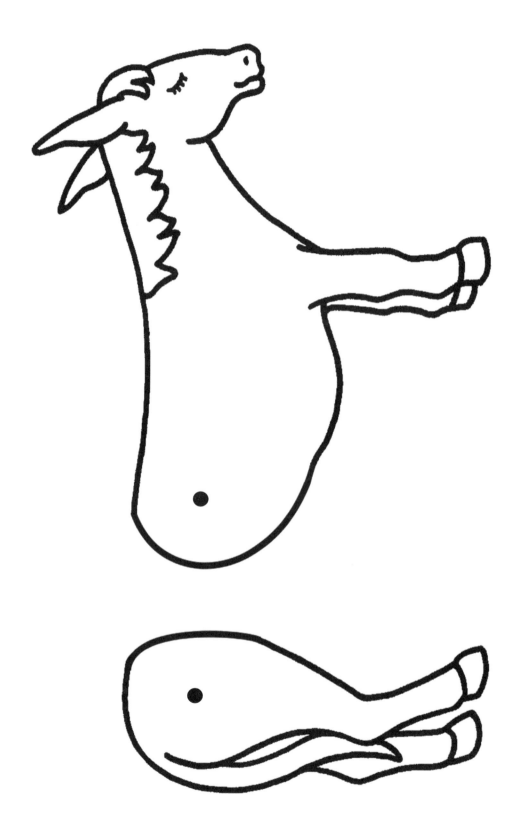

# Deuteronomy

## Remember God's word

Bible story
Deuteronomy 6:4–9

Bible point
**God wants us to remember his words.**

## Activity

### Fluorescent phylacteries

Make phylacteries.

● **You will need**

Shoe laces or knitting yarn, fluorescent-coloured felt-tipped pens, fluorescent-coloured paper, a hole punch, snack-size resealable plastic bags, a chalkboard or piece of paper

● **Preparation**

Cut 2cm x 10cm rectangles from the coloured paper, one for each child. Write 'Love the Lord your God with all of your heart, soul, and strength' (Deuteronomy 6:5) on a chalkboard or piece of paper for children to copy.

● **Handy hint**

For extra fun, substitute neon-coloured plastic lacing for the shoe laces.

● **Step-by-step**

1. Give each child two plastic bags. Using a hole punch, make a hole in all four corners of both bags.
2. Give each child four shoe laces. Help the children to thread a shoe lace through both holes on one side of one of their bags. Repeat on the other side. Do the same thing with the other bag.
3. Help the children to copy the Bible verse on to two squares of coloured paper. Show them how to place one of their verse papers into each bag. Zip the bags shut.

4. Tie one phylactery around the children's wrist as a bracelet. Tie the other around each child's head as a headband.

Love the Lord your God with all your heart and with all your soul and with all your strength.

## Teaching point

Choose a few children to help read Deuteronomy 6:4–7. Explain that God told his people that they were supposed to talk about his word constantly. He even told the people to wear God's word around their wrists and around their heads. Then ask:

- What is God trying to tell his people about his word?
- How would life be different if we thought about God's word all day?
- How can we remember God's word throughout the day?

Finish by saying that God commands his people to remember his word. God knows that if we think about his word, we'll remember what God is like and what makes him happy. Then we can begin to make better choices, too.

# Joshua

## God gives victory over Jericho

> Bible story
> Joshua 6:1–20
>
> Bible point
> **We can obey God.**

## Activity

### Let the trumpets sound

Make collages of trumpet shapes.

### ● You will need

Coloured paper, magazines, aluminium foil, scissors, PVA glue, felt-tipped pens or pens, sheets of A4 card

### ● Preparation

Lay out all supplies on a table.

### ● Handy hint

You may want to have a few templates of different sized trumpets for the children to use.

### ● Step-by-step

1. Split the children into groups of seven and create one collage per group.
2. Cut seven trumpet shapes out of the different materials (one per child in each group).
3. Lay the trumpets on the card in a creative design. Then use the glue to attach the trumpets, overlapping each other like a collage. Be creative and glue a few tiny pieces of card under some of the trumpets to give them a three-dimensional effect, use glue to give selected trumpets an even glaze, or outline a few trumpets with lines of glue.
4. Entitle the finished artwork, 'We can obey God'.

## Teaching point

When the children have finished their trumpet collages, read the Bible story about the trumpets being used to obey God. Then ask:

- Why did the priests carry trumpets and blow them?
- How did the people win in the end when the trumpets were blown?
- What kinds of things can we do to obey God?

Explain that the priests listened to Joshua because they wanted to obey God. The walls of Jericho fell down so that the people could help the city become a city for God. Point out that the collages have seven trumpets on them just like the seven days that the priests obeyed God. The trumpet collages remind us to obey God seven days of every week.

# The sun stands still

Bible story
Joshua 10:1–15

Bible point
**We can trust God for help.**

## Activity

### Let the sun shine!

Make suns as a reminder of the day when God made the sun stand still for Joshua and his men to win the battle.

### ● You will need

Large paper plates (18cm round), yellow balloons, scissors, yellow felt-tipped pens, coloured felt-tipped pens, hole punches, knitting yarn

### ● Preparation

Create two working areas as you set out the supplies. Set the paper plates, scissors and yellow felt-tipped pens in one area, with the balloons, hole punches, yarn and a few more scissors in the second area. This will help to provide a more comfortable working area for this project.

### ● Handy hint

Create a child-friendly, exciting atmosphere for Bible stories. Ask the children to leave their suns in the room for you to use as decorations. After the session or during the following week, use a sturdy ladder and hang the suns from the ceiling with either nylon thread and drawing pins, or tape.

### ● Step-by-step

1. Cut a circle in the centre of the paper plate to create an outer ring for the sun. Then cut triangular-shaped sun flares on the outside ring.
2. Use the yellow felt-tipped pens to add colour to the front of the ring. On the back of the ring write, 'I can trust God for help' with the coloured felt-tipped pens. Then list the things you want God to help you do (such as 'be more patient with a friend').
3. Blow up a balloon and gently push it halfway into the centre of the paper plate ring.

4. Cut a piece of yarn about as long as your friend's arm. Punch a hole at the top of the paper plate ring and thread the yarn through the hole. Tie the yarn so that the sun can be hung up.

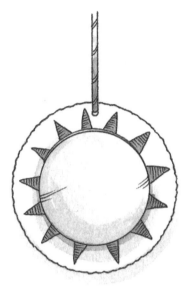

## Teaching point

When the children have finished their suns, read or review the Bible story. Then ask:

- What problem was Joshua having?
- How did Joshua's problem get solved?
- How did our friends help us with our creations?
- How can God help us with our problems?

Explain that working with a friend made it a lot easier to cut the yarn the right length. In our Bible story, Joshua asked God for help. God was Joshua's friend in battle. He helped Joshua solve his problem by keeping the sun from setting and holding it still for a whole day. If God can make the sun stand still, God can handle our problems, too.

Invite the children to take turns prayerfully sharing one thing they listed on the back of their balloons. Close the time of prayer by saying together, 'In Jesus' name. Amen'.

# Judges

Age guide: 7–11s

## Deborah takes responsibility for the battle

Bible story
Judges 4:1–16

Bible point
God gives us responsibilities to honour him.

## Activity

### Responsibility reminder board

Make bulletin boards for posting reminders of daily responsibilities.

● **You will need**

PVA glue, clothes pegs, cardboard, fabric, fabric ribbon, small slips of paper or notelets

● **Preparation**

Cut a piece of cardboard 28cm x 36cm, a piece of fabric 30cm x 38cm, eight 46cm pieces of fabric ribbon and a 10cm piece of ribbon for each child.

● **Handy hint**

Use the clothes pegs to hold the fabric and ribbons in place while the glue sets.

● **Step-by-step**

1. Lay a piece of fabric, wrong side up, on the table in front of you. Centre a piece of cardboard over the fabric, as if wrapping a gift.
2. Folding the corners neatly, glue the extra fabric around the cardboard.
3. Turn the cardboard over and place four ribbons diagonally across the cardboard. Making sure the ribbons are held tightly across the cardboard, glue the ribbons to the back of the board.

4. Glue the other four ribbons in the opposite diagonal direction, weaving them over and under the first ribbons.
5. Glue the 10cm ribbon to the top of the board for a hanger.

## Teaching point

When the children have finished their boards, tell the story from Judges 4:1–16. Then ask:

- How did Deborah know that the Israelites were to fight their enemies?
- Why did Barak refuse to lead the army by himself?
- What would we have done if we had been Barak?
- What kind of leadership qualities did Deborah have?

Explain that Deborah knew God wanted Barak to lead the Israelites into battle. God even promised to deliver the enemies right into their hands! When Barak refused to lead the army by himself, Deborah took the responsibility. God may not ask us to lead an army but he has given us responsibilities at home, at school and in other activities. When we ask him, he will help us.

Ask several volunteers to share about some of their responsibilities. Using a sample board, demonstrate how little notes can be tucked under the ribbons to be posted on the board.

# God helps Gideon defeat the Midianites

Age guide: 5–7s

---

Bible story
**Judges 7:1–22a**

Bible point
**God can use something small to do something big.**

---

## Activity

### Roly-poly painting

Use a marble to make paintings, showing that God can use something small to do something very big.

● **You will need**

Newspaper, crisps canister, piece of plain paper measuring 22cm x 25cm, marbles, washable paint, paint-brushes, pencils, painting aprons, water, paper towels or damp flannels, sheets of card slightly larger than the plain paper, PVA glue

● **Preparation**

Line a table with newspaper and set the canister, marbles, paint and paper on it. Have water and paper towels or damp flannels available for a quick clean-up afterward.

● **Handy hint**

The painting part of this project goes very quickly, so it is easy to share canisters. If your group is large, use one canister for every two to three children.

If you have time, let the children place five or six marbles in the can to create their first picture, then only one marble in the can to create the second picture. Then let them compare the two effects.

● **Step-by-step**

1. Help the children to put on the painting aprons and then write their name on the back of their paper. Turn the paper over. Show the children how to place about five or six big drops of paint in different places on their paper.

2. Roll the paper with the paint on the inside. Place the rolled sheet inside the canister, then place a marble inside the canister and replace the lid.
3. Experiment with different ways of shaking the canister. Roll it on the table, or shake it up and down. After a few minutes, remove the lid and marble. Take out the paper and see what the marble did.
4. Let the painting dry and then glue it on to a larger sheet of card to complete the work of art.

## Teaching point

As the paintings dry, tell the story of Gideon's army from Judges 7:1–22a. Then ask:

- How might Gideon have felt as he watched the army get smaller and smaller?
- How might Gideon's soldiers have felt, knowing there were only 300 of them, fighting a much bigger army?
- Is anyone too small to be used by God? Why or why not?

Finish by saying that God planned for a small Israelite army to defeat the large, fierce army of the Midianites. God wanted the Israelites to learn that it was his power, not the size of the army, that won the victory. Just as we used something small—only one marble—to make an exciting picture, God can used just a few people to do something big.

# Ruth

Age guide: 6–10s

## Ruth is faithful

Bible story
Ruth 1:1–18

Bible point
God wants us to show kindness.

## Activity

### Cup of kindness

Make 'cups of kindness' cocoa as a gift.

● **You will need**

For every child: four teaspoons of drinking chocolate, two teaspoons of milk powder, one teaspoon of granulated sugar, a spoon, a resealable plastic bag, a paper cup, an index card. For each pair of children, you will also need a mixing bowl, a measuring cup, pencils, felt-tipped pens, stickers

● **Preparation**

Have all the food-related items arranged at one large table or several smaller tables. Set the index cards, pencils and stickers on a separate table. Let the children wash their hands before beginning and then choose a partner and work together in pairs.

● **Handy hint**

If possible, arrange for your group to deliver their cups of kindness personally to elderly members of the church family, or to a care home for the elderly in your community. With the latter, check with the nursing staff ahead of time to be sure that the gift is suitable for the intended recipients from a dietary point of view.

● **Step-by-step**

1. Working with their partner, ask the children to choose who will measure four teaspoons of milk powder and who will measure two teaspoons of sugar into the bowl.

2. Ask each child to measure four teaspoons of drinking chocolate mix into the bowl, and mix all ingredients together.
3. Carefully spoon half of the mix into one resealable plastic bag, and the other half into another bag. Zip them closed. Let the children take one bag and give the other to their partner.
4. On an index card, write, 'Cup of kindness cocoa: place two tablespoons of mix into a cup and add hot water, stirring well'. Ask the children to decorate their recipe cards and paper cups with stickers and felt-tipped pens. Tuck the recipe card and the 'bag of kindness' cocoa inside the paper cup.

## Teaching point

Using a children's Bible or easy-to-understand version such as the CEV, read Ruth 1:1–18 to the children. Then ask:

• How did Ruth show kindness to Naomi?
• What are some ways we can show kindness to someone?
• Who can we show kindness to this week?

Explain that, in Bible times, women who had lost their husbands didn't go to work. Unless they had someone to care for them, they were very poor. Ruth didn't want to see Naomi left alone. God used Ruth's kindness to provide for Naomi's needs.

Even though we have many ways of taking care of elderly people today, many older people spend time alone, as Naomi did. The 'cups of kindness' we made today are gifts for elderly people. They will enjoy the cocoa mix but, even more, they will appreciate knowing that we put our creativity and love into making the gift. God will use us to show kindness to them.

# Ruth marries Boaz

Bible story
Ruth 2:2–23

Bible point
**We can worship God with our work.**

## Activity

### Grainy wreaths

Make wreaths containing wheat and barley (the grains that Ruth gleaned from Boaz' fields).

### ● You will need

White paper plates, a hole punch, string, scissors, pencils, plastic bowls, plastic spoons, plastic knives, PVA glue, food colouring (optional), shredded wheat cereal, uncooked barley (found in the health food section of most grocery stores), glue pots

### ● Preparation

Arrange three workstations. At the first, set out the paper plates, pencils, hole punch and string. At the second, set out some plastic knives for spreading and some plastic spoons. Pour some PVA glue into a bowl. Crush enough shredded wheat cereal into the glue to make a thick mixture. Do this just before the children arrive so that it doesn't dry ahead of time. At the last station, set out the glue pots, some more plastic knives and bowls of barley.

### ● Handy hint

To add some colour to the wreath, mix a few drops of food colouring into the glue before adding the crushed cereal.

### ● Step-by-step

1. Punch a hole near the edge of a paper plate. Thread a small length of string through the hole and tie a knot.
2. Cut out the centre circle of the paper plate. Turn the plate upside down and draw pencil lines from the centre outward to divide the wreath into six to eight sections.
3. Show the children how to spoon some of the shredded wheat mixture on to some sections of their wreath. Use fingers or a plastic knife to flatten and even out the mixture.
4. At the next station, use a plastic knife to spread glue over the remaining sections. Arrange barley kernels over the glued sections. Then let the wreath dry.

## Teaching point

Explain that, in Bible times, farmers left the fallen parts of their crops in the fields so that poor people could collect the leftovers. This gathering of leftover crops was called 'gleaning the fields'. Our Bible story tells how Ruth gleaned the barley and wheat fields. Tell the story or read Ruth 2:2–23 from a children's Bible or an easy-to-understand version such as the CEV. Then ask:

- Did it take a lot of work to finish our wreaths?
- How might God feel when he sees our hard work?
- How might Ruth have worshipped God through her hard work?
- Why was Ruth willing to work so hard?
- Were we worshipping God as we worked on our wreaths?

Next, comment that some of the children may have felt that making their wreaths was hard work: it took patience to line up all of those barley kernels, and it took perseverance to keep working until it was done. Working can be a way to worship God because it makes God happy to see us use the abilities he has given us. Another verse of the Bible says, 'Do your work willingly, as though you were serving the Lord himself' (Colossians 3:23). That's what Ruth was doing. Besides providing food for herself and Naomi, Ruth was worshipping God with her work. When we hang up our wreath at home later, we remember that our work—whatever it is—can be used to worship God.

# 1 Samuel

Age guide:
6–10s

## Saul becomes king

> Bible story
> 1 Samuel 9:22—10:1
>
> Bible point
> **We can do important things for God.**

## Activity

### Jars of oil

Make small jars of bath oil.

● **You will need**

Baby food jars, baby shampoo, baby oil, inexpensive perfume or cologne, 12cm circles of fabric, coloured ribbon cut in 46cm lengths (or coloured rubber bands), felt-tipped pens, newspaper, paper towel, sticky-backed labels

● **Preparation**

Create two workstations as you set up the supplies. Protect a table with newspaper. Set the baby food jars, shampoo, baby oil and perfume in this area. Put the fabric and ribbon in another area. This will prevent the fabric from getting wet in case of any accidental spills.

● **Handy hint**

Younger children may need to use coloured rubber bands instead of ribbon around the jar. They could draw a picture of something they might do for God instead of writing words on their jar, or they could ignore the felt-tipped pens and just talk about what they could do for God.

● **Step-by-step**

1. Use a felt-tipped pen to write your name on the bottom of a baby food jar. Be very careful with the glass jar so it doesn't accidentally fall and break while you are working with the oil.

2. Pour some baby oil into the jar until it is one-quarter full. Add several drops or sprays of perfume. Pour shampoo into the jar until it is full.
3. Seal the jar tightly with the lid, then put a fabric circle on the top. Use a partner to help you hold the jar as you tie the ribbon.
4. Wipe the jar off with a paper towel so that it's not slippery from the oil.
5. On the sticky-backed labels, ask the children to write or draw something they would do for God that is important, such as being kind, helping others, sharing and so on. Stick the labels on to the jars.

## Teaching point

When the children have made their bath oil, place the jars on a table in a group where everyone can see them. Read the Bible story and then repeat the verse about Samuel pouring oil on Saul's head (1 Samuel 10:1). Ask:

- Why was pouring oil an important job for Samuel?
- What are some things we can do for God?
- Who has done something important in our lives?

Invite some of the children to share what they wrote on their jars and talk about how many important things they can do. Explain that pouring oil on someone's head was a special act a long time ago. Samuel poured oil on Saul's head to show that Saul had been chosen by God to do an important job. It showed that Saul would be the first king of Israel.

We could give our jars of bath oil to someone important in our life and tell that person that he or she was chosen by God to do important things, just like we were.

# God chooses David to replace Saul

> Bible story
> 1 Samuel 16:1–13
>
> Bible point
> It's what is in our hearts that counts.

## Activity

### What is inside my heart counts

Make thumb-print hearts to help us remember that outward appearances are not as important as what is in our hearts.

### ● You will need

Red paper, pencils, felt-tipped pens or crayons, scissors, white paper, glue

### ● Preparation

Place all the supplies on the table.

### ● Handy hint

Display the hearts on a bulletin board for other church members to guess who they belong to. Title the board, 'Can you guess what's in our hearts? God can!' Use drawing pins so that the papers can be turned over to see the names.

### ● Step-by-step

1. Show the children how to fold the red paper in half and hold the folded side with their thumb.
2. Ask them to draw around their thumb, but making the outline about 2cm to 3cm bigger, so they make the shape of half a heart. Make at least three of these shapes along the fold, and cut out the hearts.
3. On the right-hand side of the outside of each heart shape (the side with the mountain fold), ask the children to write or draw one thing that people can see by looking at them.
4. On the inside of each heart shape, ask them to write or draw one thing about themselves that they are proud of, that people cannot see by looking at them.
5. Glue the left-hand side of each heart shape on to a piece of white paper so that the hearts can be

opened and closed. Write, 'What's inside our heart counts' on the top of the paper. Ask the children to write their names on the back of the paper.

## Teaching point

When the children have finished gluing the hearts on the white paper, collect the papers. Read the story of Samuel from an easy-to-read version of the Bible or from a children's Bible. Then ask:

- What is the first thing we notice when we look at a person?
- What things does God notice when he looks at us?
- What are some ways we can find out what is in a person's heart?

Explain that sometimes we look at people and see lots of things about their appearance. We see hair colour, eye colour and size, but that is not what God looks at when he sees us. God sees our heart. What is in our hearts counts most to God. Let's see if we can guess what is inside some of our friends' hearts.

Take the papers and read what is on the inside of the hearts. Encourage the children to try to guess who is being described. Give them clues by reading what's on the outside of the hearts. Explain that it is very hard to see what is inside a person, but God does it every day. The better we get to know our friends from the inside, the more we too can see their heart.

# David defeats Goliath

Age guide: 6–10s

Bible story
1 Samuel 17:1–50

Bible point
**Faith helps us to win.**

## Activity

### Faith conquers

Make David and Goliath figures.

● **You will need**

At least 25 split-pin paper fasteners for each child, aluminium foil cut in pieces about 15cm square, scissors, felt-tipped pens, rubber bands, sheets of thin card

● **Preparation**

Put out pieces of aluminium foil with felt-tipped pens or crayons, paper fasteners, scissors and card. Put one box of paper fasteners aside in case someone uses too many in their creations. (Everyone will need one more fastener after they have created their Goliath figure.)

● **Handy hint**

Create a life-size Goliath in the room for everyone to work on, with aluminium foil on a piece of rolled-out newspaper. Foil can be attached with extra paper fasteners and staples. Goliath was about three metres tall. A life-size visual will make the story have more impact. Display the figure for others to see.

● **Step-by-step**

1. Use felt-tipped pens to draw a large giant figure on the right-hand side of the card.
2. Cut pieces of aluminium foil to make armour for the giant. Use the paper fasteners to attach the armour to the giant's body. Use extra fasteners to let the children create any further pieces of armour.
3. Use felt-tipped pens to draw a small boy figure on the left-hand side of the card. Use a paper fastener to add a rubber band to the boy's hand for a catapult.
4. Cut the card in half, separating the figures. Then secure the two pieces back together by overlapping the halves by about 3cm and attaching a paper fastener close to the bottom of the card.

## Teaching point

Faith — Conquers

When the children have finished their pictures, invite them to share their pictures with the group. Read the Bible story or tell it in your own words. Then ask:

• Why was David not afraid to battle Goliath?
• How did David's faith in God help him?
• How could we show someone we have faith in God?

Explain that Goliath was a very big giant who wore scales of armour. Explain that you think the children's Goliaths look scary with all their scales of armour. Point out that the real Goliath was scary-looking to many people, but David was not afraid because he had faith that God would help him. He knew that faith would help him to win. Ask the children to turn to a partner with their pictures and make David say, 'Faith helps us win!' Then twist the Goliath side of the card down to make Goliath fall to the ground. Make sure each partner gets a turn.

# Jonathan warns David

Age guide: 6–10s

> Bible story
> 1 Samuel 20:1–42
>
> Bible point
> Friends reach out to each other.

## Activity

### Friends for ever

Make two friends to hang over a doorframe or a computer monitor.

● **You will need**

Medium-weight card, light-weight card, crayons or felt-tipped pens, scissors, rulers

● **Preparation**

Put all supplies on a table.

● **Handy hint**

Ask the children to hold their paper friends by the head and get in a circle. Everyone should have one paper friend that can touch another person's paper friend. Take turns telling the name of one friend they have, who they would like to reach out to. Pray that the children will be able to reach out to that friend in some way this week.

● **Step-by-step**

1. Take a piece of medium-weight card and fold it in quarters. This will be used for a template.
2. Lay the template in the middle of a piece of light-weight card. Trace around it. Draw two outstretched arms about 3cm in width and 10cm in length. Add hands and draw a head around one corner. Make another one on the opposite corner (see illustration).
3. Write 'Friends' on one arm and 'for ever' on an arm of the other one.
4. Draw faces on the two friends and colour in as desired. Then cut out the middle of the frame as shown.

## Teaching point

When the children have finished making their door hanger, tell them the story of Jonathan and David from 1 Samuel 20, either in your own words or from a children's Bible. Then ask:

- What are some ways in which Jonathan showed his friendship to David?
- Why is it important for friends to reach out and help each other?
- Can you think of one way we should show someone that he or she is our friend?

Explain that Jonathan and David were very close friends who reached out to each other whenever one of them needed something. They were friends for ever. Tell the children that they can take their paper friends home and hang them from a door handle or around a computer monitor to remind them that friends always reach out for one another.

# 2 Samuel

## David becomes king

Bible story
2 Samuel 1:1–7

Bible point
God always keeps his promises.

## Activity

### Crown him king

Make puzzles of King David's crown

### ● You will need

White cardboard, coloured pencils, felt-tipped pens, scissors, resealable plastic sandwich bags, gold or silver spray paint

### ● Preparation

Cut the cardboard into rectangles measuring 18cm x 22cm. Place the cardboard, felt-tipped pens and scissors in a work area where all materials are easily accessible to the children.

### ● Handy hint

Provide the children with coloured cellophane, wrapping paper, wallpaper scraps, sequins or beads to create a more three-dimensional look.

### ● Step-by-step

1. On the cardboard, design and decorate a large crown. Make it as detailed and colourful as desired using the coloured pencils and felt-tipped pens.
2. Draw lines across the crown like a puzzle and then cut the pieces out.
3. Place the puzzle pieces into a resealable plastic bag. Then find a partner and complete each other's puzzles.

## Teaching point

When the children have completed their puzzles, read the Bible story to them and then ask:

- What have we ever had to wait a long time for?
- How might David have felt when he finally became king?
- What dreams do we have that we need patience to wait for?

Explain that, just as it takes patience to create and put together puzzles, David had to wait many years before he became king. Samuel had anointed David to become king as a young boy, but it wasn't until he was a grown man that God chose David to take the role of king. No matter how long we have to wait, God always keeps his promises.

# David is merciful to Mephibosheth

---

Bible story
2 Samuel 9:1–13

Bible point
**God wants us to be kind.**

---

## Activity

### Weaving kindness

Make placemats.

### ● You will need
Binca tapestry canvas, narrow ribbon, scissors, safety pins

### ● Preparation
Cut the canvas into pieces measuring 28cm x 43cm. Cut strips of ribbon 46cm long and 30cm long. Lay the canvas pieces on the floor, forming a circle for the children to sit and work in. Lay a 46cm and 30cm ribbon on top of each piece of canvas.

### ● Handy hint
Remind the children to pull the canvas threads gently yet firmly. If time permits, you could remove the canvas threads ahead of time so the children only have to weave the ribbon.

### ● Step-by-step
1. Remove a few threads from the centre of the canvas in a vertical line. Then remove a few more threads in a horizontal line, creating a cross shape.
2. Place a safety pin at one end of a 46cm ribbon and weave it through the empty vertical line in the canvas. Then remove the safety pin, place it at the end of the 30cm ribbon, and weave it through the horizontal line in the canvas.
3. Trim any leftover ends of ribbon.

## Teaching point

When the children have completed their placemats, read the story from a children's Bible or an easy-to-understand version, such as the CEV. Then ask:

- Why was David kind to Mephibosheth?
- How did David show kindness to Mephibosheth?
- How can we weave kindness into someone else's life?

Explain that the Bible tells us that David was kind to Mephibosheth. Mephibosheth was the son of Jonathan, who had been one of David's special friends. The placemats remind us that God wants us to be kind to others. We can weave kindness into other people's lives just as we wove the coloured ribbons into the placemats. Finish by encouraging the children to remember to serve others with kindness.

# 1 Kings

## Solomon rules wisely

Bible story
1 Kings 3:5–15; 4:29–30

Bible point
God's blessings are beyond measure.

## Activity

### Bountiful blessings

Make measuring cups as a reminder that God's blessings are without measure.

#### ● You will need

Plastic cups, wide craft sticks, black marker pens, stickers, water, bucket, measuring cups, sticky tape, scissors

#### ● Preparation

Bring in a bucket of water and several measuring cups of varying units. Line the craft tables with plastic tablecloths to minimise the mess.

#### ● Handy hint

When the crafts are dry, ask each child to bring his or her cup, and ask several children to share with the group some of the blessings God has given to them.

#### ● Step-by-step

1. Use a black marker to write 'God's blessings are beyond measure' on a craft stick. Carefully cut a small slit in the top of the plastic cup. Insert the craft stick and secure with tape.
2. Show the children how to use the measuring cups provided to pour water into their cups. Using a black marker, help them to create measuring lines on their cups to correspond with the level of water achieved by each measuring cup. Empty and repeat until the entire cup is complete. Measurements should include ¼, ½, ¾ and 1 cup.
3. Decorate the cups with stickers.

## Teaching point

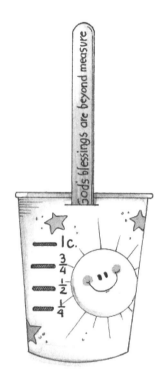

Introduce or review the Bible story. Reread 1 Kings 4:29–30. Then ask:

• Why was God so pleased with Solomon's request?
• What things can we ask God for?
• How has God blessed us more than we expected?

Explain that Solomon was David's son and succeeded him as king of Israel. God appeared to Solomon in a dream and offered to give him anything he desired. Solomon chose wisdom. Wisdom is seeing things as God sees them. While other kings may have chosen money or fame, Solomon wanted an understanding mind. This choice pleased God, so God blessed Solomon with wisdom and also gave him wealth and fame. God wants to bless all of his children beyond measure. We learn that God's blessings are beyond measure.

# The Queen of Sheba visits Solomon

Age guide: 6–10s

Bible story
1 Kings 10:1–13

Bible point
**We can honour God with our gifts.**

## Activity

### Great gifts

Make treasure boxes.

### ● You will need

Empty tissue boxes, aluminium foil or shiny wrapping paper, glue, white paper, card (optional), scissors, index cards, jewel or coin stickers, pens

### ● Preparation

Arrange the seating so that children can easily share the foil and stickers. If supplies are limited, modify the craft by having the children work together to decorate one or two large boxes.

### ● Handy hint

Modify this craft for older children by providing coloured foil papers or ceramic tiles and having them apply the shapes in a mosaic design with glue.

### ● Step-by-step

1. Cover a tissue box with foil and mould it into place.
2. Write 'We can honour God with our gifts' on a piece of white paper. Cut out and glue this on to the foiled box. Apply the stickers and decorate the box. (If you don't have stickers, use card to make shapes of jewels and coins.)
3. Write on an index card something that you can give to King Jesus, and slip the card inside the box.

## Teaching point

Introduce or review the Bible story from 1 Kings 10: 1–13. Then ask:

- What are some reasons people give gifts to one another?
- What gifts did the Queen of Sheba present to Solomon?
- How can we honour God with our gifts?

Finish by saying that the Queen of Sheba came to see King Solomon after hearing of his incredible wisdom and all the great things he'd done. She presented the king with her best gold, jewels and spices. Encourage the children, when they look at their treasure boxes, to remember to give God their best offering. Just as the Queen of Sheba honoured Solomon with her gifts, we can honour God with our gifts.

# 2 Kings

## God heals Naaman's leprosy

> **Bible story**
> 2 Kings 5:1–16
>
> **Bible point**
> Trust God for help.

## Activity

### Jumping in the Jordan

Make Naaman figures.

### ● You will need

Polystyrene cups, medium-weight card, craft sticks, blue tissue paper, felt-tipped pens, glue, scissors

### ● Preparation

Set out the required supplies.

### ● Step-by-step

1. Draw a simple figure to represent Naaman on the card, colour him in and cut him out. Be sure his size is small enough to fit inside the cup. Glue the figure on to the top of a craft stick.
2. Using the point of the scissors, carefully make a slit in the bottom of the cup. The figure will be moved up and down through this hole.
3. Cut pieces of blue tissue paper and glue them to the outside of the cup to create the Jordan River.
4. Insert the Naaman figure, stick first, through the hole in the bottom of the cup. Get ready to tell the story of Naaman!

## Teaching point

Introduce or review the Bible story from 2 Kings 5:1–16. Encourage the children to use their Naaman figures while you tell the story. Then ask:

- Why did Naaman need help?
- How would it feel to be so ill that even the doctors couldn't help us?
- Can we think of a time when we trusted God?

Explain that Naaman was an army commander who was well known and admired. Although he had many successes, he also had a big problem. Naaman suffered from a terrible disease called leprosy. Following his young servant's advice, Naaman went to God's prophet, Elisha. Elisha told him to bathe in the Jordan River seven times and he would be healed. When Naaman obeyed, he was healed. God wants each of us to have faith in his ability to help us, just as Naaman did. We must not be too proud to trust God for help.

# Hezekiah removes the idols

Age guide: 7–11s

---

Bible story
**2 Kings 18:1–7**

Bible point
**Jesus can clean away the wrong things we do, say and think.**

---

## Activity

### Squeaky-clean cross sculptures

Make soap sculptures as a reminder of how King Hezekiah 'cleaned out' idolatry from Judah.

● **You will need**

Bars of white soap, plastic knives, plastic tablecloths

● **Preparation**

Line the tables with the plastic tablecloths for easy clean-up. Designate a place for the finished crosses to be displayed. If weather permits, you may wish to try this craft outside.

● **Step-by-step**

1. Take a bar of soap. Use a plastic knife to gently scratch into the soap the outline of a cross.
2. When the design is ready, begin carving the soap with the plastic knife by gently chipping away the soap little by little, following the outline. Brush off excess soap particles as the sculpture progresses. Then display the cross in the designated area.

## Teaching point

Introduce or review the Bible story from 2 Kings 18: 1–7. Tell the children the story of how King Hezekiah removed idols because he wanted to put God first. Remind them that when we ask Jesus to forgive us, he washes away the wrong things we do, say and think. Then ask:

- What are some 'idols' that keep us from putting God first?
- How can we get rid of the things that separate us from God?
- Why is our obedience important to God?

Explain that King Hezekiah helped people turn back to God by obeying God and following his decrees. The king 'cleaned out' the country by removing pagan temples and destroying idols. An idol is anything that we put before God. We need to follow Hezekiah's example and remove the things that stand between God and us.

Invite the children to take their sculptures home and display them in their bathrooms. Encourage them to let the sculptures remind them to keep their hearts clean and to put God first.

# 1 Chronicles

Age guide: 7–11s

# The prayer of Jabez

> Bible story
> 1 Chronicles 4:9–10
>
> Bible point
> **God honours prayers that bring him glory.**

## Activity

### Personal prayer plaque

Make personal prayer plaques as a reminder that God honours prayers that bring him glory.

### ● You will need

Craft foam squares, calligraphy pens, ribbons, hole punch, glue, white index cards, pencils, paper, stickers

### ● Preparation

Write a few sample prayers to give the children some ideas to follow. Be sure to set out some spare paper and pencils, so that the children can draft their personal prayers before writing them on the index cards. Children may also want to practise using the calligraphy pens.

### ● Handy hint

Enhance this craft by gluing the prayers on to wood plaques instead of craft foam, and by adding a coat of lacquer to finish. Invite the children to take their prayer plaques home and display them in their bedrooms. Encourage them to use the plaque as a reminder to pray for things that will bring honour and glory to God.

### ● Step-by-step

1. Ask the children to use the pencils and paper to write their own one- or two-sentence prayer to God. When they have finished, ask them to copy the prayer on to an index card with a calligraphy pen.

2. Show them how to glue the card (face up) in the centre of the craft foam, then punch a hole at the top of the foam and string a ribbon through it to hang on a doorknob or in a window.

3. Decorate the plaque with stickers and display.

## Teaching point

Read the story of Jabez from 1 Chronicles 4:9–10. Then ask:

- Why is prayer important?
- What types of things can we pray about?
- Why was Jabez mentioned in this story?

Explain that the book of 1 Chronicles provides a family history of the nation of Israel. It traces family roots and shows God's influence upon his people's lives. Many people are named, some for their faith and others for their failures. Jabez is remembered for his prayer life. We can learn from this story that God honours a genuine prayer life and will reward prayers that bring him glory and are in his plan.

# 2 Chronicles

## Jehoshaphat trusts God for victory

Bible story
2 Chronicles 20:1–20

Bible point
Look to God for victory.

## Activity

### Saviour scope

Make telescopes as a reminder to keep our focus on God.

### ● You will need

Tall empty crisp canisters, black card, stickers, glitter, glue, paper, felt-tipped pens, can opener

### ● Preparation

Prepare the canisters by removing the bottoms with a can opener. Make sure any jagged edges are removed. Gently wipe out the cans with a towel.

### ● Handy hint

Encourage the children to use their Saviour scopes to read their Bibles. Remind them that knowing and obeying God's word helps us to be victorious.

### ● Step-by-step

1. Glue a piece of black card around the canister. Write 'Look to God for victory' on a strip of paper and glue it to the outside of the telescope.
2. Use the glue, glitter, stickers and remaining supplies to decorate the telescope.

## Teaching point

Introduce or review the Bible story from 2 Chronicles 20:1–20. Then ask:

- What can we do when we face trials?
- How did Jehoshaphat respond?
- Why should we look to God for our victory?

Explain that the nation of Judah faced a terrible crisis. As enemy armies closed in, declaring war, King Jehoshaphat immediately looked to God for solutions. He sought God's help, knowing that the battle was his. When we face hard times in our lives, we need to remember Jehoshaphat. Encourage the children to look through their Saviour scopes and remember to trust God for victory.

# Ezra

## Service to God

Bible story
Ezra 3:1–6; 6:12

Bible point
Serving others pleases God.

## Activity

### Kingdom tools

Make tool belts as a reminder that serving others pleases God.

### ● You will need

A4 manila envelopes (one per two children), hole punch, knitting yarn, card, scissors, pens or felt-tips, cardboard (optional)

### ● Preparation

Prepare the envelopes in advance by sealing each one and cutting them in half lengthwise. You may wish to use cardboard to make templates of various tools, for the children to trace around and cut out.

### ● Step-by-step

1. Take one envelope half and hold it so that the opening faces up. Punch a hole at each top corner of the envelope.
2. Insert a piece of yarn through each of the holes to create a tool belt. Secure each end with a knot.
3. Use card to draw or trace various tools, such as a hammer, saw and screwdriver. Cut out the tools and insert them into the pocket of the tool belt.
4. Write 'Serving others pleases God' on the outside of the tool belt. Show the children how to wear the belt by tying it around the waist.

## Teaching point

Introduce or review the verses from Ezra. Then ask:

- What are some ways we can serve others?
- Why is our service important to God?
- How did Ezra use his talents?
- How can we use our talents?

Explain that a tool belt reminds us of hard work. Ezra was a man who wasn't afraid of serving God and others. Ezra led a group of people to Jerusalem to rebuild the temple. He also worked to teach God's word to the people of Israel. When you see a tool belt, think about Ezra. When we serve others, we serve God. Serving others pleases God.

# Ezra devotes himself to studying scripture

> Bible story
> **Ezra 7:6 and 10**
>
> Bible point
> **Study God's word.**

## Activity

### Devotion diaries

Make a devotion diary.

### ● You will need

A4 card, hole punch, ribbons, stickers, felt-tipped pens, scissors

### ● Preparation

Prepare a sample of this craft in advance. This will give children some ideas and help them visualise the end result.

### ● Handy hint

Have a few simple Bible verses that most children might know, such as John 3:16, written down on paper. Encourage the children to select one of their favourite Bible verses and share it with the group. The children can make a page in their diary entitled 'Friends' favourites' and write down their friend's verses to study later.

### ● Step-by-step

1. Take several sheets of A4 card and fold them in half. Stack them together. Punch three holes in the folded end of the card. Insert ribbons and tie them to look like a book.
2. Design a creative cover with a title such as 'Michael's devotion diary'. Use the stickers and felt-tipped pens to decorate both the outside and inside pages of the diary.
3. Encourage the children to use their diaries to record favourite scriptures and things God teaches them.

## Teaching point

Introduce or review the verses from Ezra. Then ask:

- How do we learn about God?
- Why is it important to study God's word?
- How did Ezra show his devotion to God?

Explain that Ezra was a priest and scribe who devoted his entire life to learning about God and serving him. Ezra meditated on scripture to know more of God and to be able to share him with others. Encourage the children to follow Ezra's example and stay devoted to reading and meditating on God's word. Tell the children that, when they read the Bible, they can use their devotion diaries to write down special verses or things God says to them.

# Nehemiah

## Nehemiah rebuilds the walls

Bible story
Nehemiah 2:11–20

Bible point
Examine your heart.

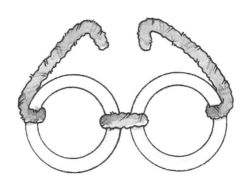

## Activity

### Inspection spectacles

Make pretend glasses as a reminder to inspect those areas in our lives that need God's repair.

● **You will need**

Plastic lids from crisp canisters (two per child), pipe cleaners, safety scissors

● **Preparation**

Prepare the craft by cutting a large slit in the centre of each plastic lid. This will help the children to get their scissors inside the lid to cut out the centre.

● **Handy hint**

Encourage the children to wear their glasses each time they read their Bibles. Remind them to ask God to search their hearts and show them any area that needs repair.

● **Step-by-step**

1. Use scissors to cut out the centres of two plastic lids.
2. Twist a pipe cleaner between the two lids, joining them together. Cut off the excess pipe cleaner and push down any protruding parts.
3. Twist a pipe cleaner on the outer edge of each circle to make the ear pieces for the glasses.

## Teaching point

Invite the children to wear their glasses while you introduce or review Nehemiah 2:11–20. Then ask:

- What are some everyday things that break down?
- How might our hearts get damaged?
- How can we solve our problems?

Explain that Nehemiah had a vision to rebuild the walls of Jerusalem. He gathered information by looking closely at the walls. He then gave his concerns to God. We often face problems just like the walls, and feel as if things are crumbling down around us. Encourage the children to remember to inspect their hearts, then look closely to God for help.

# Dedication of Jerusalem's walls

Bible story
Nehemiah 12:27–43

Bible point
**We can praise God with music.**

## Activity

### Individual instruments

Make original musical instruments.

### ● You will need

Items such as empty cream cheese boxes, sticky tape, knitting yarn, small bells, plastic combs, craft sticks, paper plates, dried beans, safety pins, card, rubber bands, scissors, drinking straws

### ● Preparation

Scatter the various materials along each table so that everyone can reach.

### ● Handy hint

The children may enjoy creating a praise band. Put on some praise music and let the children play their instruments in time with the music. Emphasise that they should listen to the rhythm of the song to gauge when and how they play their praise instrument to God.

### ● Step-by-step

1. Invite the children to use the supplies to create and decorate their own unique praise instrument. Encourage them to be as creative as possible, and be prepared to demonstrate how their instruments work.
2. For example, they could make a rattle by putting some beans in an empty cheese box, taping it shut and decorating the outside.
3. Make a comb chime by attaching bells to the comb with rubber bands, then using a craft stick to rub across the comb's teeth. Encourage the children to use their imaginations and have fun!

## Teaching point

Introduce or review Nehemiah 12:27–43. Then ask:

- Why was music so important in the celebration?
- How do we praise God for what he does?
- Why is praise so important to God?
- How can we praise God through music?

Explain that when the walls of Jerusalem were completely repaired, the people celebrated with a dedication ceremony. There was music, singing and praise to God. The people were joyous because God had given them the ability and strength to complete a difficult task. Encourage the children to remember to be like the Israelites and give God praise for his help in their lives. We can praise God with music.

# Esther

Age guide:
7–11s

## Esther saves her people

Bible story
Esther 2:1–18

Bible point
God can use us.

## Activity

### Mirror, mirror on the wall!

Make wall decorations reminding us that God can use us.

#### ● You will need
5–10cm frameless mirrors (two per child), narrow fabric ribbon, glass paint pens, low-temperature glue guns, PVA glue, scissors, beads

#### ● Preparation
Arrange two separate centres. In one area, place the mirrors and the glue guns. In the other area, set up the ribbon, PVA glue, glass paint pens and beads.

#### ● Handy hint
Small mirrors can be purchased at craft stores or glass shops. Because the ends are unfinished, it is very important to show the children how to handle them safely.

#### ● Step-by-step
1. Using the glue gun, bond two mirrors together back-to-back.
2. Starting at one corner, glue the ribbon along the side edges of the mirrors. At the very next corner leave a 5cm loop to be used as the hanger. Continue gluing the ribbon along the remaining three sides until the starting point is reached.

3. Glue beads or additional ribbon next to the loop for decoration. On the mirror, along the top in small letters, use glass paint pens to print the words 'Look who God can use'.

## Teaching point

When everyone is finished, ask the children to bring their crafts and form a circle on the floor. Introduce or review Esther 2:1–18. Then ask:

- What kind of a person was Esther before she became queen?
- What kind of people does God use to do his work?
- How might God use us?

Explain that sometimes we might not feel very special or capable, but we are very special to God. God uses ordinary people and events every day to do wonderful things, just like he used Esther. Encourage the children, when they look into their mirrors and read 'Look who God can use', to smile and say, 'Me!' Finish by taking time for each child to share what they hope to be or do when they grow up. Encourage ideas that prove nothing is impossible with God.

# Esther and the king's decree

> ### Bible story
> Esther 3:10–12; 8:8
>
> ### Bible point
> **No one can separate us from God.**

## Activity

### I decree thee!

Make signet rings to understand better the certainty of having Jesus in our hearts.

### ● You will need

20-gauge gold craft wire, beads with holes large enough to slide on to wire, long-nose pliers, felt-tipped pens, modelling clay, slips of paper

### ● Preparation

Cut the wire into 12cm strips. Place the wire strips, felt-tipped pens and small bowl of beads in the middle of the table. Be sure enough elbow room is allowed to twist and turn the wire. On a piece of paper, use a felt-tipped pen to write, 'Dear Jesus, I believe you are my Saviour. Thank you for living in my heart. Help me to always serve you and tell others about you.' Place a small rounded piece of clay, the size of a penny, under the decree. Make one for each member of the group.

### ● Handy hint

The children may choose to design a more elaborate ring, perhaps shaping their initial on the top. Boys may choose to twist two wires together to form a more masculine-looking ring.

### ● Step-by-step

1. Use a thick crayon or felt-tipped pen to use as a model for a finger. Lay the felt-tip on the centre of the wire. Bring the two ends up together and twist the wire twice so it fits snugly around the pen.
2. Twist and shape the two wire tails into a design of your choosing. String a bead on to one of the ends. Be creative and loop and tuck the wires to form a

shape that doesn't stick out and catch on things. Then use the long-nose pliers to bend the ends of the wires to avoid injury or snagging on objects.

3. Remove the ring from the felt-tip and place it on your finger for size. If the ring needs to be made smaller, just twist the top a few more times.

## Teaching point

When the children have finished their rings, ask them to join you sitting in a circle on the floor. Have the slips of paper with the 'decree' in front of you. Read the verses from Esther 3:10–12 and 8:8. Explain that when the king made a decision, he would stamp his signet ring on it, and the law could not be changed. Then ask:

• If we were the king today, what kinds of laws would we stamp with our signet rings?

Explain that the one thing that no one can ever change or take from us is our decision to follow God. Like the king in the book of Esther, we have full authority over that decision. Our decision to follow Jesus is far stronger than any power that the king's signet ring had. This will never change!

Show the children the slip of paper with the decree written on it. Allow them to punch their signet ring into a piece of clay if they agree with what the decree says. When everyone is finished, thank God for teaching us about taking ownership of what is right, and in unison say, 'In Jesus' name. Amen'.

# Esther saves her people

Age guide: 5–7s

---

Bible story
Esther 4:10–17

Bible point
**Be courageous for God.**

## Activity

### 'C' stands for courage!

Make badges of courage.

### ● You will need

10cm square piece of cardboard, foil, PVA glue, scissors, hole punch, black paint, paintbrushes, newspaper, painting aprons, box of tissues, sticky tape, safety pins

### ● Preparation

Organise two working areas. In one area, have the square of cardboard, foil, yarn, glue, scissors and hole puncher. Spread newspaper over the other area, where the paint and paintbrushes will be located. Have tissues available in both areas.

### ● Handy hint

To avoid paint messes on clothing, have painting aprons available for the children. Another alternative could be tucking long paper towels under their chins like a bib.

### ● Step-by-step

1. Help the children to put on painting aprons. Then cut out a large circle from the cardboard.
2. In the middle of the circle, glue a piece of yarn into the shape of a 'C'. Glue additional yarn and leftover cardboard shapes around the edge to make a design.
3. Cover the front of the cardboard with foil. Use a tissue to gently rub out the creases and find the definition of the yarn. Fold the foil edges towards the back and stick down with glue. Punch a hole at the top.
4. Paint over the foil with black paint. Using the tissue, dab over the wet paint to absorb most of it. This leaves a weathered, antique look.
5. Attach a safety pin to the back of the badge.

## Teaching point

With their finished badges, ask the children to join together in a circle. Introduce or review the Bible story. Then ask:

- What does it mean to be courageous?
- When are the times at school or home that we need to be courageous?
- What can we do to act more courageously?

Explain that it is not always easy to have courage. It is hard to be brave when we have to stand up for someone or forget our fears. Esther could have stayed out of Mordecai's problems and minded her own business, but Esther loved God. She knew it was the right thing to try to protect God's people. When we need courage to be brave, we can pray to God and he will give us what we need to face anything.

# Job

## Job remains faithful in suffering

> **Bible story**
> Job 1:1—2:10; 42:10–17
>
> **Bible point**
> **We can trust God when bad things happen.**

## Activity

### God-is-with-me comfort bags

Make comfort bags.

### ● You will need

Pre-cut felt square, scissors, felt-tipped pens, low-temperature glue gun or fabric glue, uncooked rice, bow, spoons or measuring cups

### ● Preparation

Set out the supplies.

### ● Handy hint

If you have a microwave available on site, have an adult helper warm the bags up to surprise the children when you toss them their bags. Since microwave oven temperatures vary, experiment with the timing and be careful not to overheat them. The heat will not soften the glue.

NB: You may want to send a note home with instructions to parents for heating and cooling the bags.

### ● Step-by-step

1. Show the children how to fold a piece of felt in half and press it down with their hands. With the felt still folded, ask them to write the words 'God is with me' on it, and then turn the folded felt over and write their name on the back.
2. Glue down two sides of the felt, leaving one end open.
3. Wait until the glue is set and then carefully fill the bag one-half to two-thirds full of rice.
4. Glue the bag closed.

## Teaching point

Invite the children to hold their comfort bags while you introduce the Bible story of how Job trusted God even when bad things happened to him. Read the story in Job 1:1—2:10 from a children's Bible or child-friendly version of the Bible. Then ask:

- What terrible things happened to Job?
- How did Job trust God?
- How did God help Job?
- What are some bad things that happen to us?
- How can we trust God when bad things happen?

Explain that, like Job, we sometimes find bad things happening to us even when we don't deserve it. Read Job 42:12–17 out loud. Emphasise that God healed Job and gave him new riches and a new family. Job tried hard to trust God and to be honest, and God was pleased with Job. We can trust God when bad things happen. Let's praise God for loving us and taking care of us when bad things happen.

Finish by explaining to the children that their bag is called a comfort bag because if their mum or dad puts it in the microwave on a low setting for a few seconds, it will get warm and comforting. They can then snuggle with it and relax. Encourage them, when they feel the warmth, to remember that God is with them. When the weather is hot, they can put their comfort bag in the freezer and use it to cool themselves. The comfort bag reminds us that, just like Job, we can trust God in all situations.

# Psalms

## Blessed are they who delight in the Lord

> Bible story
> Psalm 1:1–6
>
> Bible point
> **God wants us to grow in him.**

## Activity

### Bubble-painting trees

Create flourishing tree paintings.

### ● You will need

Sheets of white A4 paper, paintbrushes, drinking straws, paper plates, small squares of sponge, brown and green paint, newspaper, felt-tipped pens (optional)

### ● Preparation

Cover two tables with newspaper. At one table, set the paper, brown paint, brushes and straws. At the other table, set the sponges, paper plates and green paint.

### ● Handy hint

If time allows, children can draw little apples, oranges, or lemons on their tree tops with felt-tipped pens when the sponge painting has dried.

### ● Step-by-step

1. Hold the paper so that the long side is vertical. Place about five or six drops of brown paint in one spot at the bottom of the paper.
2. Show the children how to place a straw just over the drops of paint and tilt the paper away from them. Ask them to gently blow the drops of paint in different directions to make 'branches'. Add more paint to create more branches. When this is done, ask them to take their paper to the next table.
3. Show the children how to dip a sponge lightly in green paint and scrape off the excess on the edge of the paper plate. Sponge 'leaves' throughout the painted branches. Set the tree aside to dry.

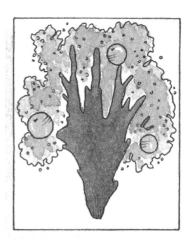

## Teaching point

While the paintings are drying, read Psalm 1. Then ask:

- What did we add to our trees to make them look as if they were growing strong and healthy?
- What kinds of things make us grow strong in our Christian faith?
- What does it mean to delight in the Lord?
- How do these verses describe someone who delights in the Lord?

Explain that trees that are well-watered grow lots of big, green leaves and juicy fruit. Psalm 1 tells us that if we delight in the Lord and in his word, we will grow strong, just like a well-watered tree. God wants us to grow in him. Invite the children to take turns sharing one way they can delight in God and his word during the coming week.

# The heavens are God's handiwork

Bible story
Psalm 8:1–9

Bible point
The heavens declare God's glory.

## Activity

### Starshine water globes

Make night-sky water globes as a reminder of God's glory as seen in his creation.

### ● You will need

Empty small plastic bottles, funnels, glycerin, distilled or cooled boiled water, blue food colouring, star-shaped table confetti, silver or gold glitter, teaspoons, glue, paper towels, newspaper

### ● Preparation

Line a table with newspaper and set out the supplies.

### ● Handy hint

Walk your group around the building and outdoors to see the effect of light on their water globes. Invite the children to contrast the look of their water globes when they walk into a darkened room with the way they look in daylight.

### ● Step-by-step

1. Place one drop of blue food colouring in the bottle. Then, using a funnel, fill the bottle with water, leaving about a thumb's length of air at the top. Replace the lid and shake to mix the food colouring.
2. Reopen the lid and pour in a level teaspoon of star-shaped confetti and glitter. Replace the lid and shake again to test the effect. Add more glitter if needed. Add a few drops of glycerin and test again. The glycerin should slow the rate of the snowfall.
3. Pour a little glue inside the bottle cap and screw it on to the bottle. When the glue has dried, shake the bottle to see the stars shine!

## Teaching point

Invite the children to sit in a circle with their water globes. Read Psalm 8. As you read verses 3 and 4, let the children shake their water globes. When you finish reading the psalm, ask:

- What was the writer thinking about when he looked at the night-time sky?
- How can the moon, stars, and planets make us think of God's glory?
- How does it feel to know that the same God who created the stars also created us?

Explain that when the psalmist looked at the night-time sky, he must have wondered what kind of a great God could create such beauty in such a huge space. No one can put any boundaries on the sky and section it off— the sky stretches around the whole world. Think about how great God is to create something so amazing.

# We are his sheep

> Bible story
> Psalm 23:1–6
>
> Bible point
> **God walks with us.**

## Activity

### Walking sheep puppet

Make puppets to use while Psalm 23 is read and discussed.

● **You will need**

White craft foam, white pipe cleaners, pens, scissors, PVA glue, cotton balls, black felt-tipped pens, wobbly eyes

● **Preparation**

Cut sheets of foam into 10cm x 12cm rectangles. Cut pipe cleaners into 5cm pieces.

● **Handy hint**

In church, the children could use their puppets to act out the verses to the congregation while you read the psalm. Also, consider inviting the children to give their puppets as gifts to a family member or friend.

● **Step-by-step**

1. Help the children to draw a large cloud shape on a piece of foam for the sheep's body, and then cut it out.
2. Take two pipe cleaners and bend each one into a U-shape. Turn the sheep over and tape the ends of these two wires to the bottom of the sheep's body. They should form loops for the children's fingers to slide through.
3. Turn the sheep over again. Near the top of its body, draw a circle for the sheep's face. Glue the wobbly eyes in place and draw a mouth and ears.
4. Glue cotton balls on the rest of the sheep's body.

## Teaching point

Demonstrate how to insert two fingers into the puppet, making it 'walk'. Help the children put their sheep puppets on their fingers. As you read Psalm 23, ask the children to 'walk' their puppets when you read words such as 'lead', 'guides', 'walk' or 'follow' (depending on which Bible version you use). Then ask:

* Which of the places where the shepherd and the sheep walked can make us feel happy?
* Which parts of this psalm can help us when we feel afraid?
* When is God with us?

Explain that the psalm is like a picture of God and us. He is the shepherd and we are the sheep. The shepherd led the sheep wherever they went and stayed with them in both the happy places and the scary valleys. God promises to be with us always, too. Even when we don't feel God's presence with us, we can know that God walks with us always.

# God's word makes us wise

> Bible story
> **Psalm 119:96–106**
>
> Bible point
> **God's word is our guide.**

## Activity

### My Bible diary

Construct covered Bible diaries.

#### ● You will need

File folders, rulers, pencils, scissors, adhesive-backed pieces of Velcro, A5 paper, stapler, felt-tipped pens, stickers or other decorations

#### ● Preparation

Cut tabs off file folders (if appropriate) and trim 8cm from the bottom of the folders.

#### ● Handy hint

List about three to five simple Bible passages on a piece of paper that the children can place in their Bible diaries and read during the week. Challenge the children to write in their diaries every day for one week. At the end of the week, ask the children to bring in their diaries and share their favourite thoughts, if they would like to.

#### ● Step-by-step

1. Place the folder with the crease to the left side. Cut 5cm from the right edge of the top layer only.
2. Fold the bottom layer of the folder (on the right side) to overlap the top.
3. Unfold the overlapping flap on the right side. Place a piece of Velcro on the inside of the flap, and its coordinating piece on the folder directly below it.
4. Open out. Staple about six pieces of paper to the top edge of the inside cover on the right side.
5. Decorate the Bible diary using felt-tipped pens.

## Teaching point

Ask the children to sit in a circle with their Bible diaries and Bibles. Ask for volunteers to help read Psalm 119:96–106. Ask:

- According to this passage, does anything in our lives need to change for God?
- What are some benefits of reading God's word?
- What comparisons does the writer use to describe God's word?

Explain that the Bible is like an instruction manual for life. Carefully reading and thinking about it will guide us in all our decisions. Encourage the children to use their Bible diaries to write down the important things God says to them as they read his word.

# God is always watching over us

> Bible story
> Psalm 121:1–8
>
> Bible point
> **God watches over us.**

## Activity

### Day-and-night mobiles

Create woven mobiles as a reminder that God watches over us day and night.

● **You will need**

Cardboard, pencils, sharp scissors, ruler, craft foam in white, light blue and yellow, narrow ribbon, PVA glue, hole punch

● **Preparation**

On cardboard, create two 20cm stencils of each of the sun, moon and star patterns shown. The children will trace these shapes on to foam. Cut ribbon into 30cm lengths.

● **Handy hint**

To reinforce the point that 'God is watching over us', glue wobbly eyes to the top of the shapes.

● **Step-by-step**

1. Help the children to trace one of the patterns on foam and cut out the shape.
2. In the large central section of the shape, draw five lines that are about 8cm long. Space the lines evenly. Slit the lines with scissors. NB: Don't allow the children to use the scissors themselves.
3. Glue five ribbons to the underside of the shape, just above the first slit line. Let the glue set for a minute or two. Carefully weave the ribbons over and under, through the slits, trying not to pull the ribbon too tightly in case the glue is not quite dry.
4. Let the remaining ribbon dangle below the shape. Trim the ribbons evenly or trim them to form a point.

5. Make a loop from a scrap of ribbon and thread it through a hole punched at the top of the shape. Tie a knot to secure.

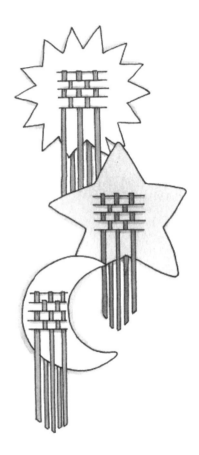

## Teaching point

Read Psalm 121 aloud and then ask:

- How does it make us feel to know that God never sleeps?
- Why is God's help better than anyone else's?
- When are the times that we might especially want to remember that God is watching over us?

Explain that the psalm reminds us that God is always with us and wants to protect us. It doesn't mean that we'll never fall down or be unwell. We have a promise from God, though, that if something scary does happen, he is with us through it and will never stop watching over us.

# Praise the Lord, everybody!

> Bible story
> Psalm 150:1–6
>
> Bible point
> **God wants us to praise him.**

## Activity

### Praise clackers

Make praise clackers (castanets) to use in worship.

### ● You will need

Jam jar lids, coloured plastic sticky tape (electrical tape), small fat rubber bands (the bands used to bind vegetables such as broccoli or asparagus work well), gift ribbon, scissors, jingle bells (optional)

### ● Preparation

Cut 38cm lengths of ribbon and run them through the scissors to curl them. If you have more than one colour, separate the curled strips by colour for the children to choose when doing their project.

### ● Handy hint

For more variety of sound, help the children to tie small jingle bells to the centre of a few of their ribbons.

### ● Step-by-step

1. Place two lids together with the inside rims touching.
2. Tape one rubber band to the middle of the top lid. Tape a second rubber band to the middle of the bottom lid. Cut a piece of tape about 10cm in length. Run the tape from the middle of the top lid to the middle of the bottom lid, creating a hinge.
3. Choose three to five curly ribbons and attach them to a new piece of tape.
4. Attach the tape with the ribbons to another piece of tape on the top lid. To play the clackers, show the children how to slide their thumb though the top band and their index finger through the bottom band. Give the clackers a try by snapping the lids together with the thumb and finger.

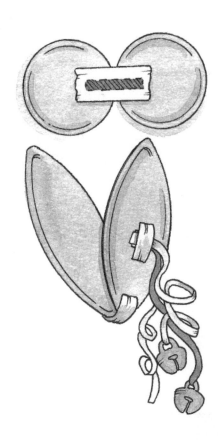

## Teaching point

Play a short, upbeat praise song or sing one with the children. Let them stand and use their clackers as they sing along. Next, read Psalm 150 and let the children play their clackers as you repeat verses 5 and 6. Then ask:

- When can we praise the Lord?
- Besides saying 'Praise the Lord!' what are some other ways we can praise God?
- How does praising God make us feel?
- How does our praise make God feel?

Explain that as we are praising God, we are thinking about how special he is. Thinking of God makes us happy even if we weren't happy when we began. This psalm tells us that God wants to hear our praises—not only when we are in a good mood or when God gives us something we want, but all the time. God is good all the time, and he is always worthy of our praise.

# Proverbs

## Wisdom wins

> **Bible story**
> Proverbs 2:1–15
>
> **Bible point**
> God's wisdom protects us.

## Activity

### Decision-makers

Make paper cube decision-makers to help make wise choices.

### ● You will need

The decision cube template (see page 67), A4 sheets of coloured card, scissors, felt-tipped pens, sticky tape

### ● Preparation

Photocopy the decision cube on to coloured card (one for each child). Set out felt-tipped pens, scissors and tape.

### ● Step-by-step

1. Ask the children to cut out the decision cube and write their name somewhere in one of the shapes. Decorate the boxes with felt-tipped pens.
2. Fold the template on the dotted lines and tape the edges to form a cube that shows the words on the outside.

## Teaching point

When the children have finished constructing their cubes, explain that the book of Proverbs was written for everyone everywhere, to help us make good choices in life. Ask the children to open their Bibles and ask a volunteer to read Proverbs 2:1–15 out loud. Then ask:

- What is one of the wisest things we might know?
- What are some ways we learn to be wise?
- Who gives wisdom?

Explain that God gave us the instructions in Proverbs to keep us safe and to help us have a good life. He wants us to be wise. He promises to give us the wisdom we need. Verse 12 says, 'Wisdom will protect you.' Explain that the cube is called a decision cube. On each face of the cube is a question we can ask ourselves when we don't know what to do. It can help us think before we act. That's wisdom—and God's wisdom always wins.

Review each of the questions on the cube. Then ask the children to think of situations that they have faced or might face. Be prepared to describe situations for them, such as sneaking off to see a film when their parents think they are at a friend's house, or joining a group of children to get back at someone they don't like. Invite them to toss their decision cubes on the floor in front of them and ask themselves the question that lands on top.

# Decision cube

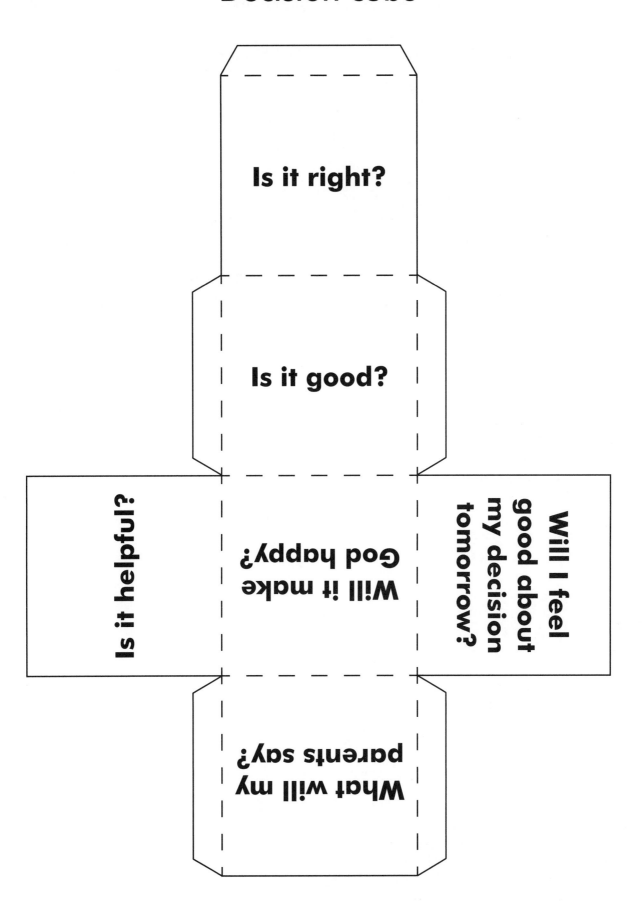

**Is it right?**

**Is it good?**

Is it helpful?

Will it make God happy?

Will I feel good about my decision tomorrow?

What will my parents say?

# Trust in the Lord

Age guide: 7–11s

## Activity

### Trusting hearts

Make fabric hearts as a reminder to trust in the Lord with all our hearts.

● **You will need**

White fabric such as a sheet, pillowcase or tablecloth, fabric pens or felt-tipped pens, scissors, self-adhesive paper, masking tape

● **Preparation**

Cut a piece of fabric for each child, measuring 12cm x 18cm. Cut the self-adhesive paper into squares and then fold the squares in half and cut heart shapes out of each one. The heart shapes need to be big enough for children to write inside. You'll need about three hearts for each child.

● **Handy hint**

For extra fun, tape the fabric squares to a piece of card slightly larger than the fabric, or glue them to cardboard for children to take home to frame and hang in their bedrooms. If you or one of the children's parents likes to sew, the pieces could be sewn together to make a banner to display in the hall or church. The children could think of ways to raise money to help church missionaries or a local charity—people who are often trusting God with their whole hearts to meet their needs.

● **Step-by-step**

1. Lay a piece of fabric on the table. Tape the corners down with masking tape to hold it in place.
2. Peel the backing off three of the heart shapes and press them on to the fabric, making a design. Overlapping the hearts a little bit or placing them at different angles makes a good design.
3. Trace, colour, draw, or scribble over the edges of the hearts with fabric pens. Work until the edges of all the hearts have ink around them.
4. Peel the self-adhesive paper hearts off the fabric. White areas will appear where the paper was. Write the words, 'Trust in the Lord' or 'Trust in the Lord with all your heart' inside the heart shapes.

## Teaching point

When the children have finished their fabric hearts, ask a volunteer to read Proverbs 3:5–6 out loud. Then ask:

- Why is it better not to trust only in our own judgment?
- In what ways can we let God lead us?
- What does it mean to do something with all our heart?
- How can we show God that we trust him with all our hearts?

Explain that these verses in Proverbs tell us to trust God with all our heart—especially when we don't understand something. We can always know that God is in control, even when it doesn't feel like it. In the end, he'll always make things turn out OK. Encourage the children to use their fabric hearts as a reminder to trust God all the time. He's trustworthy! We can trust the Lord all the time.

# Ecclesiastes

Age guide: 7–11s

## Only God satisfies

Bible story
**Ecclesiastes 2:24–26**

Bible point
**God helps us to feel satisfied.**

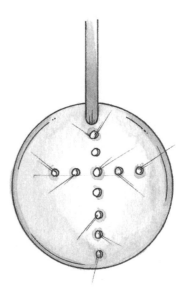

## Activity

### Satisfaction hangers

Make satisfaction hangers.

### ● You will need

Jam jar lids, paper, pencils, scissors, sticky tape, old magazines, hammer, thin nails, ribbon or knitting yarn, a torch

### ● Preparation

Create two working areas as you set out the supplies. Provide an area for drawing and a separate area for hammering. Prepare one of the lids beforehand as a sample.

### ● Step-by-step

1. Trace around a lid on a piece of paper and cut out the circle.
2. On the circle draw a simple shape that represents God to you, such as a cross, a heart or sunshine. Then tape your drawing to the metal lid.
3. Set the lid on top of one or two old magazines to protect the table and then make nail holes with the hammer and a nail, following the lines of your drawing. Leave a little bit of space between each hole. When your design is finished, turn the lid over and flatten any rough edges with a hammer. Ask an adult for help with this part if you need it.
4. Make a hole in the top and string a length of ribbon through it to make a hanger.

## Teaching point

When the children have finished making their hangers, ask everyone to hold them up for each other to see. Praise the children for their efforts. Read Ecclesiastes 2:24–26 out loud and then explain that God wants to help us be happy with our work. That feeling is called satisfaction. Maybe our hangers aren't perfect or didn't turn out as we wanted, but trying is the way we learn. Our efforts are pleasing to God and he wants us to be satisfied and happy, too. Ask:

- What does it mean to be satisfied?
- Where does true satisfaction come from, according to these verses?
- How can God help us to be satisfied?

Explain that sometimes we work really hard at something and we are happy with the results, but sometimes we work really hard and things don't turn out the way we wanted. We are disappointed and not satisfied. Encourage the children to use their hangers as a reminder to let God shine through their lives so that they can be satisfied with their work when they've tried hard, even if the results aren't perfect. Invite the children to take turns passing the torch around and, shining it through their hanger, say a simple 'thank you' to God for helping them to feel satisfied.

# A time for everything

Bible story
Ecclesiastes 3:1–8

Bible point
**God gives us time for everything.**

## Activity

### My time is his time

Create sundials as a reminder that God has a time for everything.

● **You will need**

The sundial template (see page 71), medium-weight card, rulers, felt-tipped pens, crayons or coloured pencils, PVA glue

● **Preparation**

Copy the sundial cut-outs on to card (one per child).

● **Handy hint**

Trace the sundial template on to balsa wood and cut out with a fret saw. Supply oil-based paint and paintbrushes to decorate the sundial. Allow to dry and then use craft jewels or beads to mark the divisions on a clock. Write the words 'A time for everything' on the triangular shape and glue in place, using wood glue. Place the sundial outdoors in a sunny position.

● **Step-by-step**

1. Give each child a sundial cut-out. Ask them to write their name on the back of the round sundial base and then turn it over. Write the words 'A time for everything' on the triangular shape.
2. Use the pencils and felt-tips to decorate both shapes.
3. Use a ruler to mark a fold line half an inch from the bottom of the triangle shape. Fold the base of the triangle up and glue the flap in the centre of the circle.

## Teaching point

When the children have finished their sundials, introduce or review Ecclesiastes 3:1–8. Then ask:

• How does it feel to know that God is in control of our lives?

Explain that the Bible says there is a time for everything. No matter how much we plan, things will happen that we have no control over. God is the only one who is in control of our lives. It is good to be organised and have a plan, but we need to remember that God is the one in control. Tell the children to place their sundial somewhere at home that gets a lot of sun, such as a sunny windowsill. Encourage them, each time they look at it, to remember that God has a time for everything. The sundial will help them to keep track of the time God has given them.

# Sundial template

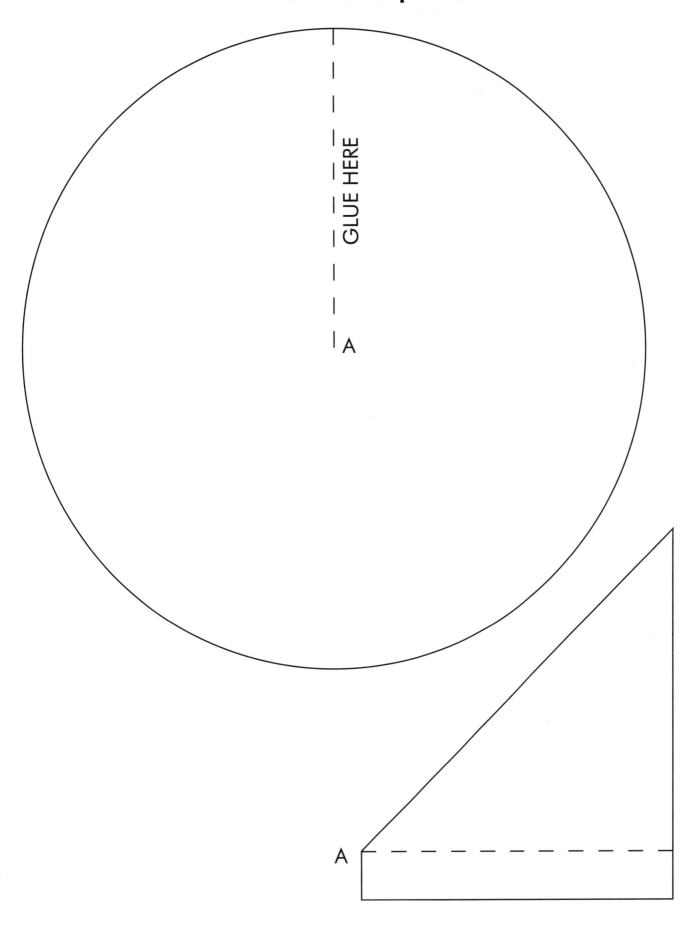

GLUE HERE

A

A

Reproduced with permission from *The Encyclopedia of Bible Crafts* published by BRF 2010 (978 1 84101 590 3) www.barnabasinschools.org.uk

# Song of Songs

Age guide: 5–7s

## God's eternal love

Bible story
Song of Songs 2:11–13

Bible point
God loves us!

## Activity

### Lovey-dovey dove

Make soft toy doves.

### ● You will need

Rectangle of white felt measuring 23cm x 30cm, cotton wadding, wobbly eyes or small piece of black felt, stick glue or a low-temperature glue gun, scissors, dove template (see page 73), thick card, pencils, glitter glue pen

### ● Preparation

Cut a few dove shapes from card for the children to use as a tracing template. Set out the supplies.

### ● Handy hint

With a needle and thread, sew a string through the top of each dove to hang from the ceiling. It will be a constant reminder of God's love and peace.

### ● Step-by-step

1. Using a pencil, help the children to trace the dove outline twice on to the white piece of felt.
2. On one dove, pour a thick line of glue all along the edges, leaving an 8cm gap to allow room for stuffing. Next, lay the other dove shape over the glued dove, matching edges and press firmly.
3. Cut out two small circles from the black felt for the eyes. Glue one on each side of the dove's head. Alternatively, glue the wobbly eyes in place.
4. When the two dove shapes are glued securely, carefully push wadding inside the dove, being sure

not to tear the two pieces apart. Be sure the wadding is spread evenly and reaches inside the tips of the wings and beak. Glue the hole shut. Use the glitter glue pen to make a line for the dove's wing. Let it dry for about ten minutes, and then make a wing on the other side of the dove to match the first side.

## Teaching point

Invite the children to join you in a circle on the floor with their doves. Read Song of Songs 2:11–13 aloud and then ask:

- What words can we use to tell someone we care for them?
- How does it feel when we show someone we love them by giving them a hug?
- What words can we use to describe how much God loves us?

Explain that a dove is a symbol of love and peace. Ask the children to imagine the freshness, newness and loveliness of spring-time. Alongside the symbol of the dove, this is a picture of God's love for us. God loves us with all the emotions we may feel towards our parents or a special pet or toy. Encourage the children, when they hold their dove in the palm of their hands, to remember that God loves us and holds us in the palm of his hand. God loves us!

# Lovey-dovey dove

Reproduced with permission from *The Encyclopedia of Bible Crafts* published by BRF 2009 (978 1 84101 590 3) **www.barnabasinschools.org.uk**

# Isaiah

## God's forgiveness

> **Bible story**
> Isaiah 1:18
>
> **Bible point**
> God forgives the wrong things we say, do and think.

## Activity

### Let it snow, let it snow!

Make snowy crosses representing God's forgiveness.

● **You will need**

Red plastic plates, felt-tipped pens, cross template, scissors, thick card, PVA glue, clean dry eggshells, clear glitter

● **Preparation**

Measure and cut out a few cross shapes for the children to trace on to their plates. Collect and wash enough eggshells so that each child can have three to four, depending on the size of the plates.

● **Handy hint**

Ask the children to cut the crosses completely away from the plate, punch a hole at the top, and thread a piece of knitting yarn through the hole so they can hang it in their bedroom window when they get home.

● **Step-by-step**

1. Show the children how to turn the red plate over and trace the cross template on to the back. Cut the cross out but leave the bottom of the cross attached to the plate. Bend the cross so that it stands up when the plate is flat. Then lay the cross back down.
2. Use the felt-tips to draw a simple picture of something personal that makes God sad. Ask for God's forgiveness and then spread a thin layer of glue all over the cross. Be careful not to get glue on the rest of the plate.
3. Crush the eggshells and sprinkle the shells over the picture. Place dots of glue on the eggshells, sprinkle the glitter over the top and then shake it off. Lift the cross up a little, making sure the glue hasn't stuck.
4. Set the plate aside to dry. When the glue is dry, stand the cross up.

## Teaching point

Invite the children to join you in a circle on the floor. Ask a volunteer to read Isaiah 1:18. Then ask:

• Are our sins really 'red'? Does God really make them white?
• When God forgives, does he also forget what it was we did wrong? How do we know?
• What do we need to do in order for God to forgive our wrongdoings?

Encourage the children, as they look at their crosses, to look at the red that stands for wrongdoing and remember the drawing. Explain that when we obey God and pray for forgiveness, God promises not only to forgive but also to forget the things we do wrong. He sees us as pure and white as snow—in the same way that the eggshells covered our drawings to hide them. What a holy and loving God we serve! God forgives us and no longer remembers the wrong things we do, think and say.

# God calls us by name

> Bible story
> Isaiah 43:1
>
> Bible point
> **God knows us by name.**

## Activity

### Name that tune

Make door chimes as a reminder that God knows us by name.

### ● You will need

Piece of thick cardboard measuring 12cm x 15cm, string, embroidery thread, acrylic paint, paintbrushes, small bells, beads or other decorative materials, felt-tipped pens, scissors, glue, darning needle or sharp nail, sheets of A4 paper, newspaper

### ● Preparation

Beforehand, type the following rhyme on to paper so that the children can just glue it to the front of their craft instead of writing it:

*When you hear these little bells, remember, for it's true, God knows you by your name and thinks the world of you.*

Set up two separate areas for this activity. Cover an area with newspaper and let this be where the children paint the cardboard. The other area will be where they use all other supplies.

### ● Handy hint

The bells can get tangled very easily. To avoid this, lay the craft down flat on a table and put a piece of tape over the strings to help keep them in place until the children get home.

### ● Step-by-step

1. Paint one side of the piece of cardboard all one colour and then set it aside to dry.
2. Thread a bell on an 18cm piece of string. Do not tie the string but lay it aside to be used later. String five to seven bells in this same way.

3. When your paint is dry, glue the poem to the very front of the cardboard. Glue beads or other decorations around the rhyme. With the felt-tip, write your name in large letters at the very top.
4. With the darning needle or nail, poke holes through the bottom of the cardboard, spacing them evenly apart. Thread the strings with the bells through each hole and tie the two ends together in a knot. Try to make each tied string the same length so that the bells will touch each other when you hold the craft upright. Poke a hole on each side near the top to tie a long string so that the name plaque can be hung on a doorknob or wall.

## Teaching point

Ask the children to place their name plaque in front of them on the floor. Ask everyone to sit together and open their Bibles to Isaiah 43. Ask for a volunteer to read Isaiah 43:1. Ask:

- Why is it so special to be called by our name?
- What things has God done that prove he knows each of us very well?
- What does this verse say about how God feels about each of us?

Explain that we are all unique and special in our own ways. We have different likes and dislikes. God not only knows us by name but he knows and cares about every little detail in our lives. God created us, formed us and saved us. Our names belong to us; they fit us. In the same way, we belong to God, and he values everything about us. God knows us by name.

# Jeremiah

## At the potter's house

> **Bible story**
> Jeremiah 18:1–17
>
> **Bible point**
> God wants to mould our lives.

## Activity

### Potter's house

Make houses of clay.

### ● You will need

Individual serving sized juice cartons, homemade clay (see recipe below), rolling pins, brown acrylic paint, paintbrushes

### ● Preparation

Clean and dry the cartons thoroughly. Make the clay before the session. (The recipe makes enough dough for two children, so you will need to adjust the amounts according to your group size.) Mix together 225g flour and 100g salt. Then add 100ml water and one tablespoon cooking oil. Flour hands to prevent dough from sticking and knead the dough for at least one minute.

### ● Handy hint

It may be a good idea to find a picture or diagram of Bible-time houses in a picture Bible or Bible encyclopedia for the children to see. Make extra clay and allow the children to mould accessories for their houses, such as pots, people or even a wheelbarrow, to make the house look more authentic.

### ● Step-by-step

1. Cut off the top of the carton and turn it upside down. Roll out enough clay to cover the four walls of the house and the roof. Place the clay over the box, pinching corners together. Using your fingers, pinch a ledge to go around the roof.

2. Bake at 250°F (130°C, Gas Mark ½) for 25 minutes (the box will not burn at this low heat). Remove from oven and allow to cool. Paint a door, a few small windows and a ladder going up to the roof.

3. If you will be letting your house dry on its own, you can paint a door and windows now (the clay will not be messy or fall apart easily, so transporting it home should be trouble-free).

## Teaching point

Leave the houses where they can be seen, but not touched. Have everyone join together in a circle to review or read the Bible story. Then ask:

- How did it feel to be the creator of a clay house?
- In what ways does God mould or shape our lives?
- What do we need to do so that God can do his work in our lives?

Finish by saying that it is always fun to work with clay: we can take a lump of nothing and turn it into a piece of art. God wants to mould and shape our lives so that through him, just like the clay, we too can be useful, beautiful people. If we have willing hearts to listen and obey him, he will do beautiful things in our lives!

# God's plans for us

Bible story
Jeremiah 29:11

Bible point
**God has good plans for us.**

## Activity

### Bible scrolls

Make Bible-times wall planners.

● **You will need**

A4 sheets of light brown or cream coloured card, small brown paper bags, dark knitting yarn, glue, sticky tape, scissors, felt-tipped pens

● **Preparation**

To save time, cut down the side seams of the paper bags and open them out flat.

● **Handy hint**

It may be helpful to bring in a wall planner to explain the purpose of keeping your daily plans organised. A calendar with events and times circled on it will also help to reinforce that a scroll would have been used in this way.

● **Step-by-step**

1. Starting at the corner and working towards the opposite corner, roll a sheet of card as tightly as possible into a thin tube. Tape in place and then make one more.
2. Gently crumple the paper bag until it feels soft and pliable. Carefully tear small pieces around the edges to give it the look of parchment.
3. Lay the bag flat and glue the top underside of the bag to one of the card tubes. Cut the tube to the desired length (approximately 5cm longer than the bag at each end). Repeat with the other tube.
4. Loosely wrap a piece of yarn, measuring 30cm in length, around two fingers. Carefully remove the yarn and string a 15cm piece of yarn through it. Tie a knot and cut through the loop to make tassels. Make four of these and tie them to each end of the card tube.

5. Write the words of Jeremiah 29:11 on the paper bag. Then invite the children to write a few ideas of the plans they think God has for them—for example, 'God plans for me to be happy' or 'God plans for me to spread his word'. Roll the scroll from each end until it meets in the middle. Secure with a piece of string.

## Teaching point

Sit the children together in a circle on the floor. Ask for a volunteer to read Jeremiah 29:11. Explain that in Bible times people did not write on paper or in books but rather on animal skin (parchment). The original books of the Bible were written on parchment. The parchment was made into scrolls and people in Bible times kept track of important dates and events on them in the same way we use a calendar or diary. Ask:

• What things do we hope to do in the future?
• How could we serve God in our plans?
• How does it feel to know that God has great plans for us?

Explain that sometimes we get so busy with all the events in our lives that we have to keep track of things on a calendar or in a diary. But we need to stop and think about the plans God has for us as well. Encourage the children, the next time they check their calendar for the day's activities, to remember to read their scrolls and take a moment to consider God's plans for their day. Finish by saying that we are all very special to God and, when we trust him, we discover what good plans God has for us.

# Lamentations

## God's mercies never end

> Bible story
> Lamentations 3:22–23
>
> Bible point
> **God's mercies never end.**

## Activity

### Circle of love

Make bracelets to remind us that, like a circle, God's mercies never end.

### ● You will need

Leather lace or embroidery silks in a variety of colours, coloured beads, scissors

### ● Preparation

Precut the leather lace or embroidery silks into 30cm lengths. It may be best to place the beads in bowls in the middle of the work area for easier access and to prevent them from rolling away.

### ● Step-by-step

1. Ask the children to find a partner. Ask one child in each pair to choose three colours of lacing and tie them together at one end. Their partner then holds the end that has been tied.
2. The children begin braiding the three strands, adding coloured beads as they go to create their own design. When they get about a finger's width from the end, they need to tie another knot to keep the bracelet from unravelling.
3. Use another strand to thread through the braided area just below both knots to connect the bracelet. Ask partners to help tie the finished bracelet on their friend's wrist and then swap round so that the first child helps his or her partner to make their bracelet.

## Teaching point

When everyone has finished and the children are all wearing their bracelets, sit down together in a circle. Point out to the children how the circle of the beads never ends. Explain that the circle shape of their bracelets tells the story of God's great mercy, which goes on and on for ever. Discuss the shape of the bracelet as a circle that never ends. Read Lamentations 3:22–23 and then ask:

- What things may we wish would never end?
- How do we feel when good things end?
- What can this bracelet always remind us of about God's love?

Explain that, on earth, everything ends at one time or another: A fun-filled special day ends when we go to sleep for the night; football games have a final whistle at the end of the game; an ice cream tastes really good but then we've eaten it and it's gone. But God's love and compassion for us is like the shape of a bracelet. There is no end to a circle and there will never be an end to his love. We are loved unconditionally for ever and ever. God's mercies never end.

# Ezekiel

## The glory of God

Bible story
**Ezekiel 1:25–28**

Bible point
**Desire God's glory.**

## Activity

### Bright light

Paint light switch covers as a reminder of God's glory.

### ● You will need

Plain white light switch covers, coloured felt-tipped pens, acrylic paint, paintbrushes, glitter glue or large sequins, a low-temperature glue gun, newspaper

### ● Preparation

Cover one table with newspapers and have paints and brushes located in that area. If you are using glitter glue and sequins to decorate, have them set up in a separate area with the glue gun. Tape the screws for the switch cover securely to the backs so that they don't fall off before the children get home.

### ● Handy hint

For younger age groups, it may be helpful to have the words written on a large piece of paper for the children to copy. NB: Remind the children that they should not replace the light switch in their room, but should ask an adult to help.

### ● Step-by-step

1. Write the message 'May the glory of God shine on me!' on to the light switch panel.
2. Add designs or small pictures with the paint or glitter glue.

## Teaching point

When the light switch panels are decorated, ask everyone to join in a circle on the floor. Introduce or review Ezekiel 1:25–28. Then ask:

- How might we describe the brightness of the sun to someone who cannot see?
- How might Ezekiel have felt when he saw the glory of God?
- How might we describe God?

Explain that, according to Ezekiel, God's glory took the form of a brilliant light. We know of God's love, kindness and compassion, but it is wise to remember that he is also as shining and bright as the brightest star, and more glorious than our eyes could ever take in. We do not serve a dull God! We can desire God's glory.

# Daniel

Age guide: 6-10s

## Daniel interprets a dream

Bible story
Daniel 2:1–28

Bible point
**God knows my dreams.**

## Activity

### My dream

Make three-dimensional pictures depicting the truth that God knows and cares about our dreams.

### ● You will need

Black, skin-tone and brightly coloured card, gel-pens, old magazines, safety scissors, pens, glue, stapler

### ● Preparation

Beforehand, cut the card in the following sizes for each child: one 30cm x 23cm piece in black; one 27cm x 13cm in white; one 24cm x 5cm strip in a bright colour.

### ● Handy hint

Younger children will need extra help drawing their profiles as large as the paper. Make a light and simple profile for them, and allow them to draw in their own sleeping eye, hair and lips. If the outline is simple, they can do the cutting out themselves.

### ● Step-by-step

1. Ask the children to lay their face down sideways on the white card and have a partner trace the outline of their head, face and neck to create a profile. Since this picture will only show half their face, ask them to draw facial features showing themselves sleeping. Then cut out the profile.
2. Ask the children to cut three small pictures from a magazine of something they might have a dream about. Glue the pictures across the top of the black

paper. Use gel-pens to draw a white circle around each picture, with smaller circles extending to the bottom of the page to depict dream 'bubbles', as you would see in a cartoon.
3. Write the words 'Only God knows my dreams' on the brightly coloured strip (help younger children with this task). Lay the head on top of the black paper and the coloured strip on top of the head. Line up all the three left sides to be flush with each other, and also so that all three are flush on the bottom. Staple once on the bottom left side. It should look as if the person is sleeping on a pillow.
4. Align the other three ends to the right side, which will cause the black paper and head to curve forward but will also make a three-dimensional look. Staple all three layers on the lower right side.

Only God Knows my Dreams

## Teaching point

When the children have finished, invite them to join you and bring their creations with them. Introduce or review the Bible story. Then ask:

* What kinds of things might we dream about?
* Why might we dream about those things?
* Why did God give the king the dreams for Daniel to interpret?

Explain that Daniel was obedient to God. He trusted God to help him understand the king's dream. God knows our dreams. God cares about what we think, dream and do. When we pray to him and trust in his love, God will help us. God knows our dreams!

# Daniel's friends are safe in the fiery furnace

> **Bible story**
> Daniel 3:1–30
>
> **Bible point**
> **God takes care of us.**

## Activity

### 'Escape the heat' pot holders

Sew pot holders to show how God protected Shadrach, Meshach, and Abednego.

### ● You will need

Scraps of cotton material, thick felt or wadding, embroidery thread, darning needles, scissors, fabric paint or felt-tipped pens

### ● Preparation

Since material is hard to cut without a good pair of fabric scissors, it would be best to have it pre-cut before the session. Each child needs two pieces of thick felt or wadding cut into a 15cm square, and two pieces of matching cotton cut into 18cm squares.

### ● Handy hint

The children will need help with this project, simply because sewing can be frustrating for beginners. Provide patient assistance, a calm environment and a 'Let's have fun!' attitude throughout, and the whole experience will be positive.

### ● Step-by-step

1. Centre the two pieces of felt or wadding on the wrong side of one of the cotton squares. Place the second cotton square, wrong side down, on top of the centred felt. (Pretend you're making a felt sandwich.)
2. Push the threaded needle down through all four pieces of material and pull the thread through, leaving about a 3cm tail. Bring the needle back up through the four layers, close to the first entry point. Cut the thread and tie the two ends into a firm knot. Do this at all four corners, in order to hold the material together.
3. Re-thread the needle with about 75cm of thread. Tie a knot at one end. Starting at one corner, do a simple 'down and up' stitch around the outside edge of the pot holder. The felt was already stitched in place in Step 2. Now you are simply sewing the two pieces of material together just next to the edge of the felt. Tie a knot in the thread after all four sides have been sewn down.
4. Using the fabric paint or permanent marker, write 'God protects us' on the outside of the pot holder.

## Teaching point

Join together in a circle and introduce or review the story of Shadrach, Meshach and Abednego from Daniel 3. Then ask:

- Why did the men in the Bible story need protection?
- When might we want to ask God for protection?
- What can we do to get this protection from God when facing tough times?

Explain that when we take out something hot from the oven, we trust that a pot holder will protect our hands from being burned. In the same way, Shadrach, Meshach, and Abednego trusted that God would be with them and take care of them. If we trust in God, God will take care of us.

Close with a song such as 'Trust and obey' as the prayer for the day.

# Writing on the wall

Age guide:
7–11s

Bible story
Daniel 5:1–31

Bible point
God wants our attention!

## Activity

### Read the writing on the wall!

Make surprise pictures.

### ● You will need

A rectangle of thick card measuring 23cm x 33cm (one per child), A4 paper, scissors, felt-tipped pens, thin black permanent marker, plastic folders (one per child), sticky tape

### ● Preparation

Have the card already folded into three equal sections.

### ● Handy hint

Until you actually do this project, it will be hard to explain to the children how it will work. It is a good idea to make one before class to show as an example.

### ● · Step-by-step

1.  On the front flap of the card, mark out a rectangle to make a picture frame.
2.  Cut away a half-moon finger-grip space through all three sections. Open the cardboard and cut out the rectangle. This is the front of the card. Draw a brick wall on this front frame.
3.  Cut a separate piece of paper the same size as one section of the card, and draw a picture of Daniel wearing his purple robe and gold chains.
4.  Slip your picture into the plastic folder with the top against a fold. Trim the plastic to the same size as the picture. Use tape to secure the back of the picture to the plastic.
5.  Use the permanent marker to draw an outline of the picture on the plastic. Completely open your card and lay it out flat so that the coloured frame side is

facing down. Fold the bottom flap into the middle. Slide the plastic-covered picture over the bottom flap. The coloured picture will go behind the bottom flap. Fold the top flap down over the plastic. Grip the plastic and coloured picture and slowly pull; the black and white picture is now in colour!

## Teaching point

Join together in a group and tell the story from Daniel 5, using either a children's Bible or easy-to-read version of the Bible. Then ask:

*   How do we get someone's attention?
*   What things might we do that are similar to what the king in today's story was doing?
*   What does God do to get our attention?

Explain that when we show someone the craft we made today, we might get a lot of attention for our craftiness! But the handwriting on the wall was a miracle. God performed this miracle to get the king's attention and warn him about his pride. Even after receiving this miracle from God, the king wouldn't listen. He was later defeated by his enemies. God wants our attention—it's in our best interest that we should give it to him.

# God protects Daniel in the lions' den

Age guide: 5–7s

## Activity

### God saves Daniel

Make lions.

### ● You will need

Craft sticks, brown felt, yellow fun foam or yellow card, safety scissors, wood glue or a glue gun, yellow acrylic paint, paintbrushes, brown fabric paint

### ● Preparation

Set up two separate workstations. At one table set up the paint and brushes and set all other supplies at a second table. Also have a 20cm x 3cm strip of felt pre-cut for each child.

### ● Handy hint

Make sure an adult is supervising the use of the glue gun. It's always a good idea to have a few extra glue guns and a few extra helpers whenever using hot glue. There are also cooler temperature glue guns available at craft shops or through the Internet.

### ● Step-by-step

1. Lay six craft sticks side-by-side horizontally to create the lion's body. Next, glue a stick on each side, going vertically, connecting the ends of the six sticks together. The top of each vertical stick should be even with the top of the body, and the remaining end of the stick will make the two legs. Cut a stick in half to make a tail and glue it to the top of the back leg. If you are using wood glue, it will take a few minutes for this to dry. While the glue dries, make a fringe along one long edge of the felt and set it aside.

2. Paint the sticks yellow. While the paint is drying, cut a circle about 7cm in diameter out of the yellow foam to create the lion's head. Glue the fringe around the lion's head. Cut off the extra and save it for the lion's tail.

3. Paint on the lion's facial features and glue the whole head to the top right-hand corner of the body. Glue the extra fringe to the end of the tail.

## Teaching point

Ask the children to join you in a circle on the floor. Tell the story of Daniel in the lions' den from a children's Bible or an easy-to-read Bible version. Then ask:

- Why was Daniel thrown in the lion's den?
- Besides being protected from the lions, what other good thing happened because of Daniel's loyalty to God?
- How can we be an example to our friends that God is real?

Explain that lions are very dangerous animals and we should never go near them. Long ago, lions were used as a cruel way to execute criminals. King Darius had made a law to make people obey him, but Daniel was loyal to God and God kept the lions from harming him. Because of Daniel's loyalty, the king saw that God was real and he, too, praised God. Just like Daniel, the way we live and the things we say can show others that God is real and is capable of helping us all.

# Hosea

## Get to know God

> **Bible story**
> **Hosea 6:3**
>
> **Bible point**
> **God wants us to know him.**

## Activity

### Memory verse holders

Make memory verse holders.

● **You will need**

Thick card, spring-loaded clothes pegs, low-temperature glue gun, poster paint, brushes, black fine-tipped felt pens, decorative stickers, index cards

● **Preparation**

Cut a 12cm card square for each child. Make a list of Bible verses that tell us something about God, such as Genesis 1:1, Psalm 18:2 and Luke 1:37. Set up two separate workstations, one with the glue, stickers and clothes pegs, the other with paint, brushes and felt-tipped pens.

● **Handy hint**

It may be helpful for younger children to have the Bible verse written out in large letters so that they can easily copy it on to their craft. While waiting for the paint to dry, ask older children if they know any Bible verses that they have already memorised.

● **Step-by-step**

1. Paint the front side of the cardboard in a solid colour.
2. When the paint is completely dry, write 'Let's do our best to know the Lord' on the front of it in your best handwriting.
3. Glue decorative stickers on the front. Give an adult the task of gluing a clothes peg to the back of the

card, using a low-temperature glue gun. The clothes peg should be lined up with the bottom of the cardboard to serve as a stand to keep the holder upright. Write on index cards verses that tell us something about God and place the index cards in the clothes peg.

Let's do our best to know the Lord. Hosea 6:3

## Teaching point

Join in a circle and ask the children to place their memory verse holders in front of them. Ask them to read the verse written on their holders. Explain that the Bible helps us to know who God is. When we talk about God, we are getting to know who he is and what he does. Ask:

- How do our friends or family members get to know us?
- What can we do to get to know God better?

Explain that we might know things about God—how he made the universe, how he parted the Red Sea, how he is a loving and merciful God and so on—but God wants us to really know him, just like we know the people in our family or a friend at school. One way to do this is to memorise what the Bible says about God. God wants us to know him better than we know our families and closest friends.

# Joel

## God will give his Spirit to everyone

> Bible story
> Joel 2:28–29
>
> Bible point
> **God gives us his Holy Spirit.**

## Activity

### Spirit whirligigs

Make whirligigs to remind us of God's gift of the Holy Spirit.

### ● You will need

Plastic canvas, pipe cleaners, beads, scissors, fishing line

### ● Preparation

For each child, cut 14 strips of plastic canvas. Each strip should measure three squares wide and 40 squares long. If possible, have the strips, one pipe cleaner and six beads on individual trays or in resealable plastic bags for each child.

### ● Handy hint

Threading the second end on to the pipe cleaner is especially difficult for younger children. Monitor closely and help them by doing the first few for them.

### ● Step-by-step

1. Thread three beads on to one end of a pipe cleaner and turn up a small portion of the end to ensure the beads won't slide off.
2. Thread the pipe cleaner through the middle end hole of each piece of plastic canvas. There will now be three beads with a stack of plastic canvas strips resting on the end of the pipe cleaner. Take the bottom piece of plastic canvas, closest to the beads, and bring the other end of that strip up on to the pipe cleaner. Again, thread the middle end hole,

to form the shape of a 'C.' Do the same for all the other strips of canvas, from the second-to-bottom piece. One by one, thread the canvas on to the pipe cleaner until all 14 of the strips have the pipe cleaner threaded through both ends.
3. Add the final thee beads to the top and wrap the tail of the pipe cleaner down to form a loop. Thread a piece of fishing line through the loop so that you can hang the whirligig up.

## Teaching point

Ask the children to bring their whirligigs and join you on the floor. Read Joel 2:28–29 and then ask:

- How do people who are filled with God's Holy Spirit act?
- How is the Holy Spirit like the wind that makes our whirligigs move?
- What do we need to do to have the Holy Spirit live inside us?

Explain that God's Holy Spirit is a gift that brings peace and wisdom to our hearts. Even though we can't see the wind that makes our whirligigs move, we know the wind is there by how it feels on our face or the sound of it rustling in the trees. In the same way, we can't see God's Holy Spirit, but when we trust in Jesus the Holy Spirit lives inside us. All we have to do is ask God for this wonderful gift, and it will be ours. God gives us his Holy Spirit.

# Amos

## Only God can change us

Bible story
Amos 9:11–15

Bible point
Only God can change us.

## Activity

### 'Changed lives' pictures

Make pictures that show how God's love removes the wrong things we do, say and think.

### ● You will need

A4 paper, coloured wax crayons including several black crayons, craft sticks or old keys

### ● Preparation

Set out the supplies, giving each child a piece of paper, several crayons, one black crayon and a craft stick

### ● Handy hint

Amos is a difficult book to share with young children as it deals with a lot of prophecies and symbolism. It is important to give children symbols that they understand. After relating a part of Amos, compare it to a situation that children may experience in their own lives.

### ● Step-by-step

1. Ask the children to cover their paper completely with many different colours. They don't need to make a pattern, just get many bright colours all over the paper without using black.
2. Now completely cover the other colours with black. Push hard so that the black goes on very thickly.
3. Using a craft stick, carefully scratch out wide letters to spell the word 'GOD' in the black crayon. As the black layer is removed, the bright colours will appear underneath. Make the letters wider to show more of the pretty colours underneath.

## Teaching point

Ask the children to bring their pictures to share with the group and then invite volunteers to read Amos 9:11–15. Ask:

- In what ways did Amos say God would restore Israel?
- If Amos came to our town today, what are some of the things he would tell us to stop doing?

Explain that Amos was someone who listened to God. He warned the people of Israel to stop doing wrong things and turn back to God, but only God is capable of removing the wrong things we do, say and think and finding the beauty that lies beneath. When we do something wrong, we feel bad. When we ask God's forgiveness, God removes the dirt and we feel bright and good inside.

# Obadiah

## God warns Edom to be humble

Bible story
Obadiah 1:1–21

Bible point
**God wants us to be humble.**

## Activity

### Mountains of pride

Make sand mountains to remind us of God's strength.

### ● You will need

Large balloons, funnels, felt-tipped pens, silver sand

### ● Preparation

Set out the craft supplies so that the children can easily reach them.

### ● Handy hint

If funnels are in short supply, cut the bottoms out of empty plastic bottles. For extra fun, give the children stickers of birds to attach to Edom's side of the mountain.

### ● Step-by-step

1. Inflate the balloon and then let the air out of it. Place a funnel in the opening of the balloon and fill the balloon with sand. Help the children to tie the end of the balloon.
2. On one side of the balloon, draw rocks, eagles and an eagle's nest. On the other side draw a crown.

## Teaching point

Tell the children the story of how the nation of Edom helped Israel's enemies to hurt Israel. Emphasise that the people of Edom thought they were so strong that they didn't need to pay attention to God, and that this is called 'pride'. Explain that the Edomites were proud. They didn't like Israel so they helped Israel's enemies. The Edomites thought they were too strong for anyone to punish them. The Bible says that they had so much confidence in their armies and strength that their pride was as big as a mountain.

Ask the children to turn their balloon mountains to the side with the eagle's nests. God said that the people of Edom hide in their pride the same way an eagle hides her nest in the rocks of a mountain. Ask:

• How did God feel about Edom's pride? Why?
• What kind of things should we be proud about?

Ask the children to roll their mountain to the opposite side. Explain that God wants us to put our pride in being protected by his strength. God's power is truly like a strong mountain in which people can hide and really be safe. The Edomites weren't truly safe by trusting in their own strength. God wants us to be humble and not put our pride in ourselves. When we are humble and trust God, he will be our protection.

# Jonah

## Jonah learns a lesson

> Bible story
> Jonah 1—2
>
> Bible point
> God forgives us.

## Activity

### Jonah in the big fish

Make big fish.

### ● You will need

Resealable plastic sandwich bags, twist ties, coloured tissue paper, scissors, copies of the template on page 89, crayons, felt-tipped pens

### ● Preparation

Photocopy the picture of Jonah praying (one per child). Cut coloured tissue paper into little squares. Place them in a pile and mix up the colours. Set up the supplies for the children.

### ● Handy hint

Ask the children to bring in small photographs of themselves to place in the fish along with Jonah, as a reminder that they also need to ask God for forgiveness. Alternatively, with permission from parents and carers, use a digital camera to take pictures of the children and have them printed out in readiness for the activity.

### ● Step-by-step

1. Colour Jonah and cut him out. Place a small handful of coloured squares in a resealable bag. Place Jonah inside and then seal the bag.
2. Lay the bag on the table so that it forms a diamond shape. A few inches from one point of the diamond, place a twist tie, and twist it so that a tail forms. Spread out the tail.

3. Using the felt-tip, draw an eye on each side of the fish.

## Teaching point

Use one of the fish to illustrate the telling of the story of Jonah 1:1—2:10. Then ask:

- What happened to Jonah when he disobeyed God?
- How did Jonah make things right with God?
- What should we do when we disobey God?

Explain that when Jonah realised that God knew he had disobeyed, he prayed and asked for forgiveness. We, too, need to remember to ask God for forgiveness when we do wrong. Often we think, like Jonah, that we can hide our wrongdoing. God knows all about us. When we do wrong, we feel bad inside. The only way to feel good inside again is to pray and ask God's forgiveness. God will forgive us.

# Jonah template

# Jonah obeys God

Age guide: 6-10s

> Bible story
> Jonah 1:1–3:3
>
> Bible point
> **God wants us to obey him.**

## Activity

### Just like Jonah

Make magnetic bookmarks.

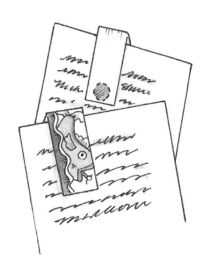

### ● You will need
Thick card, felt-tipped pens or crayons, scissors, adhesive-backed magnet strips, decorative stickers

### ● Preparation
Cut the card into strips measuring 20cm x 5cm. Cut the magnetic strips into 2cm lengths. Set up enough supplies so that each child will have one strip of card, two magnet pieces and crayons, felt-tips or stickers to decorate their bookmarks.

### ● Handy hint
Have the Bible verse written out on pieces of paper so that younger or less able children can simply copy it on to their project. If you want to save time, you can type the verse on your computer and print it on address labels that the children simply stick on the bookmark.

### ● Step-by-step
1. Fold the strip of card in half. On one side, write 'Jonah obeyed the Lord' (Jonah 3:3).
2. On the other side, draw a picture of what happened when Jonah didn't obey God.
3. On the inside of the strip, glue a magnetic piece on each end by the open edge. The bookmark can be folded around a page in a book and the magnets will hold it together.

## Teaching point

When the children have finished their bookmarks, let them put them in their Bibles and join you for Bible time. Tell the story of Jonah, using a children's Bible or an easy-to-read version. Then ask:

- What happens when we disobey someone who has asked us to do something?
- What did God want Jonah to do?
- What happened when Jonah obeyed?

Explain that when Jonah disobeyed, a big storm came and frightened many people. A big fish also swallowed Jonah. When we disobey, there are often consequences that follow, and sometimes our disobedience affects other people too. Good consequences also follow when we choose to obey. When Jonah obeyed God, many people were saved by the wonderful news about God. When we remember to be obedient, we also shine God's light on the people around us. God wants us to obey him. Invite the children to share ways they can be obedient at home and school.

# Jonah complains about God's compassion

Bible story
Jonah 3:1—4:11

Bible point
**God cares for us.**

## Activity

### Caring trees

Make fig trees as a reminder of the ways God cares for us.

● **You will need**

A4 sheets of green card, A4 sheets of yellow card, sticky tape, scissors, black felt-tipped pens or pencils, glue sticks

● **Preparation**

Set out the supplies. Take a piece of paper and trace the fig template (see illustration) several times. Photocopy on to yellow card. Now the children can simply cut out the figs.

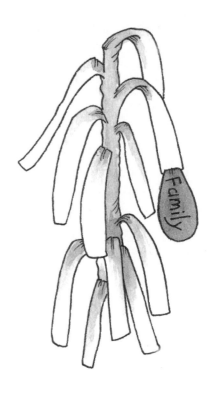

● **Step-by-step**

1. Tape two sheets of green card together, end to end, so that there is one long strip.
2. Starting at one short end, roll up the strip and tape it securely.
3. At one end of the tube, cut three-quarters of the way down. Make another three-quarter cut about 2cm from the first one. Continue making cuts until you have gone all the way around the tube.
4. Pull the inside layer of paper from the tube and your tree will grow.
5. Cut figs out of the yellow card. Write one way in which God cares for us on each fig. Glue the figs to the ends of the branches.

## Teaching point

Bring the group and their trees together. Tell the story in Jonah 3:1—4:11. Then ask:

- How did God care for Jonah?
- In what ways might we complain like Jonah?
- How does God care for us?

Explain that God sent Jonah a shady tree to cool him off, but Jonah was still angry with God for forgiving the people of Nineveh. Jonah grumbled. He didn't take care of the tree and it withered. (At this point in the story, show the children how to push their trees down into the tube to make them 'wither'.) Many times we get wonderful things from God but, instead of rejoicing, we grumble. We think we want something else or something more. We need to be thankful for what God has given us and look for ways to use it to his glory. Instead of grumbling, we should count all the ways God cares for us. (Show the children how to make their trees 'grow' again.)

# Micah

## God promises to remove our sins

Bible story
Micah 7:18–19

Bible point
God removes our sins.

## Activity

### Bottom of the sea

Make miniature oceans.

### ● You will need

Plastic bottles with lids, small pebbles, silver sand, coloured felt-tipped pens, funnels, water, washing-up bowls

### ● Preparation

Set out the supplies in two areas. In one area have the empty bottles, sand and coloured felt-tipped pens. Place the funnels and water in an area with the washing-up bowls. Keep the pebbles to one side.

### ● Handy hint

For extra fun, bring in small shells and large fish-shaped sequins for the children to add into their oceans.

### ● Step-by-step

1. Take a plastic bottle and draw pictures of fish all over the outside.
2. Remove the lid, place the funnel in the hole and pour a small amount of sand in the bottom of the bottle. Fill the bottle two-thirds full of water. Then tightly screw the lid on to the bottle.

## Teaching point

When the children have finished, ask them to sit in a circle. Ask a volunteer to read Micah 7:18–19. Then ask:

- What should we do when we know we have done, thought or said something that is wrong?
- How does it feel to know that God removes our sins?

Explain that Micah had just finished telling the people that God knew about their sins and that God was not happy, but God was also willing to forgive his people and forget about their sins. Set the pebbles on the floor in the centre of the group and ask the children to think about one thing that they have done, thought or said this week that they know is wrong—this is called a sin. Pause. Explain that Micah said that God forgives us and then throws our sins away to the bottom of the sea. Have the children carefully remove the lid from their oceans, drop a pebble down to the bottom and then replace the lids. Finish by saying that it is a great feeling to know that God throws away our sins and removes them far, far away.

# Nahum

## God brings peace

> ### Bible story
> ### Nahum 1:15a
>
> ### Bible point
> ### God sends us good news.

### Activity

#### Festive feet

Make painty footprints.

#### ● You will need

Flour, salt, water, poster paint, disposable aluminium pie dishes (one per child), measuring cups, plastic spoons, sheets of A4 paper, baby wipes, newspaper

#### ● Preparation

Mix equal parts of water, flour and salt and distribute the mixture into the pie dishes (one per child).

#### ● Handy hint

This craft would make a suitable gift for Mothering Sunday.

#### ● Step-by-step

1. Cover the floor with newspaper.
2. Invite the children to choose a colour of poster paint and add that colour to their dish. Help the children to stir the paint in with a plastic spoon.
3. Ask the children to take off one shoe and sock (roll up trouser legs if necessary). Write the child's name on the back of a sheet of paper and set it on the floor in front of him or her. Show the child how to step into the dish of paint and then step firmly on to the piece of paper.
4. Wipe off the child's foot with a baby wipe. Set the paper aside to dry. The paint will dry with a puffy texture.

### Teaching point

Read Nahum 1:15 to the children, using a child-friendly Bible version. Explain that God made all of our feet differently—our feet can do some amazing things. Then ask:

- What is some good news that we might run to tell our friends?
- What sort of things can we do for God by using our feet?
- Who can we run to and tell about God's good news?

Explain that in the Bible story, someone used his feet to tell sad people good news. God's people were sad because their enemies were hurting them. God told Nahum that he would tell his messengers to use their feet to give them good news. God would rescue them! God sends us good news to tell others.

# Habakkuk

Age guide: 7–11s

## Habakkuk complains about God's punishment

Bible story
Habakkuk 1:12–17; 2:4

Bible point
**God is too pure to tolerate wrongdoing.**

## Activity

### Eye care

Make cool sunglasses.

### ● You will need

Empty green-tinted plastic bottles (one per child), sandpaper, sharp scissors, sticky tape, felt-tipped pens (coloured and black), sunglasses template (see page 95)

### ● Preparation

Photocopy the sunglasses template (one per child) and set the supplies out on a table.

### ● Step-by-step

1. Cut the neck and bottom off the bottle and then cut a straight line vertically down the side of the cylinder.
2. Tape the sunglasses template to the table. Then tape the green plastic over the top of the template. Use a black felt-tipped pen to trace the sunglasses template on to the plastic. Decorate the glasses with coloured felt-tipped pens.
3. Remove the tape and carefully cut out the glasses with scissors. Smooth away any rough edges around the sunglasses with the sandpaper. The sunglasses are now ready to wear!

## Teaching point

Ask the children to wear their sunglasses and sit down in a circle. Read Habakkuk 1:12–17 and 2:4 and then ask:

- What is sin?
- Why doesn't God tolerate sin?
- What do you think sin does to our relationship with God?

Explain that God was punishing the people of Israel for their sin—but he used a nation that did worse things than Israel did, to do the punishing. This confused Habakkuk because he knew how God felt about sin. God's answer was that, in his own time, he would punish the Babylonians too. Because God is holy, he will never tolerate wrongdoing. God was showing Israel that they needed a Saviour to forgive their sins. That's why God later sent Jesus to die for us and remove our many sins. God sees all that we do. Just as the sun hurts our eyes, God is too pure to tolerate wrongdoing.

# Sunglasses template

# Zephaniah

# God gives his people hope for the future

> Bible story
> **Zephaniah 3:11–13**
>
> Bible point
> **God can use us to heal the world.**

## Activity

### Pure lips

Make homemade lip balm.

### ● You will need

Petroleum jelly (such as Vaseline™), small resealable plastic bags, a variety of flavoured essences (such as peppermint, vanilla, lemon, strawberry or cherry), plastic spoons, paper cups, paper towels

### ● Step-by-step

1. Place six level spoonfuls of petroleum jelly into a cup.
2. Invite the children to choose their favourite flavouring and add a few drops to their cup. Mix vigorously, being careful not to splash the mixture. Tell the children to use an index finger to apply the balm to their lips to test for taste. Add small amounts of flavouring at a time, if they need more.
3. If they like the taste, ask them to place their cup in a resealable plastic bag to keep it from drying out, and seal the bag shut.

## Teaching point

Start by saying that lip balm is used to heal our dry lips and keep them moist. Then read Zephaniah 3:11–13 and ask:

- What kinds of spoken words might feel dry and hurtful to others?

- How does it make us feel when someone says something kind to us?
- What kind words might make people feel soft and nice inside?

Explain that Zephaniah told God's people that, after God had disciplined them for their sins, he would help them do the right things. Zephaniah said that God would give the people lips that refused to tell lies (v. 13). God promises to help us be people who can make him and others happy. God is on our side and works to help us think, say and do things that will cause others to soften and turn to God. God knows that we say things that are bad, so he promises to purify us and help us be more like Jesus.

Each time our lips get dry, we can remember that God has provided help for us to be kind to others through his Son, Jesus, who is like a healing balm to the world. God can use us to soften people's hearts and heal the world.

# Haggai

Age guide: 6–10s

## God promises to use Zerubbabel

Bible story
**Haggai 1:1—2:9**

Bible point
**God gives us strength to complete his work.**

## Activity

### Completion of God's temple

Create ideas for remodelling the front of a church.

### ● You will need

Sheets of A4 paper, pencils, coloured pencils, rubbers, pencil sharpeners, rulers, coloured card, glue sticks, clipboards or trays (optional)

### ● Preparation

Gather the supplies you need (including this book) and place them in a bag or box. Take the supplies and lead the children outside to sit in front of your church to draw their ideas.

### ● Step-by-step

1. Ask the children to look at the front of the church and notice the overall shape of the building. It might be rectangular or square. Draw shapes to create an outline of the church building. Add features such as doors, windows or paths.
2. Notice the material that the church is made of, such as wood, brick or stone. Notice features such as trees, bushes or shrubs. Ask the children to think about what they would keep and what they would want to change to make it look nicer and glorify God.
3. Draw the changes and then use coloured pencils to enhance the drawing. When the children are finished, ask them to write their name at the bottom of the paper. Glue the drawings to a large sheet of card to make a display.

## Teaching point

Talk to the children about their drawings and let them share their ideas with the rest of the group. Ask for volunteers to read Haggai 1:1—2:9 and then ask:

- How does it feel when a job takes a long time to complete?
- How did it feel to redesign the front of the church on paper?
- What makes us carry on when things are difficult? What makes us give up?

Explain that God's people had begun rebuilding the temple about 16 years before, but they had become discouraged and had given up. God used Haggai to encourage the people and to remind them that he was still with them and could give them the strength to finish the work.

# Zechariah

## The Lord reigns

Bible story
Zechariah 14:20–21

Bible point
**Everything we have belongs to God.**

## Activity

### Posted notice

Make bag tags as a reminder that everything we have is to be used for God.

### ● You will need

Embroidery silks, decorative stickers, crisp canister lids (one per child), card circles measuring 8cm in diameter (one per child), glue sticks, felt-tipped pens, hole punch, masking tape

### ● Preparation

Cut the embroidery silks into 30cm lengths. Set out the supplies.

### ● Handy hints

If you have children who haven't learnt how to plait, check your local library and bring in a few books with simple diagrams for them to follow.

### ● Step-by-step

1. Glue a card circle to a plastic lid. On the circle, write the words 'For God's use'. Then decorate the circle. Don't forget to include your name.
2. Punch three holes close together below the words on your lid. Thread a length of embroidery silk through each hole and tie the silks in a knot behind the lid.
3. Tape the lid to a table with masking tape and plait the three pieces of embroidery silk, referring to the diagram if necessary. Knot the plait at the end to prevent it from unravelling.
4. Tie the bag tag on to a bag.

## Teaching point

Explain that the book of Zechariah is about what life will be like when Jesus is in charge. Zechariah said that even the everyday pots and pans would have signs on them that said, 'Set aside for God's use'. Nothing will be too ordinary to be used by God. Ask the children to get into groups of three. Ask each group to think of ways they can use the things they own for God's use. Read Zechariah 14:20–21 and then ask:

- How can we use the things we own for God?
- Is there anything that we own that we can't use for God? Why or why not?

Explain that one of the ways we can show we understand that God is in charge is to use everything we own to make him happy. That means we share with others. It also means that we don't pay more attention to our possessions than we give to God. Encourage the children to tie their tag to a bedroom door knob or a bag as a reminder that we should use our possessions for God.

# Malachi

Age guide: 7–11s

## God is coming

> **Bible story**
> Malachi 4:1–3
>
> **Bible point**
> Watch for the day of the Lord.

## Activity

### Marking time

Make calendars as a reminder that Jesus is coming back.

### ● You will need

Thick card, calendar pads (from stationers or the internet), glue sticks, felt-tipped pens, decorative stickers

### ● Preparation

Cut one 10cm x 15cm piece of card and one 10cm square of card for each child.

### ● Step-by-step

1. Glue the back of the calendar pad to the 10cm square card.
2. On the other piece of card, write the words 'Maybe today' at the top. Attach the calendar to the cardboard frame. Decorate as desired.

## Teaching point

Encourage the children to use their calendars to keep track of what day of the month it is. Suggest that one fun thing they could do with a calendar is keep track of special days, such as their birthday or the last day of school. Invite a few volunteers to read Malachi 4:1–3. Then ask:

- How does it feel to wait for a big day like Christmas or a birthday?
- What do we do to get ready for special days?
- What can we do to get ready for the special day when Jesus comes back?

Explain that Malachi's friends could not wait for the time when God would send someone to rescue them from their enemies. They called this day the 'Day of the Lord'. God promised to bring healing to all of his people who were hurting. God promised that the people who loved him would jump for joy. When Jesus comes again, it will be the 'Day of the Lord'. We don't know when that will be—but we can watch for the 'Day of the Lord' and pray it will be soon.

# God promises joy when Jesus comes again

Bible story
**Malachi 4:2**

Bible point
**God brings joy.**

## Activity

### Spin for joy!

Make toy cows that leap for joy.

### ● You will need

Medium-thickness rubber bands (two per child), medium-weight card, copies of the joyful cow template on page 101, stapler, greaseproof paper, cardboard tubes, crayons, scissors, pencils, craft sticks, glue sticks

### ● Preparation

Before the session, photocopy the template (one per child). Cut the cardboard tubes into lengths of about 12cm. Cut the greaseproof paper into 8cm circles. Set out the supplies.

### ● Step-by-step

1. Securely staple a rubber band to the bottom inside of a cardboard tube.
2. Place the greaseproof circle over the opening at the opposite end to the stapled rubber band. Secure the greaseproof paper with another rubber band.
3. Use a pencil to poke a small hole in the centre of the greaseproof paper. Thread the other end of the rubber band through the hole and staple the rubber band to the centre of a craft stick.
4. Cut out the cow and glue it to a piece of card. Trim around the card and decorate the cow with crayons. Glue the bottom of the cow to the craft stick.
5. Gently twist the cow until the rubber band is tight. Let the cow go and watch it spin for joy!

## Teaching point

Read Malachi 4:1–6 to the children. Explain that God's people were sad because many bad things were happening to them. Evil people were hurting them, and they wondered if it would ever get better. Ask the children to think of difficult times. With each hard time that the children suggest, invite them to turn their cows two full rotations. Encourage the children to continue suggesting ideas until the rubber bands are tight and are difficult to turn any further. Then ask:

- How does it feel when things are difficult? What can we do?
- In what way is the tight rubber band similar to how we feel when things are difficult?

Explain that sometimes, when things are hard, we feel tense inside. Through Malachi, God promised the people that he would send his chosen helper, the Messiah, to rescue the people. God said the people would be so happy that they would jump for joy like a cow released from its pen. Ask the children to hold their rotated cow by the base and then let go. Explain that now God has sent the Messiah, Jesus, to help us when things are difficult. We have a reason to be joyful. Jesus is our wonderful helper. God brings us joy through his Son, Jesus.

# Joyful cow template

# Matthew

## Wise men find Jesus

Bible story
Matthew 2:1–12

Bible point
**Show the way to Jesus.**

## Activity

### Spicy stars

Make star ornaments as a reminder of how the wise men and shepherds found the baby Jesus.

### ● You will need

Brown self-hardening clay, greaseproof paper, plastic knives, pencil, ribbon, paper plates, resealable plastic bags

### ● Preparation

Ahead of time, knead the clay until it is pliable but not too dry, and then store in resealable plastic bags (one per child). Cut the ribbon to 25cm lengths for each child. Set out the supplies so that each child will have a piece of greaseproof paper, a plastic knife and a length of ribbon.

### ● Step-by-step

1. Roll the lump of clay into a ball and flatten it into a large round circle that is flat and smooth.
2. Using the plastic knife, design and cut out a star shape, removing the outside pieces.
3. Use the pencil to put a hole near the top of the ornament. Leave to dry, and then carefully lift the star and thread the ribbon through the hole. Ask the children to write (or help them to write) their name on a paper plate. Place the star on the plate to take home. Let the star dry out for about five days before hanging it up.

## Teaching point

Bring the children together. Tell the story from Matthew 2:1–12 and then ask:

- How did the wise men know how to find the baby Jesus?
- How did they feel once they found Jesus?
- What are some ways we can show or tell others about Jesus?

Explain that the wise men followed a star to find the baby Jesus. They knew he was important because they had been studying the scriptures that told of his coming. God has given us the Bible to help us find Jesus. He has also given us church, teachers and family members to show and tell us about Jesus.

# Jesus is baptised

> Bible story
> Matthew 3:1–17; Mark 1:9–11;
> Luke 3:21–22
>
> Bible point
> **We are part of God's family.**

## Activity

### Heavenly doves

Make soap-on-a-rope doves as a reminder of how baptism symbolises that we belong to God's family.

### ● You will need

White bars of soap, small graters, water, vegetable oil, greaseproof paper, knitting yarn

### ● Preparation

Grate the soap until you have approximately three cups full. Add a quarter of a cup of water and knead until you have the consistency of modelling dough. Store in an airtight bag until ready for use. At each child's place, lay out a large piece of greaseproof paper and a length of yarn about 20cm long. Have each child rub a few drops of vegetable oil on their hands and then give them a portion of the soap clay.

### ● Handy hint

If the children have difficulty moulding the clay into a dove shape, let them flatten their clay slightly and then lay a simple dove template, cut out of card, on top and cut around the silhouette. Then they can mould and soften the edges by rounding them slightly.

### ● Step-by-step

1. Mould your clay into the shape of a dove.
2. Take a piece of yarn, fold it in half and knot it together.
3. Gently push the knotted end into the top of the soap dove. Let the dove dry overnight.

## Teaching point

When the children have finished, provide the means for them to wash and dry their hands and then gather together for the story of Jesus' baptism. Ask:

- What happened just after Jesus was baptised?
- How might the people watching have felt when they saw God's Spirit coming down in the form of a dove?
- How does it feel to belong to God's family?

Explain that Jesus shows us how important baptism is. When Jesus was baptised, God sent his Spirit like a dove. Also, God spoke to Jesus. When we're baptised, we're telling everyone who knows us that Jesus has invited us to be part of God's wonderful family.

# Jesus teaches about God's blessings

> ### Bible story
> Matthew 5:1–11
>
> ### Bible point
> **God wants us to give his blessings to others.**

## Activity

### Wheel of wonder

Make a wheel of the qualities that God finds beautiful.

### ● You will need

White card, scissors, crayons, split-pin paper fasteners, circle templates (see page 105)

### ● Preparation

Photocopy enough circle patterns so that each child has one. Set out the crayons, scissors and paper fasteners.

### ● Handy hint

Create a list of traits that highlight each of the blessings and mark the corresponding verse beside each trait. Post the list so that everyone can see it. If there is time, let the children identify the list.

### ● Step-by-step

1. Cut out the circles. Cut out the window on one circle.
2. Choose your favourite blessings, draw a picture of what attitudes they show and then write the blessing inside your picture spaces.
3. Place the circle with the window on top of the other circle and use a paper fastener to attach the two circles together. Turn the outer circle to view the various blessings.

## Teaching point

Ask the children to bring their circles to the group. Read Matthew 5:1–11. As you read each of the blessings, let the children turn their wheels to the correct picture. For each of the blessings, ask:

- What blessings does God want us to give others?
- What are some ways we can show others God's blessings at home or school?

Explain that when Jesus saw all the people who came to listen to him, he knew that he needed to teach them how God wanted them to act toward each other. Jesus gave the people a list of blessings that God wants his people to show others. When we display these traits in our lives, people are able to see God in us. God wants us to show others his blessings.

# Circles template

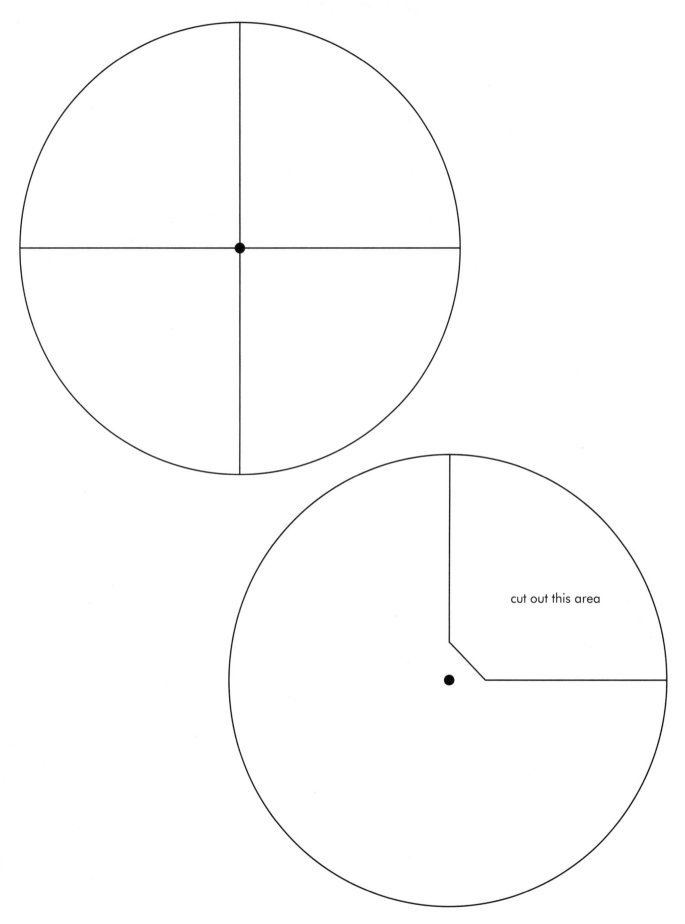

cut out this area

# Jesus teaches that we are to be like salt and light

> Bible story
> Matthew 5:13–16
>
> Bible point
> We are like salt for everyone on earth.

## Activity

### Salt painting

Make salt paintings that crystallise and glitter.

### ● You will need

World template (see page 107); table salt; green, yellow and blue food colouring; PVA glue; paintbrushes; thick card; resealable sandwich bags; paper plates

### ● Preparation

Place 100g salt in a sandwich bag. Add a few drops of green food colouring and close the bag. Knead the bag until the salt is a uniform colour. Prepare two more bags of salt in the same way, using yellow and then blue food colouring. Copy the world template on to card. For each child, set out the template, a paintbrush and a small container of glue.

### ● Step-by-step

1. Paint glue on to the ocean areas of the picture, and then sprinkle blue salt over the area. Gently shake the extra into a paper plate for someone else to use.
2. Paint glue on to the different continent areas of the picture and then sprinkle green salt over the separate areas. Gently shake the excess into a different paper plate for someone else to use.
3. Squeeze lines of glue to create sunrays around the earth. Sprinkle these with yellow salt. Set the picture aside to dry.

## Teaching point

While the pictures are drying, gather the children and read Matthew 5:13–16. Ask:

- What two things did Jesus say we are?
- What good things do salt and light do for us?
- In what ways might people act to be like salt and light at home or at school?
- How can our actions shine for Jesus?

Explain how Jesus taught that people who follow his ways are like salt and light. He showed us that, because of our example, people will know about God. If we don't share what we believe about Jesus and God with other people, it is like letting the salt lose its flavour or hiding a light where no one can see it. We need to let people see Jesus in us just as we can see the sparkle of the salt through the colours on our pictures. We are like salt for everyone on earth.

# World template

Reproduced with permission from *The Encyclopedia of Bible Crafts* published by BRF 2010 (978 1 84101 590 3) **www.barnabasinschools.org.uk**

# Jesus teaches us to pray

Bible story
Matthew 6:5–15; 7:7–11

Bible point
**We can talk to God.**

## Activity

### Prayer pockets

Make prayer pockets.

● **You will need**

Craft sticks, felt-tipped pens, A5 sheets of card, staplers, hole punches, knitting yarn, large sheet of paper

● **Preparation**

On the paper, clearly print the words from Matthew 7:7, 'Ask, and you will receive' and place the paper on the wall or in the centre of the work area for the children to copy. Set out the rest of the craft supplies.

● **Handy hint**

As a group, learn and pray the Lord's Prayer together. In closing, ask God to help each child to remember to have a daily prayer time.

● **Step-by-step**

1. Fold the short end of the card up three-quarters of the way. Staple it on two sides so that it makes a pocket.
2. On the outside of the pocket, copy the words from Matthew 7:7: 'Ask, and you will receive.'
3. On each craft stick, write one thing that you want to pray for and then decorate the craft sticks.
4. Place the craft sticks in the pocket. Using a hole punch, punch two holes at the top of the pocket. Cut a piece of yarn about 30cm in length and thread it through the holes on the prayer pocket so that the pocket can be hung by the child's bed at home.

## Teaching point

Ask the children to bring their finished sticks to the circle and together read what Jesus told us about prayer. Ask:

- What are some of the things we can pray for?
- Why does God want us to pray?
- How can we talk to God through prayer?

Explain that prayer is having a conversation with God. God wants us to talk to him every day. When we pray, we should remember to thank God for all the good things he has done in our lives. We need to ask God's forgiveness for the wrongs we have done. Finally, we should talk with God about the things we need. We can pray for our family and friends. We can talk to God through prayer about anything and everything. Encourage the children, each time they pray, to take out one stick, pray for what is written on it, and repeat with the next stick.

# Jesus walks on the water

Age guide:
7–11s

## Activity

### Walking on water

Illustrate the Bible story using paints and glitter pens.

#### ● You will need

Black craft foam, white card, brown and blue poster paint, sponges, clothes pegs, shallow dishes, gel pens, glitter glue pens, pens, glue sticks

#### ● Preparation

Before the session, cut the craft foam into 20cm squares. Cut several simple boat templates out of the white card. The boats should be approximately 12cm in length and 8cm high. Cut sponges into small pieces and attach the clothes pegs to the sponges to make handles for the children to hold. This will reduce the mess on fingers! Pour out small amounts of the paint into shallow dishes. Set up a designated area where children can place their pictures to dry.

#### ● Handy hint

Bring in an electric fan and, under supervision, allow the children to hold their pictures in front of it to dry the sponge painting quickly. That way, they won't drag their arms across the paint while finishing the rest of the picture.

#### ● Step-by-step

1. Stick a boat shape on to a black foam square approximately 5cm from the bottom of the square. Use a sponge to paint the boat.
2. Use the blue paint and sponge to paint the water.
3. Use the gel pens and glue pens to draw the disciples in the boat, Jesus walking on the water and other details such as the night sky and the waves. Then place your picture in the designated area to dry.

## Teaching point

When the children have finished their pictures, read the Bible story together. Then ask:

- How might it have felt to have been one of the disciples in the boat?
- What things make us afraid?
- How can we show that we trust in Jesus the next time we face something scary?

Explain that the disciples were very afraid when they were in the boat. They weren't sure who, or what, was walking on the water. When the disciples realised that it was Jesus, they were amazed. Jesus reminded them that they could put their trust in him and be brave—there was nothing to be afraid of. Trusting in Jesus makes us brave, too. When we are afraid, we can ask Jesus to help us.

# Not just seven times

Bible story
Matthew 18:21–35

Bible point
Get hooked on forgiving others.

## Activity

### The forgiveness game

Make a fun, repetitive game.

### ● You will need

Polystyrene cups, crayons, string, large beads, sticky tape, pair of compasses

### ● Preparation

Use the pair of compasses to punch a small hole carefully in the bottom of each cup. For each child, have a cup, a bead, some crayons and a length of string that is two and half times the length of the cup.

### ● Handy hint

Threading beads and tying them may be difficult for younger children. You may want to pre-string the bead and tie a knot on both sides of the bead so that it won't fall off while the children are completing the craft.

### ● Step-by-step

1. On the outside of the cup, ask the children to write, 'How many times should I forgive?' (Younger children will need help.) Then write, '70 x 7'. Let the children decorate the cup in their own unique way.
2. Tie the bead to one end of the string. Push the other end of the string through the hole in the bottom of the cup, from the outside in.
3. Tie a knot and tape the end of the string on to the inside bottom of the cup.
4. Holding the cup in one hand, swing the bead up and around and try to get it in the cup.

## Teaching point

Ask the children to bring their forgiveness games and sit in a circle. Ask them to keep count of how many times in a row they can catch the bead. Read the Bible story and then ask:

• How might the man have felt when the king forgave his debt?
• How might the friend have felt when the man wouldn't forgive his debt?
• Would we have been as angry as the king? Why or why not?

Explain that forgiving people is not always easy. Sometimes we are too hurt or angry to forgive. Sometimes we are too selfish. Whatever the reason, Jesus told us to forgive over and over again. Our game doesn't end when we get the ball in the cup—that just makes us want to try again to get the ball inside one more time. That is how we are supposed to forgive: to forgive others repeatedly. Ask each child to repeat the following statement, inserting their top number of catches in the blank. 'This week I will forgive not just …… times, but over and over again and again.'

# People rejoice as Jesus enters Jerusalem

Age guide: 5-7s

Bible story
Matthew 21:1–11; Mark 11:1–11; Luke 19:28–44; John 12:12–19

Bible point
We can praise Jesus.

## Activity

### One-man-praise band

Make one-man-band instruments.

### ● You will need

Small plastic containers with lids, thin white card, coloured pencils, blue or yellow corrugated paper, glue sticks, sticky tape, uncooked popcorn, plastic spoons, rubber bands

### ● Preparation

Before the session, wash and dry the containers. Using the white card, cut one 24cm x 12cm strip of paper for each child. Cut one 28cm x 5cm strip of the corrugated card for each child.

### ● Handy hint

Let the children use their one-man-band instruments during singing time.

### ● Step-by-step

1. Fill the container with enough popcorn to make a rattling sound when it is shaken, put on the lid and tape it firmly shut.
2. Using the coloured pencils, draw a picture of the Bible story on the white card.
3. Tape one end of the card to the container, wrap the card around the container and then secure the other end with tape.
4. Tape one end of the corrugated strip to the container, below the Bible story picture, wrap it around and glue the other end with the craft glue. Hold the ends down and count slowly to ten to let the glue set.

5. Place a rubber band around the container. The spoon will make a grating sound when rubbed on the corrugated trim, or you can use it to tap the top or bottom of the container. The container can also be shaken, or the rubber band can be plucked.

## Teaching point

When the children have finished their craft, read the Bible story together. Then ask:

- What would have been the most exciting part about being in Jerusalem the day Jesus came riding in on the donkey?
- How could we have praised Jesus that day?
- In what ways can we praise Jesus today?

Talk about the ways that we can praise Jesus. Explain that the Bible even says it is our job to praise Jesus. It makes Jesus so happy when we praise him.

# The last supper

> Bible story
> Matthew 26:26–30; Mark 14:12–26;
> Luke 22:7–38; John 13:1–38
>
> Bible point
> **Remember Jesus.**

## Activity

### 'Remember me' tags

Make lunchbox or backpack tags.

### ● You will need

A4 card, clear self-adhesive paper rectangles, felt-tipped pens or crayons, scissors, hole punch, ribbon or knitting yarn

### ● Preparation

For each child, you will need to cut one 5cm x 10cm card rectangle and two 7cm x 12cm self-adhesive paper rectangles. Set out the supplies, giving ample room for the children to work.

### ● Handy hint

Invite your minister to come and share with the children what Holy Communion means in your church.

### ● Step-by-step

1. On one side of the card, write 'Eat this as a way of remembering me!' (Luke 22:19). On the other side, draw a picture of a loaf of bread and a cup. Then decorate your card.
2. Peel the backing from one piece of self-adhesive paper and lay it sticky side up. Lay your card face down on the self-adhesive paper. Then remove the backing on the other piece of self-adhesive paper, and place it over the top. Keep the paper smooth so that there are no wrinkles. Trim around the edges.
3. Punch a hole in the top of the card. Cut a piece of yarn about 20cm long, fold it in half, and thread the loop end part-way through the hole. Put the two cut ends through the loop and pull gently. Tie the tag to a lunchbox or backpack.

## Teaching point

Gather the children into a group and review the Bible story. Then ask:

- How did Jesus tell his disciples to remember him?
- What are some ways we can remember how Jesus saved us?

Explain that sometimes we only remember about Jesus when we're in church, doing church things. Jesus wants us to remember him all the time—that he died so that we can be friends with God. Every time you see your lunchbox tag, remember that Jesus wants us to remember him, and that we'll eat with him in heaven some day.

# Mark

## Disciples follow Jesus

> **Bible story**
> Mark 1:16–20; Matthew 4:18–22; Luke 5:27–32; John 1:35–51
>
> **Bible point**
> We can tell others about Jesus.

## Activity

### Fishing game

Make fishing games.

### ● You will need

Medium-weight card, photocopies of the fishing game templates (see page 114), coloured pencils, black felt-tipped pens, scissors, paperclips

### ● Preparation

Photocopy one fishing game template for each child. Then set up the supplies in the craft area.

### ● Handy hint

Sing the song, 'I will make you fishers of men'. When you sing the word 'fishers', let the children show their craft fish.

### ● Step-by-step

1. Cut out the fish and decorate each one differently with the coloured pencils.
2. Open two paperclips, leaving a large hook at one end. Poke one paperclip through the mouth of a fish and one through the tail. Repeat this for all of your fish.
3. Find a partner. Drop all of your fish in a pile and take turns trying to hook as many fish together as you can. Each time you hook a fish, tell one thing you know about Jesus to your partner.

## Teaching point

When the children have finished their fish, ask them to bring their work and join you. Introduce or review the Bible story. Then ask:

- What did Jesus mean when he told his disciples that they would be fishing for people?
- What can we tell others about Jesus?

Explain that Peter, Andrew, James and John were all fishermen before they met Jesus. They spent all their time catching fish. When Jesus called them to follow him, he asked them to spend their time with him and tell others about him. We can tell others about Jesus too. We can be fishers of people.

# Fish template

Reproduced with permission from *The Encyclopedia of Bible Crafts* published by BRF 2010 (978 1 84101 590 3) www.barnabasinschools.org.uk

# Jesus chooses his first disciples

Age guide: 7–11s

> ### Bible story
> Mark 1:16–20; Matthew 4:18–22; Luke 5:27–32; John 1:35–51
>
> ### Bible point
> **Jesus wants us to be his disciples.**

## Activity

### Disciples wanted

Make 'situation vacant' posters to help Jesus find disciples.

### ● You will need

Newspaper 'situation vacant' ads, black card, gel pens

### ● Preparation

Cut newspaper ads to measure 23cm x 33cm. (You'll need one per child.) Gather the supplies and set them out for the children to use.

### ● Handy hint

Let the children display their posters in church for all to see.

### ● Step-by-step

1. Tear the edges of a black piece of card to make it look a little old-fashioned and then glue it on to the newspaper.
2. Use the gel pens to create a 'situation vacant' poster. Be creative and describe yourself as the person Jesus is looking for to be his disciple.

## Teaching point

When the children have finished their posters, ask them to join you, bringing their posters with them. Ask volunteers to read the Bible story. Then ask:

- What do you think it means to be a disciple?
- What kind of people did Jesus choose to be his disciples?
- If you saw and heard Jesus, would you want to be his disciple? Why or why not?

Explain that disciples are people who want to be like their teacher. They listen, watch and learn all they can from the teacher. Jesus wants us to be his disciples, too. When we believe that Jesus is God, and want to learn all about him and how he wants us to behave, we become his disciples. Jesus doesn't care if you're always right or do good things, because he wants to teach you his ways. Jesus wants us to be his disciples.

# The parable of the mustard seed

---

Bible story
Mark 4:30–34; Matthew 13:31–32;
Luke 17:5–6

Bible point
**We can help God's kingdom grow.**

## Activity

### Watch it grow

Make planters for seeds.

### ● You will need

Cardboard egg cartons (four squares per child), felt-tipped pens, potting soil, fast-growing seeds (such as mustard and cress seeds), cocktail sticks (four for each child), white paper, sticky tape

### ● Preparation

Beforehand, cut apart the egg cartons. Also cut four 5cm x 8cm pieces of the white paper for each child.

### ● Handy hint

Over the next few weeks, take a few minutes to allow children to report on how things are going with the people they are trying to tell about Jesus. Encourage successes, but equally encourage children who may be having a difficult time, by allowing the other children in the class to offer helpful suggestions.

### ● Step-by-step

1. Use the felt-tipped pens to decorate the outside of the egg carton.
2. Fill the egg cups with soil and plant some seeds in each cup.
3. Make flags out of the white paper and cocktail sticks by folding over the edge of the paper and taping it. Write the name of someone you will tell about Jesus on one of the flags, and then poke the flag into the soil of one of the egg cups. Repeat for each flag.

## Teaching point

When the children have finished their crafts, introduce or review the Bible story. Then ask:

- Who told each one of us about Jesus?
- What is one way that we can help someone else learn about Jesus?

Explain that the mustard seed is a very tiny seed and yet it grows into a bush big enough for birds to rest in. When we tell others about Jesus, we are like a little mustard seed that gets planted and then begins to grow. It starts with us and then we tell someone about Jesus, then they tell someone and soon many people know about Jesus. We can help God's kingdom grow by doing our part and telling others about Jesus. As you watch your seeds grow, let them be a reminder to you that you are helping God's kingdom grow by telling that special person whose name is on the flag about him.

# Jesus heals the blind man

> Bible story
> Mark 10:46–52; Matthew 20:29–34;
> Luke 18:35–43
>
> Bible point
> **Jesus wants us to see the truth.**

## Activity

### No more darkness

Make light switch plate covers.

### ● You will need

Sticky tape, light switch plate covers, fine-tipped felt pens in a variety of colours

### ● Preparation

Beforehand, tape the screws to the back of the switch plate cover. For younger children, pre-write the words 'I want to see!' on the front of the cover.

### ● Handy hint

Take the children to a room without windows and turn out the light. Ask the children what they can see. Turn on a torch and talk about how you can see a bit more. Finally, turn on the main light and talk about how you can see everything. Remind the children that when Jesus healed Bartimaeus, he healed him completely. Bartimaeus could see everything!

### ● Step-by-step

1. Ask the children to write their names on the back of the cover and the words 'I want to see!' on the front.
2. Decorate the front of the cover by drawing things that we would want to see if we had been blind.

## Teaching point

When the children have finished their switch plates, introduce or review the Bible story. Then ask the children to form groups of three or four and share the answers to the following questions in their groups. Ask:

- What might we have wanted to see if we had been blind?
- What is one truth that we can see—that we know about Jesus?

Explain that when it's dark we can't see anything, but when we turn on the light we can see everything—the truth is revealed. Being blind is like being in the dark. In our story, Bartimaeus could not see. Because he believed in Jesus, he was healed. When his eyes were opened, Bartimaeus saw the truth. Jesus wants us to see all the truths in the Bible. Tell the children to ask their parents to help them put their light switch cover on a light switch. Each time that they turn on the light, invite them to think about how Bartimaeus saw the truth when he saw Jesus.

# Jesus notices a widow's giving

Bible story
Mark 12:41–44; Luke 21:1–4

Bible point
**We can give to Jesus.**

## Activity

### My offering box

Make offering boxes.

### ● You will need

Empty cocoa containers, a sharp craft knife, coloured fine-tipped felt pens, art foam cut-outs, sequins, craft glue, acrylic paints and brushes, two pennies for each child

### ● Preparation

Beforehand, wash and dry the containers. Cut an opening in the lid of each container, large enough for a penny to drop through. Paint the containers and, if making this craft with younger children, pre-write the words 'my offering box' on the lids. Set up a designated area where children can place their offering boxes to dry.

### ● Handy hint

Encourage older children to think of ways that they may be able to earn some money this week, such as helping with extra household chores or doing jobs for a neighbour. Then talk with them about giving a portion of that money to Jesus.

### ● Step-by-step

1. Ask the children to write their name on the bottom of the container and 'my offering box' on the lid.
2. Use the foam cut-outs, sequins and felt-tipped pens to decorate the offering boxes. Paint a thin layer of glue on to the cut-outs and sequins and then stick them on to the container.
3. Place the offering boxes in the designated area to dry.

## Teaching point

When the children have finished their crafts, introduce or review the Bible story. Then ask:

- What might the widow have been thinking about when she gave all she had to the temple?
- How might we have felt if we had been one of the rich people and Jesus said we hadn't given as much as the widow?
- What is something that we can give to Jesus?

Explain that Jesus and his disciples were watching the people give their offerings. The rich people were putting in lots of money, but Jesus said that the widow who gave only two small coins had given the most. Jesus meant that, even though the amount she gave was less, she had given the greatest gift because she had given everything she had. We can give to Jesus, too. Not only can we give our offering, but we can give our praise and worship, our time and our talents. Give each child two pennies to put in his or her offering box as a reminder of the story. During the week, suggest to the children that they could put in more money and then bring the box back next week to share during offering time.

# Mary brings a gift to Jesus

> **Bible story**
> Mark 14:3–9
>
> **Bible point**
> **We can give gifts to others.**

## Activity

### A gift for you

Decorate oil bottles to be given as gifts.

### ● You will need

Felt-tipped pens, small plastic bottles with cork tops (from craft suppliers), cooking oil, funnels, paper towels, paper plates, multi-shaped sequins, craft glue, paintbrushes

### ● Preparation

Beforehand, divide the sequins on to paper plates. Set out plates for the glue to be squeezed on to before starting the project. Set up a designated area where the projects can be left to dry.

### ● Handy hint

After pouring the oil into the bottles, add a few drops of food colouring. Put the cork in the top of the bottle and shake to mix the oil and colouring. This will make the gift even more special!

### ● Step-by-step

1. Ask the children to write their name on the bottom of a bottle.
2. Use the funnel to fill the bottle with oil. Push the cork into the top as far as it will go. Wipe the entire bottle with the paper towel to remove any oil that may have spilled.
3. Paint a section of the bottle with a layer of white glue and add sequins. Continue this process until the bottle is completely decorated.
4. Set the bottle in the designated area to dry.

## Teaching point

When the children have finished making their crafts, introduce or review the Bible story. Then ask:

- What might our reaction have been to Mary's gift?
- How do we feel when someone gives us a special gift?
- How is that the same as, or different from, Jesus' feelings?

Explain that Mary gave Jesus a special gift by pouring a lovely-smelling oil over his head. Some of the disciples who were there, and saw what Mary was doing, were not very happy. Jesus told them that they should leave her alone because she was giving him a very special gift. We can give gifts to others, too. Suggest that the children could give their oil bottle to someone and tell him or her the story of Mary's special gift. The bottle can be used as a paperweight or just a decoration as a reminder of the story of Mary.

# Jesus rises from the dead

Age guide: 6–10s

> ### Bible story
> Mark 16:1–20; Matthew 28:1–7;
> Luke 24:1–12; John 20:1–31
>
> ### Bible point
> Jesus is alive!

## Activity

### Resurrection rolls

Make edible crafts that will illustrate the miracle of the resurrection.

### ● You will need

An oven, small bread rolls, cinnamon and sugar, large marshmallows, melted butter, spatula, baking sheet, greaseproof paper, small plates, serviettes, bowls, washing-up bowl of soapy water and a towel

### ● Preparation

Put the melted butter and cinnamon sugar in bowls. Preheat the oven to 350°F, 180°C or Gas Mark 4. Give each child a workspace that has a sheet of greaseproof paper on it. On the paper, place one bread roll and one large marshmallow.

NB: Be aware of food allergies. Be sure to read food labels carefully, as hidden ingredients can cause allergy-related problems.

### ● Handy hint

When children are working with food, make sure that they touch only their own ingredients. Make a piece of paper that is the same size as your baking sheet. As you put each child's 'tomb' on the sheet, write their name in the corresponding spot on your sheet. When you are ready to serve, you can be sure that each child gets his or her own 'tomb'.

### ● Step-by-step

1. Ask the children to wash and dry their hands.
2. Just like the women went to put spices on Jesus' body, let the children dip their marshmallow in butter and then roll it in the cinnamon and sugar mixture.
3. Next, carefully split the bread roll open. Put the marshmallow inside, mould the bread around the marshmallow and seal it up tight. (Be sure the edges of the roll are tightly pinched together.) Remind the children of how the guards sealed Jesus' tomb.
4. Place the rolls on the baking sheet and bake in the oven for 15–20 minutes.

## Teaching point

After the activity, ask the children to wash their hands again, and then gather together to review the Bible story. Serve the rolls on paper plates and ask someone to pray before eating. (The rolls will be puffed up, just like they were when they were placed in the oven, but when the children bite into them they will be empty on the inside.) Then ask:

- How might the women in the Bible story have felt when they saw the empty tomb?
- What might we have done if we had gone to visit Jesus' tomb and he wasn't there?

Ask the children if they were surprised to bite into their roll and find it empty. They knew they had put something in it. It was still sealed when it came out of the oven, but it was empty! Imagine how surprised and excited we would be if we had visited the tomb and found it empty. How thrilling it would be to realise that everything that Jesus had said and done really was true. Only the Son of God could conquer death. Jesus died to open the way to heaven for us. He rose again and went to prepare a place for us so that we can be friends with God for ever. Jesus is alive!

# Preaching the good news everywhere

Age guide: 5–7s

Bible story
Mark 16:15–17; Matthew 28:18–20;
Luke 24:44–49

Bible point
**Tell everyone about Jesus.**

## Activity

### I'll tell the world

Make globe magnets.

### ● You will need

Medium-weight card, scissors, ink pens, blue and green craft foam, adhesive-backed strip of magnet, craft glue, a globe or a picture of a globe

### ● Preparation

Beforehand, make several 15cm circles for the children to use as patterns. Cut the strip of magnet into two 2.5cm pieces per child. Photocopy the Bible verse from Mark 16:15 for each child and cut it out.

### ● Step-by-step

1. Using an ink pen, trace the circle template on to the blue foam and cut it out. Put the magnet strips on the back of the blue circle.
2. From the green foam, cut out pieces of land in any shape you want. If you wish, use the globe as a guide.
3. Lay the pieces of land and the Bible verse on the blue circle.
4. Glue the pieces in place using a thin layer of glue.

## Teaching point

When the children have finished their craft, introduce or review the Bible story. Then ask:

• Why is it important to tell others about Jesus?
• How do we feel when we tell someone about Jesus?
• Who can we tell about Jesus this week?

Explain that the Bible is very clear that we are to tell others about Jesus. It was not just a job for the first disciples or the people who lived during the time of Jesus. It is our job, too!

# Luke

## Jesus is born

Bible story
Luke 2:8–20

Bible point
**We can share the excitement of Jesus' birth.**

## Activity

### Shepherd pop-up cards

Make pop-up cards to share the excitement of Jesus' birth.

● **You will need**

Sheets of white A4 paper, pencils, scissors, crayons or felt-tipped pens

● **Preparation**

Fold a piece of paper in half. In the centre of the paper, from the fold outwards, draw two vertical lines, 5cm long and 2.5cm apart. Repeat so that you have one paper ready for each child.

● **Handy hint**

Provide large gold envelopes in which to place the cards. Arrange to deliver the cards, as a group, to other children or people in the community.

● **Step-by-step**

1. Use the scissors to cut slits along the two lines on the paper. Open the paper, push the centre piece in the opposite direction so it is on the inside of the card, and crease the fold line. This will be the 'pop-up' part of the card.
2. Take another sheet of paper and fold it in half. Glue the 'pop-up' paper inside the other whole sheet of paper.
3. With the paper's fold on top or on the left hand side, decorate the outside of the paper.

4. Open the paper. Draw a shepherd figure (about the size of your finger) on another sheet of paper and cut it out. Glue the back of your shepherd to the 'pop-up'.
5. Write an exciting message for your shepherd to share.

## Teaching point

Bring the children together in a circle. Explain that they have just made cards to share the excitement of Jesus' birth with others. When Jesus was born, the shepherds were the first people to spread the good news. Ask the children to act out the shepherds' emotions and actions as you read Luke 2:8–20 aloud. Then ask:

- How might the shepherds have felt when they saw baby Jesus, just as the angel had described?
- Why did the shepherds tell everyone what they had seen?
- How do we share good news with other people?

Finish by saying that after seeing and hearing the angel's announcement, the shepherds knew that Jesus was the promised Messiah—God's Son, whom they had been waiting for. We know even more about Jesus than the shepherds did because we have the Bible. We know that Jesus came to open the way for us to be friends with God so that we could live with him for ever. Like the shepherds, we can share the excitement of Jesus' birth.

# Simeon and Anna greet Jesus

Age guide: 5–7s

Bible story
Luke 2:22–40

Bible point
Jesus is the light to all people.

## Activity

### 'Light for all people' lanterns

Make lanterns.

### ● You will need

Coloured A4 paper or light-weight card, scissors, stapler, metallic stickers, baby food jars, votive candles, matches

### ● Preparation

Draw the cutting lines for the children to follow. Set up the supplies in your designated area. Keep the matches out of reach until you're ready to use them.

### ● Step-by-step

1. Hold the paper horizontally. Fold the top of the paper down to meet the bottom.
2. Cut slits in the paper from the fold to within an inch of the edges. Cuts should be about two finger-widths apart.
3. Unfold the paper and wrap it around to form a cylinder. Staple the ends together. Randomly place stickers on the outside of the lantern.
4. Place a votive candle inside a baby food jar, and set the lantern over the jar.

## Teaching point

Light one lantern to show the children how theirs will look. Turn off the lights to demonstrate the brightness of the lantern. Ask:

- What effect does light have on darkness?
- What would happen if I blew out this candle?

Tell the story of Jesus' presentation in the temple, and read Luke 2:22–32 from an easy-to-understand translation. Then ask:

- How is Jesus like a light?
- How does Jesus bring light to all people on earth?

Explain that Simeon predicted that Jesus would be a light for all people. This was important news because people of the Jewish faith believed that God's Saviour would only help them—not everyone else. When Jesus came, though, he showed everyone that he loved them and wanted them to know him.

# Jesus grows up

> Bible story
> Luke 2:41–52
>
> Bible point
> We can grow just like Jesus.

## Activity

### Growing-with-Jesus photo keepsake

Design photo keepsakes to display children's pictures of themselves growing as Jesus did.

### ● You will need

Heavy-weight cardboard, craft foam, ruler, scissors, pencils, glue, black permanent marker, measuring tape, alphabet stamps or stickers, gold glitter, smile stickers, 5cm wide ribbon

### ● Preparation

Cut the cardboard and craft foam into rectangles, each measuring 14cm x 18cm. Each child will need four rectangles of each material. Cut ribbon into 80cm lengths.

### ● Handy hint

Allow a few minutes for the children to share the kinds of photos they plan to put in each frame of their keepsake. Discuss what kinds of photos would be appropriate for each frame title.

### ● Step-by-step

1. Measure a 2.5cm border around one foam rectangle and cut out the middle. Use this to trace frames on three more foam rectangles. Cut out the middles of all of them.
2. Glue only the bottom and sides of each foam rectangle on to a cardboard rectangle so that the photos will slide through the top.
3. Write each of the following phrases on a separate frame: 'growing big', 'growing wise', 'loved by God', 'loved by others'. Then decorate each of the frames.
4. Fold over the top of the ribbon to form a loop. Space each frame equally throughout the whole length of the ribbon. Glue in place.

## Teaching point

Tell the story in Luke 2:41–51 and read verse 52 in an easy-to-understand translation. Then ask:

- How was Jesus different from any other child?
- Why is it important to know that Jesus obeyed his parents?
- How does it make us feel to know that Jesus grew in all the same ways that we grow?

Explain that the Bible tells us that Jesus grew physically, mentally, spiritually and socially—all the ways that we grow. Even though Jesus was truly God, he was also truly a human being. He was perfect in every way, yet he developed in the same way that we do.

# Satan tempts Jesus

Age guide: 7–11s

> Bible story
> Luke 4:1–13; Matthew 4:1–11;
> Mark 1:12–13
>
> Bible point
> **God helps us when we're tempted.**

## Activity

### Desert drawings

Make stained-glass window pictures.

### ● You will need

Fine sandpaper, crayons, an electric iron, white A4 paper

### ● Preparation

Plug in the iron and turn it on to medium high heat. Make sure it is in an out-of-the-way place and is supervised by an adult so that children don't get burnt.

### ● Handy hint

Bring in one or more children's Bibles and show the children how to look up an issue they may be struggling with, to find Bible passages that can help them. Help the children learn to use God's words as their defence, just as Jesus did.

### ● Step-by-step

1. Ask the children to use the crayons to draw a picture on the sandpaper of a time when they were tempted. Tell them to press down firmly and use lots of crayon.
2. Take the paper to the ironing area. Place the sandpaper drawing face-up on the ironing surface and lay the white paper on top. Iron the paper until the crayon picture can be seen showing through the paper.
3. Hold the finished picture up to a window to let the light shine through, giving it a stained-glass effect.

## Teaching point

When the children have finished their picture, introduce or review the Bible story. Then ask:

- When Jesus was in the desert being tempted by Satan, which temptation may have been the hardest one for him to fight?
- How did God help him turn from temptation?
- What is something that tempts us? Why?
- How can God help us when we are tempted?

Explain that today we drew on sandpaper. Explain that the sandpaper reminds us of the time Jesus spent in the desert, being tested by Satan. When we are being tempted by Satan, we can remember that God helps us. The best way we can do that is by following Jesus' example and using the Bible to fight Satan's temptations. When Satan tempted Jesus, Jesus quoted Bible verses. Each time we are tempted, we need to stop and ask God to help us remember the words we've read in the Bible. God helps us when we're tempted.

# The wise and foolish builders

Age guide: 5–7s

## Activity

### Solid rock texture pictures

Make texture rubbings to design an original picture.

### ● You will need

Sheets of A4 paper or newspaper, crayons, bricks or large stones, blocks of wood, scissors, glue, card, trays of silver sand

### ● Preparation

Have one table set with the paper, large stones or bricks, and a few blocks of wood. Set up another table with scissors, glue and card. Have crayons available at both tables.

### ● Handy hint

Before children do the stone rubbings, set out a tray of sand and let them attempt to do a sand rubbing. Afterwards, let the children compare how it felt to rub the sand and to rub the rock. They will find that the sand shifts, making it hard to rub; the stone is much firmer. Use this contrast to reinforce the concept that rock is strong and unmovable—a good illustration of Jesus' strength.

### ● Step-by-step

1. Remove the paper from the outside of the crayons if necessary. Place the paper over the stone or brick. Rub the side of a crayon over the paper and watch the texture appear.
2. Place the paper over a wooden block and do a crayon rubbing over it. Do this several times across the paper, so that there is a large area of wood texture. Ask the children to move to the next table.
3. Draw the outline of a house over the wood rubbings and cut it out. Cut out a section of the stone rubbing to use as ground.
4. Glue the stone rubbing near the bottom of a piece of card, then glue on the house so that it looks as if the house is built on stone.
5. Invite the children to draw a picture of themselves near the house. Add other details like trees, pets or other people.

## Teaching point

Set a tray of sand and a tray of stones in front of the children. Create a mound of sand and a mound of stones. Then place a plastic block on top of each of the mounds. Explain that the blocks represent houses. Ask:

• What will happen if the wind blows on these houses?

Let a few volunteers blow on the houses. Some sand may blow around the tray, but both houses should still be standing. Then ask:

• What will happen if it rains on these houses? Why?

Pour water on the houses. The house in the sand should shift a little. Explain that the Bible tells us about two houses just like these. Read the story from Luke 6:47–49. Then ask:

• How is sand different from the rocks we used in our rubbings?
• Why might Jesus have compared himself to a strong rock?

Explain that Jesus said that believing in him and obeying him is like building our house on strong rock. Although everything else is shaky like sand, we know that Jesus is the same for ever. We can know for sure that Jesus will hold us up—like a strong rock—no matter what happens.

# The farmer and the seeds

Age guide: 5–7s

## Activity

### The good brown soil

Make tactile pictures that tell the Bible story.

### ● You will need

White card, photocopied story picture (see page 128), yellow felt, coloured crayons, thick white craft glue, seeds, small rocks, small pompoms, perfume

### ● Preparation

Photocopy the story picture on to the white card. Pre-cut circles out of the yellow felt to represent suns.

### ● Handy hint

When doing multi-step crafts with younger children, it is always best if you are well organised. To help you keep everything for each square of the picture together, place all supplies for an individual square in a plastic zipper bag and label the bag. Only hand the children the supplies that they need to complete one square. When all the children have finished one square, choose the next bag and start the process all over again. You could do this craft as you tell the story, completing each square as you tell that section.

### ● Step-by-step

1. Colour the picture.
2. Glue the seeds on to the farmer's hand and on the path for the birds to eat.
3. Glue on the rocks and sun.
4. Glue the pompoms on as flowers and use a marker to draw a stem down into the good soil; then put perfume on the pompom flowers.

## Teaching point

When the children have finished their pictures, let them point to the appropriate square as you introduce or review the Bible story. Then ask:

- If we were seeds, where would we like to be thrown? Why?
- What are some ways we can grow in God?

Explain that when Jesus told this story, he was saying that the different soils were a bit like different people. Jesus was always telling fun stories like this. Jesus said that God wants us to grow. We grow strong when we listen to or read the Bible, pray, and go to church. When we do these things, we are like the good soil.

# The farmer template

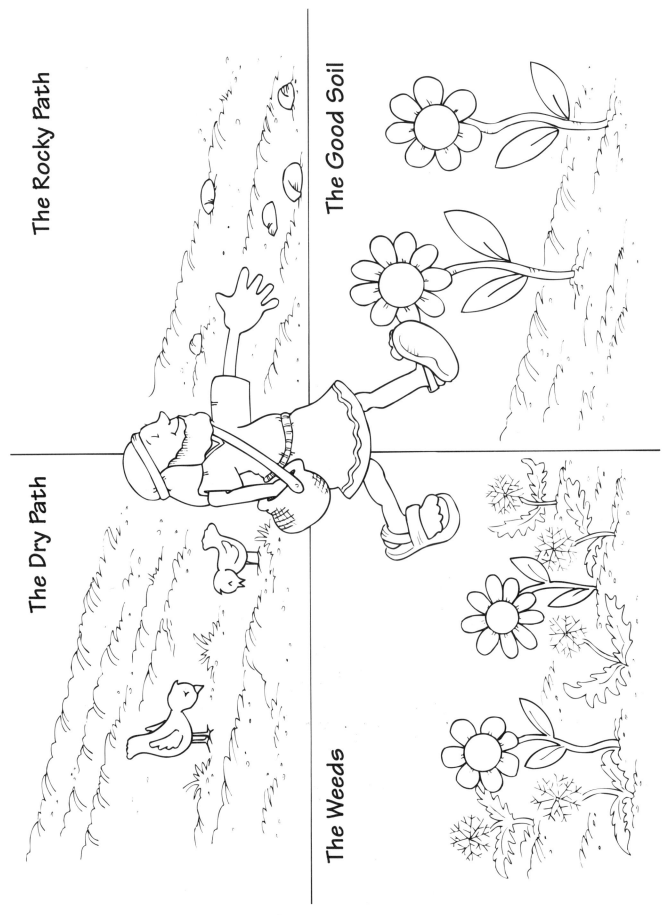

The Rocky Path

The Good Soil

The Dry Path

The Weeds

# Jesus tells about the good Samaritan

Bible story
Luke 10:30–37

Bible point
**We can help others in need.**

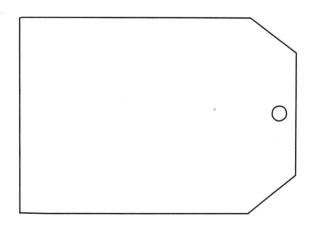

## Activity

### On-the-go first aid kit

Make simple 'first aid kit' key rings.

#### ● You will need

Thick card, craft foam, scissors, hole punch, plastic lacing or thick yarn, key rings, non-allergenic first aid plasters, individually packaged hand wipes

#### ● Preparation

Cut several 6cm x 10cm rectangles and several 6cm x 10cm tag shapes from the card. The children will use these as stencils.

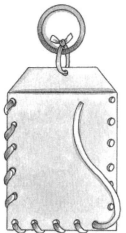

## Teaching point

#### ● Step-by-step

1. Give each child a tag shape and a rectangle. Trace each stencil once on to craft foam. Then cut out both pieces.
2. Punch holes around three sides of the foam tag, plus one more hole at the point of the tag. Holding the foam rectangle on the bottom, punch holes in the same places around three sides of the rectangle.
3. Use plastic lacing or yarn to sew three sides of these foam pieces together.
4. Tuck a hand wipe and a few first aid plasters inside the sewn tag.
5. Slip a small piece of lacing or yarn through the point of the tag and through a key ring. Then knot it.

Bring the children together in a circle. Then ask:

• When might a first-aid kit come in handy?

Tell the story of the good Samaritan in Luke 10:30–37. Then ask:

• How was the Samaritan different from the first two men, who walked past the man lying in the road?
• Why might Jesus have told this story?
• Are there times when any of us have been helped by someone we wouldn't have expected to help us?

Explain that, in Bible times, the Jewish people and Samaritans didn't get along with each other. It surprised Jesus' listeners to hear that the person showing compassion in this story was a Samaritan, rather than the priest or Levite. Jesus told this story to show us that we, too, can care for anyone in need. Invite the children to attach their on-the-go first-aid kits to their bags, so that they will be ready to help others in need.

# Jesus visits Mary and Martha

Bible story
Luke 10:38–42

Bible point
**Jesus wants our hearts more than our work.**

## Activity

### 'Hearts and hands' bunting

Make bunting to represent both Martha's and Mary's friendship with Jesus.

### ● You will need

Yarn or jute, card, pencils, scissors, hole punch, heart-shaped biscuit cutters, wooden beads, strips of cotton fabric, black marker pens

### ● Preparation

Cut the yarn or jute into one-metre lengths. Place paper, pencils, scissors and hole punches at one table. At a second table, place the pieces of yarn, beads and strips of cotton fabric.

### ● Handy hint

If the bunting isn't going to be sent home straight away, tie it end to end to use as a garland to decorate the church.

### ● Step-by-step

1. Let the children trace each of their hands on to card and cut out the shapes. (It may help to have a friend help trace the 'writing' hand.)
2. Trace the heart-shaped cutter three different times. Cut out the heart shapes.
3. Punch two holes, side by side, near the top of the hand and heart shapes.
4. Thread the hearts and hands alternately on to the yarn. Separate each cut-out shape by stringing on a few beads or tying on some cotton strips.
5. On the centre heart, write 'Hands to work, hearts to God'.

## Teaching point

Review the story of Mary and Martha from Luke 10: 38–42. Then ask:

* How were both Martha and Mary trying to show their love for Jesus?
* Why did Jesus say that Mary had chosen 'what is better'?
* Did Mary's love for Jesus mean that she never did any work?
* Which of us are more doers (like Martha) or listeners (like Mary)? Why?

Explain that sometimes we have to work—as Martha did—but our greatest love, our time, and attention must be given to Jesus. He loves us to spend time with him—reading his word, talking to him in prayer, and listening for him to speak. Jesus wants our hearts more than our work.

# Jesus heals a crippled woman

Age guide: 5–7s

## Activity

### 'Breaking free' crackers

Make 'breaking free' celebration crackers.

#### ● You will need

Assorted colours of tissue paper, rulers, scissors, cardboard tubes, parcel ribbon, clear tape, sweets or small toys (such as whistles, tops or plastic rings), a large basket

#### ● Preparation

Cut the cardboard tubes into 5cm pieces. Cut pieces of tissue paper into rectangles measuring 18cm x 30cm. Then set out the supplies.

#### ● Handy hint

For even more celebration, let the children add a small handful of confetti or streamers to their breaking-free surprises before tying them shut.

#### ● Step-by-step

1. Lay two sheets of tissue paper flat on a table. Place a cardboard tube in the centre of the tissue paper. Roll the paper around the outside of the tube and tape in place.
2. Tie one end of the tissue paper with parcel ribbon. Take a sweet or small toy and put it inside the tube.
3. Tie the other end of the cracker in place with ribbon. The tissue paper should extend 5–8cm beyond the edge of the cardboard tube.
4. Decorate the cracker with scraps of other tissue paper or stickers. Set the cracker to one side until later.

## Teaching point

Explain that as today's Bible story is read, the children need to try to guess which people need Jesus to free them. Ask for volunteers to read Luke 13:10–17 in an easy-to-understand version. Then ask:

- How might Jesus have felt when he first saw the crippled woman?
- How did Jesus set the woman free?
- From what did the synagogue ruler need to be freed?

Explain that some of the synagogue teachers during Jesus' time liked to make themselves feel important by making people follow lots of rules. Jesus knew that their hearts were bad, even though they may have done good deeds and looked good on the outside. Jesus freed the crippled woman from her disease and he wanted to free the synagogue ruler from his pride. Jesus can free us from all sorts of things that keep us from growing closer to him. Ask:

- From what might we like Jesus to free us?

Explain that the crackers are a symbol of breaking free. Show the children how to pull them open—break them—and receive a surprise. Let children pick a cracker, making sure that they don't choose their own. On a given signal, let the children break open their surprises in celebration of the freedom Jesus gives.

# Jesus looks for the lost lamb

Age guide: 5–7s

Bible story
Luke 15:3–7; Matthew 18:10–14

Bible point
**Jesus always finds us.**

## Activity

### Lost-and-found lamb

Create hiding lambs.

#### ● You will need

Three different sizes of white pompoms, craft glue, small movable eyes, black pipe cleaners, string, paper cups, small beads, pens

#### ● Preparation

Cut the pipe cleaners into four equal-sized pieces. Cut string into 35cm lengths.

#### ● Step-by-step

1. Glue a medium-size pompom to a large one. This forms the head and body of a sheep. On the opposite end of the body, glue a small pompom to form the tail.
2. Glue two eyes to the head. Cut a small piece of pipe cleaner into two pieces. Bend each in a loop to form ears, and then glue them in place.
3. Bend two more pipe cleaners to form U-shapes. Glue the bent part of both pieces to the body to form the legs.
4. Tie a piece of string around the lamb where the body and head are glued together.
5. Use a pen to poke a small hole through the bottom of a paper cup. Thread the free end of the string through this hole so that the end of the string is on the outside of the cup. Then tie a bead to the end of the string so that the string doesn't slip through the hole.

## Teaching point

Let the children try scooping the lamb into their cup. Explain that the paper cup is like the sheepfold that holds a large flock of sheep, but the lamb keeps running away. Read the story in Luke 15:3–7. Then ask:

- Are there times when any of us have been lost for a little while? How did it feel?
- What did the shepherd do when he realised that a lamb was lost?
- What might happen if the lamb is left on its own?
- How might the lamb have felt when it was found and carried home?

Explain that Jesus told this story so people would understand that Jesus is like the shepherd who searched for the lost lamb. Jesus searches for people who are far from God. Just like the lost lamb, these people seem unable to find him. Jesus rejoices to find those who are lost and brings them back home—to himself. Jesus always finds us.

# Zacchaeus climbs a tree to see Jesus

Age guide: 5–7s

Bible story
Luke 19:1–10

Bible point
**Jesus can help us change.**

## Activity

### Sticky Zacchaeus pictures

Make a picture that will change by adding hand-made stickers.

### ● You will need

Large sheets of white or manilla-coloured card, A4 paper, crayons, scissors, PVA glue, vinegar, plastic bowls, spoons, paintbrushes, greaseproof paper, damp sponge or cloth, newspaper

### ● Preparation

Mix together half a cup of glue and two tablespoons of vinegar. Pour into several plastic bowls. Have one table prepared with the paper, scissors and crayons. Have another table covered with newspaper. Set the glue mixture and paintbrushes on this table.

### ● Handy hint

When all the stickers have dried, let the children swap their picture and sticker kits with a friend. This will allow everyone the 'surprise' element of completing a different sticker picture.

### ● Step-by-step

1. On a large sheet of card, draw an outdoor background scene that includes a tall tree. Leave the picture open so that more details can be added later.
2. On a piece of paper, draw a picture of a small man (Zacchaeus) and a picture of Jesus. Let the children also draw other details if they wish to add to their picture, such as birds, sunshine or other people. Colour and cut out these figures.
3. At the next table, turn the cut-out figures over and brush the glue mixture all over the reverse sides. Then place the figures on greaseproof paper to dry.
4. When the figures have dried, let the children dampen them with a wet sponge or cloth and stick them on the background of their picture.

## Teaching point

Explain that the pictures the children have made change when more details are added. The picture becomes more colourful and exciting. Jesus can help to change our lives, too. Ask the children to listen to the story of how Jesus helped to change one man's life. Take turns reading the story of Zacchaeus in Luke 19:1–10. Then ask:

- At the beginning of the story, what was the most important thing in Zacchaeus' life?
- How might Zacchaeus have felt when he finally saw Jesus?
- How had Zacchaeus changed by the end of the story?

Explain that in Bible times, tax collectors were known for cheating innocent people out of their money. Zacchaeus was one of these rich tax collectors. After meeting with Jesus, though, Zacchaeus decided to change. He promised to give to the poor and repay over and above the amount he had cheated from others. When we come to love Jesus, we want to obey him and become more like him. Jesus can help us change, too.

# John

## God lives with us

Bible story
John 1:4–5

Bible point
**Jesus will light the way for us.**

## Activity

### Jesus ahoy!

Make lighthouses to remember that Jesus is the light that shines in the darkness.

### ● You will need

Cardboard tubes, additional cardboard, white paper, rulers, black electrical tape, small yellow stickers, red felt-tipped pens, glue, two bottle tops from large plastic bottles for each child

### ● Preparation

Use a tube as a guide to trace and cut out one cardboard circle about 2cm larger than the tube for each child. Cut white paper into 11cm x 15cm pieces (one per child). Set out one cardboard tube, one piece of cardboard, two bottle tops and one sheet of white paper per child. Then set up the rest of the supplies for the children to share.

### ● Step-by-step

1. Glue the cardboard circle to the top of the tube, and glue the white paper around the tube.
2. Attach two bottle tops together with black tape, then glue them to the top of the tube. Cut tiny squares out of the yellow stickers and attach them to the bottle tops to create window effects.
3. Draw red stripes on the lighthouse with a felt-tipped pen.

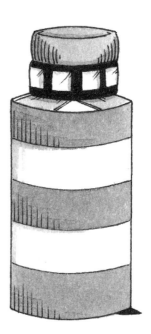

## Teaching point

When children have finished their lighthouses, ask them join you. Ask for volunteers to read John 1:4–5. Then ask:

- How do lighthouses help people at sea?
- How can Jesus' light help us?
- Who is Jesus' light shining for?

Explain that when people are lost at sea, lighthouses can help them find their way home. Jesus is like a lighthouse for us because he gives us the light of hope that helps us through life. When we feel lost, confused or alone, all we have to do is read the Bible and ask Jesus to show us what to do next.

# Jesus performs his first miracle

Age guide: 5–7s

Bible story
John 2:1–10

Bible point
Jesus can make amazing things happen.

## Activity

### Water or wine?

Make 'stone' water pots as a reminder of Jesus' miracle at Cana.

### ● You will need

Yoghurt pots, white paper, glue, paintbrushes, sponges cut into strips (one strip per child), black or grey paint, purplish-red acrylic paint, paintbrushes, aprons

### ● Preparation

Cut strips of white paper into 6cm x 10cm lengths (two per child). Set out one yoghurt pot, one paintbrush, two pieces of white paper and one sponge strip per child. Set out the rest of the supplies for the children to share.

NB: Open windows for proper ventilation when working with acrylic paints.

### ● Handy hint

If you have time, create a water pot of your own ahead of time so that you can demonstrate the water-into-wine illusion for the children. Suggest that children use their 'water pots' at home as small vases or containers for coins, pencils and so on.

NB: Remind the children *not* to drink from the cups, because of the acrylic paint.

### ● Step-by-step

1. Let the children put on an apron to protect their clothing. Glue the white pieces of paper around a yoghurt pot.
2. Paint the inside of the pot with the purplish-red paint, leaving about one inch of white space at the top. Then paint the outside of the cup with black or grey paint by dipping the end of the sponge strip in the paint and gently pressing it to the cup all over for a rough, clay-type effect.
3. When the pot is dry, let the children find a partner and take turns telling the Bible story to each other.

## Teaching point

When the children have finished painting their water pots, ask them to join you in a circle. Introduce or review the Bible story and then ask:

- Who gave Jesus the power to do miracles?
- Why might Jesus have done the miracle at Cana?
- What would happen if we poured water into the water pots we just made?

Explain that if we pour water into our 'water pots', it will look like wine because of the purple paint. This will help us remember Jesus' miracle at Cana. Jesus miraculously changed the water in the water pots into wine. Jesus helps us with *all* our problems, no matter how big or how small, if we ask him for help. Invite each child prayerfully to share one 'small problem' to ask Jesus to help them with. Ask the children to join you in closing the prayer by saying, 'In Jesus' name. Amen'.

# Jesus explains eternal life to Nicodemus

Age guide: 5–7s

## Activity

### Butterflies are beautiful!

Create paintings of butterflies to remember Jesus' promise of eternal life to all who believe in him.

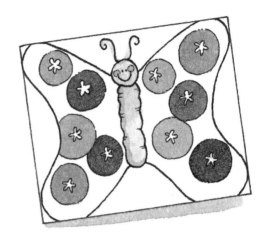

#### ● You will need

Large sheets of white paper, apples (one for every two children), knife (for leader), black plus several bright colours of acrylic or poster paint, paintbrushes, pencils, felt-tipped pens (optional)

#### ● Preparation

Cut the apples in half horizontally so that the star in the centre of the core is revealed. Set up the supplies, leaving plenty of room for each child to paint and print.

#### ● Handy hint

Younger children may do better if the teacher sketches the outline of the butterfly for them. You may want to discuss the 'eternal life' represented by the apple seed stars. When seeds fall to earth, they are 'buried', but later they bring forth new life.

#### ● Step-by-step

1. Draw the outline of a butterfly (body, head with face, and wings) with a pencil, using up most of the space on the paper. Go over the outline with paint or felt-tipped pen.
2. Use the apples to print colours inside and design your butterfly's wings. Swap to a different colour when the first is finished. Continue until the butterfly is filled with colour.

## Teaching point

When the children have finished, ask them to join you. Choose a volunteer to read John 3:16. Then ask:

- How did God show his love for the world?
- Why did God send Jesus to our world?
- How can we have the freedom of eternal life?

Explain that God loved the world so much that he sent us his only Son, Jesus. All we need to do to have eternal life is believe in Jesus. Caterpillars make a cocoon around themselves and later burst out in freedom as beautiful butterflies. This is like Jesus' wonderful promise to us: when we die, we will have beautiful new lives in heaven with Jesus for ever. Jesus gives the promise of true life with him here on earth and the freedom of eternal life.

# Jesus talks with a Samaritan woman

Age guide: 5–7s

> Bible story
> John 4:1–26
>
> Bible point
> **Jesus gives us the water of eternal life.**

## Activity

### It's raining, it's pouring!

Make water-drop people as a reminder of the water Jesus gives us.

● **You will need**

Small blue balloons, felt-tipped pens, sticky tape, blue parcel ribbon

● **Preparation**

Blow enough air into the balloons to create a water-drop shape (one balloon per child). Make a few extras for visitors or to replace any balloons that may burst. Set out the supplies.

● **Handy hint**

Suggest to children that they can display their water-drops near a sink at home. Whenever they go for a drink of water, their water-drop will remind them that water gives us life and refreshes us, but Jesus gives us life that lasts for ever.

● **Step-by-step**

1. Use the felt-tipped pens to draw facial and body features on the water-drop balloons.
2. Cut and tape the ribbon on to the base of the water-drop to create a watery effect.

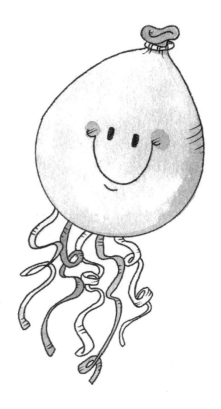

## Teaching point

When the children have finished their water-drop people, ask them to join you in a circle. Play an upbeat Christian CD that is familiar to the children and let them toss their water-drops up in the air and watch the watery effect as the balloons come down. At the end of the song, turn off the CD and ask the children to recite the Bible point: Jesus gives us the water of eternal life. Introduce or review the Bible story. Then ask:

• Has anyone ever felt sad? What happened?
• What special promise did Jesus give the woman at the well?
• What might Jesus have meant by 'water that gives eternal life'?

Explain that the woman at the well was sad until she met Jesus. Water from a fountain moves and is refreshing. When we look around at all the things God does for us each day, it makes us feel happy and refreshed.

# The feeding of the 5000

Age guide: 7–11s

Bible story
John 6:1–15; Matthew 14:15–21;
Mark 6:34–44; Luke 9:10–17

Bible point
**Share with others.**

## Activity

### Loving lunch boxes

Make lunch boxes as a reminder of the miracle.

### ● You will need
Photocopies of the lunch box template (see page 139), sheets of A4 card, felt-tipped pens, stickers, glitter, scissors, ribbon

### ● Preparation
Photocopy the template on to card (one per child). Gather up stickers, glitter, felt-tipped pens and any other things that would be fun to embellish the boxes with. Cut the ribbon into 20cm lengths.

### ● Handy hint
When sharing, children generally think of sharing material things such as food or toys. Help them think of other ways people can share with each other. Give the children some suggestions that they can try at home and school, such as helping others or letting someone go first. During the session, affirm children for sharing with each other.

### ● Step-by-step
1. Cut out the lunch box template. Then decorate the box as a reminder of Jesus' love.
2. Fold along all the dotted lines, and glue the long sides together.
3. Fold tab 1 down, and tuck tabs 2 and 3 in the slot. Tuck tab 4 in the slot.
4. Punch two holes over the circles on each side.
5. Tie the ribbon to each hole so that it forms two handles.

## Teaching point

Bring the children together and review the story. Ask:

- What miracle did the people see?
- How might the people have felt when they saw all the food left over?
- How might the boy have felt when he saw what Jesus did with his lunch?
- What are some ways we can share with others, as the boy did in the story?

Explain that the little boy in the story gave away all he had to help Jesus. Sometimes it is hard to give away something that we really want for ourselves. Jesus gave his life for us. We need to remember that when we don't want to share. Every time we put someone else's needs before our own, we are sharing the miracle of Jesus' love. Jesus wants us to share with others. Let the children think of ways in which they can share in the coming week.

# Lunch box template

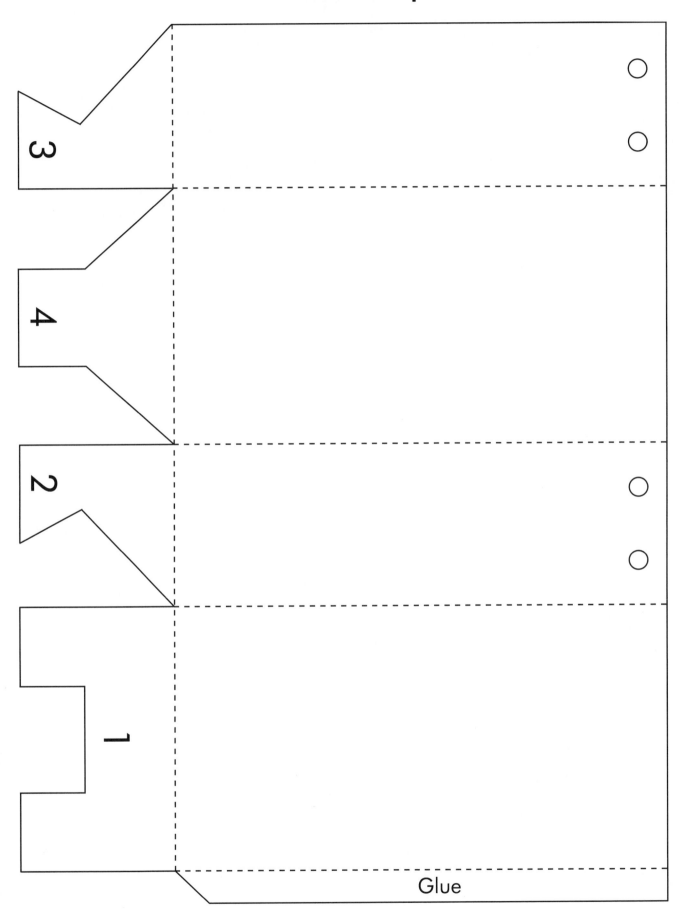

3

4

2

1

Glue

# Jesus is the bread of life

Age guide: 5–7s

Bible story
John 6:35

Bible point
Jesus is the bread of life.

## Activity

### Have a slice of life!

Make bread pictures to remember that Jesus is the bread of life.

● **You will need**

White or brown card, crayons or felt-tipped pens, scissors, glue, stalks of wheat or yellow wax paper straws

● **Preparation**

Cut the wheat stalks or straws into 8cm lengths. Each child will need ten stalks. Set out one piece of paper for each child. Other supplies can be shared from a central location.

● **Handy hint**

Bring in magazine pictures of different kinds of breads that children can cut out and glue to their pictures. Encourage children to display their bread pictures in the kitchen or dining room at home to help their families remember Jesus' promise of eternal life.

● **Step-by-step**

1. Draw a large outline of a slice of bread on the paper, using up most of the space of the paper.
2. On the top half of the slice of bread, write 'Jesus is the bread of life'. Give help where needed.
3. Arrange the wheat stalks or straws at the bottom of the bread slice to spell the word 'LIFE'. Then glue to the paper.

## Teaching point

When the children have finished their pictures, ask them to join you. Ask a volunteer to read John 6:35. Then ask:

• What is bread made of?
• How does it help our bodies?

Explain that in the Bible verse, Jesus is talking about a new kind of bread—the bread of life. We need food every day, and we need Jesus every day, too. The bread of life is Jesus. We can invite Jesus to be a part of our lives each day by praying, reading the Bible, saying grace before meals, and by thinking about him throughout the day.

# Jesus is the good shepherd

Bible story
John 10:11–16

Bible point
**Jesus is the good shepherd.**

## Activity

### Jesus, the good shepherd

Make shepherd puppets as a reminder that Jesus is the good shepherd and we are his sheep.

### ● You will need

Scraps of fabric, empty lemonade bottles, glue, scissors, 6cm diameter polystyrene balls (one per child), wobbly eyes, aluminium foil, parcel tape, felt-tipped pens, knitting yarn

### ● Preparation

Set out the supplies so that children can reach them.

### ● Step-by-step

1. Cut the label off the bottle. Take a polystyrene ball and press it firmly down on to the top of the bottle to create the shepherd's head. Cut knitting yarn to glue on to the shepherd's head and create the facial features by gluing on the wobbly eyes and creating a mouth with yarn or felt-tipped pens.
2. Mould foil to create two arms, then attach the arms to the shepherd's upper body with pieces of tape.
3. Cut a large rectangular piece of fabric that will reach from the back of the shepherd's feet, up over his head and down to the front of his feet. Fold the rectangle in half and cut a hole in the centre of the fold to create space for his head. Slide the fabric over the shepherd's head. Cut a smaller rectangle and place it on the head of your shepherd for his head covering.
4. Cut two thin strips of fabric, one to tie around the head and another longer one to use as a belt.
5. Mould a shepherd's staff out of the aluminium foil and attach it to one of the shepherd's hands.

## Teaching point

When the children have finished their craft, ask them to join you, bringing their shepherds with them. Choose volunteers to help read John 10:11–16. Then ask:

- What does a shepherd do?
- How might the shepherd have felt about his sheep?
- Why might Jesus have said that he is like a good shepherd to us?

Explain that a shepherd takes care of his sheep, feeds them, makes sure that they're healthy and leads them to good pasture. He also protects them from wolves and other animals that might harm them. The sheep trust their shepherd. They love him and follow him. Jesus is our shepherd because he loves and protects us. Let the children take turns making their shepherds tell each other how Jesus takes care of them or their families.

# Acts

## Jesus ascends to heaven

Bible story
Acts 1:9–11; Mark 16:19–20;
Luke 24:50–53

Bible point
**Jesus promises to return.**

## Activity

### Splatter sky pictures

Make splatter paintings depicting the ascension.

### ● You will need

White card; pencils; scissors; newspaper; shades of blue, purple and some yellow paint in separate shallow bowls; toothbrushes; craft sticks; large washing-up bowls

### ● Preparation

Place some card, pencils and scissors on one table. Cover another table with newspaper and place the washing-up bowls, card, paint, craft sticks and toothbrushes on it.

### ● Step-by-step

1. Draw and cut out two or three cloud shapes. The clouds should be about the size of the child's hand or smaller.
2. Take the cloud shapes to the next table. Put a full sheet of paper in a washing-up bowl. Place the clouds in different places on the paper. Leave space between the clouds.
3. Dip a toothbrush into one of the colours of paint. Point the toothbrush at the area to be painted and slowly draw the craft stick toward you along the bristles of the toothbrush. Fill the whole paper with a 'splattered' sky.
4. Remove the clouds discard them. Look at the sky on the paper!

## Teaching point

Tell the story of Jesus' ascension from Acts 1:9–11. Then ask:

- How do you think the disciples felt, watching Jesus go higher and higher up to heaven? What did they do?
- How might we have reacted if we had been there? What might we have said? How might we have felt?

Explain that Jesus went to heaven in a way that no one else could. Besides giving the disciples an incredible memory of him, Jesus wanted to show them again that he was truly God. He promises to return in the same amazing way. When he does, everyone will know that he is God.

# Jesus sends power from God

Age guide: 5-7s

---

Bible story
Acts 2:1–4

Bible point
God gives us the power of the Holy Spirit to tell others about him.

## Activity

### Tongues of fire

Paint tongues of fires as a reminder of Pentecost.

#### ● You will need

White card; powder paint in red, yellow and orange; clear glue; water; spray bottles; clingfilm; sticky tape; painting aprons; paper towels; a plastic tablecloth; a waste bin

#### ● Preparation

Make flame paint by mixing each of the three powder paints with glue and enough water to make a thin, gluey mix. Pour into small spray bottles and shake vigorously until mixed. Lay the tablecloth across a table. Set out the card, pens, clingfilm, waste bin, sticky tape, paper towels and a bowl of soapy water for cleaning up.

#### ● Step-by-step

1. Help each child to put on a painting apron and write their name on the back of a piece of white card.
2. Spray a few drops of each colour on the card. Cover the card with clingfilm. Press down on the paints to blend and smear the colours to make different flame designs.
3. When the artwork is finished, remove the clingfilm and throw it in the waste bin.
4. Use soapy water to clean hands and any spills or splatters of paint that may have occurred.

## Teaching point

When the children have completed their painting, invite them to join you. Introduce or review the Bible story. Then ask:

- If we were news reporters that day, what would we have told our audience?
- Why does God give us his Holy Spirit?

Explain that the Bible tells us that God sent his Holy Spirit to fill us with God's power so we can boldly tell others about him. When the Holy Spirit came, tongues of fire appeared over the disciples' heads. Just as we spread the paint around our pictures, God gives us the power of the Holy Spirit to spread his good news to others.

# Christians care for one another

Bible story
Acts 2:42–47

Bible point
Share what you have with others.

## Activity

### Faithful friends

Exchange beads and make friendship bracelets.

● **You will need**

Assortment of beads, shoelaces, snack-size resealable plastic bags, plastic containers

● **Preparation**

Make bags for each child containing ten assorted beads and a shoelace.

● **Handy hint**

Play a fun exchanging game before the children begin creating their friendship bracelets. Tell them that when you say 'share', they will have 15 seconds to exchange one bead with a friend. When 'stop' is called, they will freeze. Continue playing for about five to ten turns. Then let children sit down and create their friendship bracelets.

● **Step-by-step**

1. Let the children swap at least five beads with each other.
2. String the beads on to the shoelace. Then, in pairs, tie it on to the arm or ankle.

## Teaching point

When the children have completed their friendship bracelets, ask them to join you in a circle on the floor. Introduce or review the Bible story. Then ask:

• How did your friendship bracelet change after you swapped beads with your friends?
• How might the people of the early church have felt, sharing everything they had with each other?
• What kinds of things might they have shared?

Explain that the Bible tells us that the believers in the early church were good friends. They prayed together, ate together and worshipped together. They even sold their own things and gave the money to those who needed it. God wants us to share what we have with others, just as we shared and swapped beads to create our friendship bracelets.

# Peter heals the lame man

Age guide: 5–7s

> Bible story
> Acts 3:1–11
>
> Bible point
> **God wants us to praise him.**

## Activity

### Praise sticks

Make jingle bell praise sticks to praise the Lord like the lame man did.

#### ● You will need

Dowel sticks, brightly-coloured pipe cleaners, jingle bells

#### ● Preparation

Designate an area for the children to sit in, and lay out a pipe cleaner and dowel stick for each child. Provide enough jingle bells for each child to have at least three.

#### ● Handy hint

Let the children march in a circle and sing one of their favourite praise songs while shaking their praise sticks. Close by saying a prayer of praise to God.

NB: Instruct the children to shake their sticks gently or the pipe cleaners will fly off.

#### ● Step-by-step

1. Weave jingle bells on to several pipe cleaners.
2. Twist the ends of the pipe cleaners in loops so that the bells don't fall off.
3. Wrap the colourful wires around the dowel stick from one end of the stick to its centre.
4. Shake the praise stick and hear the bells jingle.

## Teaching point

When the children have completed their praise sticks, invite them to bring their sticks with them as they join you. Introduce or review the Bible story. Then ask:

- How might we have felt if we had been the man in the Bible story?
- What did the man ask Peter and John to give him?
- What might we tell people if we had just been healed? How would we act?

Explain that the Bible tells us that Peter and John met a lame man. He asked them for money. Peter told him to stand up and walk in the name of Jesus Christ. The lame man was immediately healed and went straight to the temple, walking, jumping and praising God. We made praise sticks to remind us to be like the lame man and to praise God for all he has done for us.

# Stephen forgives his accusers

Age guide: 5-7s

Bible story
Acts 6:9—7:60

Bible point
God wants us to tell others about him.

## Activity

### Preaching puppet

Make finger puppets to remind us that we are to share God's word.

● **You will need**

Cardboard tubes, scissors, glue, felt-tipped pens, card, knitting yarn

● **Preparation**

Prepare a work area with plenty of room for the children to cut and glue. Each child will need a cardboard tube and access to the card, glue, yarn and felt-tipped pens.

● **Step-by-step**

1. Choose some card for the face, wrap it around the top third of the cardboard tube and glue it in place.
2. Trace around the cardboard tube, making a circle from the same colour card as the face, and glue this to the top of the tube.
3. Choose another piece of card for the body. Wrap it around the rest of the tube and glue in place.
4. Cut out two rectangles for arms and glue them to the sides of the tube.
5. Cut out hands and attach them to the arms.
6. Use felt-tipped pens to draw a face on the puppet.
7. Cut yarn pieces and glue on to the top for hair.

## Teaching point

When the children have completed their puppets, invite them to join you. Introduce or review the Bible story. Then ask:

- Why was Stephen telling people about God?
- Why don't some people want to know about God?
- What can we tell others about God?

Let the children use their puppets to tell two friends what they know about God. Explain that the Bible tells us that Stephen told others about God. He didn't care if they didn't agree with him. Stephen knew that he had to tell the people what was right. We also need to remember to tell others about God. We can use our finger puppet to remind us to tell others about God. Close in prayer and ask God to give everyone the courage to do what's right and to tell others about him.

# Philip tells the Ethiopian official about Jesus

> **Bible story**
> Acts 8:26–40
>
> **Bible point**
> Share God's love with everyone.

## Activity

### Circle of friends

Make circles of friends to remind us to share God's love all around the world.

### ● You will need

Magazines or coloured wrapping paper, A4 card (two sheets per child), felt-tipped pens, scissors

### ● Preparation

Designate a work area in which each child will have a sheet of paper and access to the felt-tipped pens and scissors.

### ● Handy hint

To give older children more of a challenge, let them squeeze coloured glue around the outside of their circle of friends to enhance the focus. Let the glue dry so that it stands out and give a three-dimensional effect. Then display the art in church for all to see. Instead of using wrapping paper, gather magazine pictures of people from all ethnic backgrounds for the children to use as the background for their collages.

### ● Step-by-step

1. Ask the children to write their names on the back of a sheet of card. Cut shapes out of the wrapping paper and glue them on to the card to make a collage.
2. Take another sheet of card and fold it in half twice, as if creating a small card.
3. Draw a person shape with the head in the folded corners (see illustration). Make sure the person-shape arm and leg extend all the way to the edges of the paper. Then cut it out, making sure you don't cut the folds at the hands. Open up the folds to reveal the circle of friends.
4. Glue the circle of friends on top of the collage. Then write 'Share God's love with everyone' in a circular shape on the circle of friends.

## Teaching point

When the children have completed their circles of friends, invite them to join you. Introduce or review the Bible story. Then ask:

- How did Philip share God's love with the Ethiopian?
- What would we do if God asked us to tell someone we didn't know about him?
- What are some different ways we can share God's love with people in our school or community?

Explain that the Bible tells us about a time when God told Philip to go to a town that he had never been to before. Philip obeyed God and met a man from another country who wanted to learn about God. Philip told him all about God. God wants us to be like Philip and share his love with people all around the world. Our 'circle of friends' cards can remind us to share God's love with everyone.

# Saul meets Jesus near Damascus

Age guide: 6–10s

Bible story
Acts 9:1–31

Bible point
The light of God changes our lives.

## Activity

### Melting hearts

Make chocolate hearts.

### ● You will need

Cooking chocolate, butter, heart-shaped moulds, glass bowls, large bowls of hot water, wooden spoons, greaseproof paper, pallet knife, pencils, paper, bowl of soapy water, paper towels

### ● Preparation

Designate two separate work areas. Place the bowl of soapy water and paper towels in one area. Place all other supplies in the other area.

### ● Handy hint

Under close supervision, you could use a microwave oven to melt the chocolate. NB: Beware of food allergies and provide alternative treats for children who are not allowed chocolate.

### ● Step-by-step

1. Let the children wash their hands before beginning their sweet-making.
2. Break up the chocolate and put it into a glass bowl. Place the bowl in the larger bowl of hot water, making sure the water does not lap too far up the side of the small bowl. Add a knob of butter.
3. Stir the mixture until melted, refreshing the hot water if needed. Pour into heart-shaped moulds. Alternatively, pour a little chocolate on to grease-proof paper and shape into a heart using a pallet knife.
4. Let the children write their names on a piece of paper and place it next to their chocolate heart. Place the chocolate hearts to one side and leave to set.

## Teaching point

When the children have completed their chocolate hearts, invite them to join you. Introduce or review the Bible story. Then ask:

- Who was Saul?
- What happened to him on the road to Damascus?
- What happened to the chocolate when we placed it over hot water?
- In what way does God melt our hearts?

Explain that the Bible tells us about a man named Saul who persecuted Christians, but he was changed and became a Christian when Jesus stopped him in his tracks. When the bowl of chocolate was placed over hot water, the chocolate melted. Just as the heat melted the chocolate, so God is able to take the hardest of hearts and melt them with his love. When we ask God to help us say nice things to others, he will give us the power to resist saying harsh words.

# An angel frees Peter from jail

Age guide: 6–10s

## Activity

### The strength of prayer

Make torn paper pictures as a reminder that there is power in prayer.

### ● You will need

A4 sheets of card, coloured paper, paperclips, PVA glue

### ● Preparation

Set out sheets of card, coloured paper, glue and paperclips.

### ● Handy hint

Check with your local library for children's picture books that use torn paper illustrations, and bring appropriate books to the session as examples of some of the challenging details children can add to make their pictures more realistic.

### ● Step-by-step

1. Ask the children to think of a time when God answered one of their prayers.
2. Tear pieces of paper and arrange them on the card to illustrate how God answered that prayer. Layer the pieces to form a three-dimensional effect and glue in place.
3. Take some paperclips, hook them together to form a chain, and glue the chain to the bottom of the page as a reminder that God broke the chains that held Peter in prison because people were praying for him.

## Teaching point

When the children have completed their pictures, invite them to join you. Introduce or review the Bible story. Then ask:

- Where was Peter?
- Might he have been afraid?
- How did Peter get out of jail?

Explain that the Bible tells us that while Peter was chained in prison, his friends were praying hard that God's power would be with him. While the guards were sleeping, an angel appeared and woke Peter up, and the chains slipped off his wrists. Peter was free. God chose to set Peter free because his friends prayed. We need to remember to pray for others, because prayer is powerful.

# Lydia becomes a Christian

Age guide: 5–7s

Bible story
Acts 16:11–15

Bible point
**God wants us to believe in Jesus.**

## Activity

### Super story strips

Make story strips as a reminder of the story of Lydia.

● **You will need**

Cardboard, gift ribbon or raffia, circular shapes, pipe cleaners, drinking glass

● **Preparation**

Use the drinking glass to make several circle patterns from cardboard. Cut ribbon into 45cm strips. Designate a work area for children to trace and cut out circles. Set up another work area for children to colour and glue.

● **Handy hint**

Let the children make the story strip circles during the telling of the Bible story.

● **Step-by-step**

1. Trace four circles and cut them out.
2. Draw a picture of Lydia on one circle. Colour the second circle purple. Draw a heart on the third circle. Draw a house on the fourth circle.
3. Lay a ribbon vertically in front of you. Glue the circles on to the ribbon in the order in which they appear in the story, from top to bottom.
4. Form a pipe cleaner into a ring.
5. Fold the top end of the ribbon through the ring and glue it in place.

## Teaching point

When the children have completed their work, invite them to join you with their story strips. Use the story strips to introduce or review the Bible story. Then ask:

- Why was Lydia important in the story?
- Why might Lydia have chosen to believe in Jesus?
- How can we show others that we believe in Jesus?

Explain that the Bible tells us that Lydia sold purple cloth and had a lot of money. She believed in God, but Jesus was missing from her life. When Lydia heard Paul's message, she opened her heart and believed. We can use our story strips to retell the story of Lydia. God wants us to be like Lydia—to open our hearts and believe in his Son, Jesus.

# Paul's jailer believes in Jesus

Bible story
Acts 16:25–34

Bible point
**Believe in Jesus.**

## Activity

### Look to the cross

Create crosses out of jigsaw pieces.

### ● You will need

Cardboard, jigsaw pieces, clear self-adhesive vinyl, glue sticks, scraps of fabric (optional)

### ● Preparation

Cut the cardboard into 8 cm squares. Then cut the vinyl into four squares. Place the cardboard pieces around a table. Have the jigsaw pieces and glue placed so that they are accessible to all the children.

### ● Handy hint

For an extra special effect, you can spray the crosses with gold or silver spray paint and let the children drape a small piece of fabric over the arms of the cross.

### ● Step-by-step

1. Remove the backing from the vinyl and lay it on the table, sticky side up. Lay the piece of cardboard on top of the vinyl and press down firmly. Cut the corners off the vinyl and fold the remaining edges over the cardboard.
2. Ask the children to write their name on the back of their card and then turn it over. The cardboard is now a base for the cross.
3. Begin sculpting the cross by gluing one puzzle piece to another, holding each one for a few seconds, until the craft is finished.

## Teaching point

When the children have completed their crosses, invite them to join you. Introduce or review the Bible story. Then ask:

- How might Paul and Silas have felt, being inside a jail, unable to get out?
- When the jailer saw that Paul and Silas had not escaped, what did he do?
- What did the jailer have to do to be saved?

Explain that we can't tell what a jigsaw puzzle looks like from just one piece. Paul and Silas didn't know how God would use them in prison, but God knew the big picture. We can look to the cross to know that all we have to do is believe in Jesus to be saved, just as the jailer looked to Jesus and was saved. We can remember this every time we look at the crosses that we made.

# Aquila and Priscilla

Age guide: 6–10s

---

Bible story
Acts 18:1–3

Bible point
**God wants us to care for our ministers.**

---

## Activity

### Caring for our minister

Create wall hangings.

#### ● You will need

Muslin squares, felt-tipped pens, a larger piece of muslin, a piece of dowel, sewing equipment

#### ● Preparation

Cut fabric into 26cm squares. You'll need one per child. Cut one piece of fabric to measure 76cm x 15cm. This will be the top of the wall hanging that will attach the dowel rod to the fabric pictures. Set aside the large piece of fabric until later. Place the fabric squares on the working area, along with the felt-tipped pens.

#### ● Handy hint

Ask someone in your congregation to sew the children's pictures together into a wall hanging, using 1.5cm seam allowances. Arrange a time with your minister for the children to present their wall hanging and pray for him or her. The best time would be during a service, so that everyone can see.

#### ● Step-by-step

1. Ask the children to use the felt-tipped pens to draw a picture on the fabric, of one way in which the minister cares for them, their family or the people in church.
2. Let the children write their name and age clearly on their picture.
3. Sew all the fabric pictures together. Finish the wall hanging by adding the large fabric strip and dowelling to create a wall hanging to give your minister.

## Teaching point

When the children have completed their sewing, invite them to join you. Introduce or review the Bible story. Then ask:

- How did Aquila and Priscilla help Paul?
- What are some ways our minister cares for the people in our church?
- What are some ways we can show we care about him or her?

Explain that the Bible tells us that Aquila and Priscilla were tentmakers. They cared for Paul by letting him stay with them and helped him make tents. God wants us to care for our minister and others, just like Aquila and Priscilla cared for Paul.

# Romans

## Free gift of grace

> ### Bible story
> **Romans 6:23**
>
> ### Bible point
> **God gives us the gift of eternal life.**

## Activity

### The gift that keeps on giving

Make cards that open up to show a cross in remembrance of God's gift.

### ● You will need

Sheets of A4 card in dark colours such as navy, burgundy, black or dark green; gel pens; scissors

### ● Preparation

Place the card, gel pens and scissors in your art area.

### ● Handy hint

If any of the children would like to give their card away, allow them to draw a gift tag with the recipient's name on the drawing of the present.

### ● Step-by-step

1. Fold a sheet of card in half. Turn the card so that the fold is at the top and the card opens from the bottom. Use the gel pens to draw a large present with a bow on the front of the card. Decorate the present, but not the bow.
2. Cut out the bow at the top of your present. Be careful not to cut the fold. Use a pencil and trace the bow very lightly to the inside of the card.
3. Open the card and create a large colourful cross inside. When the card is closed, the bow will be filled with colour, but the cross won't be seen until the card is opened.
4. On the front of your card, write 'God's gift is for me!' Then, on the inside of your card, write 'God gives eternal life because of Jesus'.
5. Give your card to someone to remind them of God's free gift for them.

## Teaching point

When the children have finished their cards, ask them to form a circle around you. Then ask:

- Why do we give gifts?
- Why did God give us the gift of eternal life?
- How do we get the gift of eternal life?

Explain that, just as we can only see part of the cross through the card when it's closed, we can only partially understand how valuable and wonderful God's free gift of eternal life is. We could never earn the right to be in God's presence, but God gives us a gift we don't need to earn. God offers eternal life to those who believe in Jesus and ask for his gift. God's gift is eternal life because of Jesus.

# Paul describes living by God's Spirit

Age guide: 7–11s

## Activity

### Proclamation posters

Create colourful posters proclaiming our heavenly heritage.

#### You will need

Drawing paper, crayons, cocktail sticks, newspaper, cups, paintbrushes, water, water pots, painting aprons, watercolour paint

#### Preparation

Spread newspapers over one work surface. Set out pots of water, watercolour paints and brushes. Place crayons and paper in another work area.

#### Handy hint

Display the posters in church to remind everyone of their eternal heritage.

#### Step-by-step

1. Invite the children to be creative and design a brightly-coloured poster proclaiming their heavenly heritage. For example, they might write in fancy letters, 'I am God's child'. Tell them to press hard with the crayons as they fill in letters or make abstract shapes.
2. Make a solid frame around the outside of the poster with the crayons. Take a cocktail stick and scratch a design on the crayon frame, such as a wood grain, shapes or stripes.
3. Paint over the entire poster with one of the watercolours, filling in all clear spaces of the paper with paint. Set the finished posters in a designated area to dry.

## Teaching point

Ask the children to open their Bibles to Romans 8:15–16 and invite a volunteer to read the words. Then ask:

- What happened to the words on the paper when we painted over them?
- How do we become children of God?
- How does it feel to be a child of God?

Explain that even when we covered the words with paint, the message never changed. We know that we are God's children, no matter what happens. We praise God for always loving and caring for us. We are all special when we believe in Jesus and accept his forgiveness. We are sons and daughters of God when we believe in Jesus. Invite the children to turn to a partner if they believe in Jesus and say, 'I am a son (or daughter) of God'.

# God's love is always there

> Bible story
> **Romans 8:38–39**
>
> Bible point
> **Nothing can separate us from God's love.**

## Activity

### Love in action

Create illusions on top of pencils.

### ● You will need

Unsharpened pencils, blank 8cm x 13cm index cards, felt-tipped pens, sticky tape

### ● Preparation

Place supplies in the centre of the work area.

### ● Handy hint

Allow the children to make a second pencil topper, showing that God's love is there for a friend.

### ● Step-by-step

1. Fold an index card in half so that each half is the same size. Turn the card so that the fold is at the top.
2. Draw yourself in the centre of one side of the card. Then turn the card over and draw a large heart on the other side so that it fills the card.
3. Open the card and tape the rubber end of the pencil in the centre of the bottom half of the card. Close the card and tape all the edges shut so that the pencil is secure inside.
4. Hold the pencil between the palms of your hands, roll it back and forth very quickly and watch the results.

## Teaching point

When the children have finished making their pencil toppers, let them play with them and then ask:

• What can we see when we roll the pencil back and forth in our hands?

Choose a volunteer or two to read the Bible verses and then ask:

• What are some ways God shows his love in our lives?

Explain that even though we can't see it, we can remember that God's love is always around us. While a pencil may separate the two drawings you made, nothing can separate us from God's love. This pencil topper is a reminder of how we need to look for God's love because, no matter what happens, it is always there. Listen to the wonderful message again—nothing can separate us from God's love!

# God makes us different

> Bible story
> Romans 9:20–21
>
> Bible point
> Our differences can bring honour to God.

## Activity

### Creation celebration

Make clay figures.

### ● You will need

Self-drying clay, paper plates, felt-tipped pens

### ● Preparation

Give each of the children a plate with a piece of clay on it, and have the felt-tipped pens available.

### ● Handy hint

Have a mini art show and then let each child give his or her friend the figure that was made of that friend.

### ● Step-by-step

1. Divide the clay in half. Make a figure of yourself with the first piece.
2. Use the second piece of clay to make a figure of a friend. Use the felt-tipped pens to draw facial features and other details such as clothing on each figure.
3. Pose your clay figures differently or add something each person likes (such as a clay football or skipping rope).
4. When your figures are finished, write your name on the plate under your clay figure, and write your friend's name under the figure you made of him or her.

## Teaching point

Invite the children to sit in a circle beside you. Read or ask a volunteer to read the Bible verse and then ask:

- What are some ways we and our friends are different?
- Why does God make us different?
- What is something we and our friends can do together that will please God?

Explain that just as we chose to make our clay figures different, so God chooses to make us different. We can celebrate being different because we know that God made us with love and we are different for a purpose. Our differences can bring honour to God. Ask children to share with a partner something they like about their friend.

# We send good news

Bible story
Romans 10:15; Isaiah 52:7

Bible point
Talk about Jesus wherever you go.

## Activity

### Good-news feet

Make key rings with foam feet.

### ● You will need

Craft foam, pens, scissors, felt-tipped pens, hole punch, key rings

### ● Preparation

Put chairs in pairs and place the supplies within easy reach of the children.

### ● Handy hint

Allow the children to exchange one foot with a friend so that there are two different feet on the key ring, reminding the children to exchange the good news and talk about Jesus wherever they go.

### ● Step-by-step

1. Put the children into pairs. Ask one child in each pair to make a fist and place it down on a piece of craft foam with the thumb on top. The second child traces around the first child's hand. Repeat with the other hand and then swap over, so that everyone has two oblong ovals to cut out.
2. Lightly draw toes at the tops of each oval and cut around the feet shapes created.
3. Write the words 'Good news' on each foam foot and then decorate the feet with the felt-tipped pens. Punch a hole in each foam heel and attach the key ring to the feet.

## Teaching point

Gather the children together in a circle and ask a volunteer to read the Bible passage. Then ask:

- How does it feel when we have good news to share?
- What good news can we deliver about Jesus?
- How can we tell others good news about Jesus?

Explain that it's exciting to share good news. Explain that God asks us to take the good news about Jesus wherever we go. The good news makes us happy—and that is the best reason to tell others about Jesus. We can talk about Jesus wherever we go.

# Love can never be repaid

Bible story
Romans 13:8–10

Bible point
**Owe everyone love.**

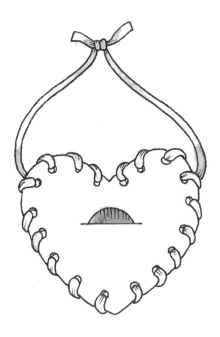

## Activity

### 'Keep the change' purse

Create purses that hold money.

● **You will need**

Craft foam, pens, cord or plastic lacing string, scissors, clear tape, small coins

● **Preparation**

Place supplies within easy reach of the children.

● **Handy hint**

Ask the children to close their eyes and imagine that each kind deed that someone did for them was a coin added to a love bank, already full of God's love. Remind the children that, no matter how much love they give to others, this bank will never be empty. Lead a prayer thanking God for his precious love and give the children an opportunity to praise God for the riches in their lives.

● **Step-by-step**

1.  On the craft foam, draw two hearts that are the same size. They should be about as tall as the child's index finger. Cut them out, then place the hearts on top of each other and trim any excess.
2.  Fold one of the hearts in half so that the top of the heart touches the bottom, and make a small slit in the centre of the heart along the fold line. The cut line should be as wide as a small coin.
3.  Cut about a 50cm length of cord. Hold the two hearts lined up together on top of each other and poke nine evenly spaced holes on each side of the hearts with a pen. Thread the cord through the holes to sew the two hearts together. Then gently pull the cord to an equal length on both sides of the heart and tie the ends together.

## Teaching point

Give each child a small coin to put in their purse. Invite the children to sit in a circle and read or review the Bible verse. Then ask:

*   What does the Bible say we owe other people?
*   Have any of us ever owed something to someone? What was it?
*   Was it paid back? How?
*   Can we ever pay back love? Why or why not?

Explain that although we can never repay God's love, we try to show love to others so that they know we have God's love in our life. It is a good feeling to repay a debt, but we can't earn or pay for God's love. God has already given it to us and it's so much more than we can imagine. We can obey God by loving others as he has loved us. We owe everyone love.

# Wake up to God's message

Bible story
Romans 13:11–12

Bible point
**God wants us to watch for him.**

## Activity

### 'Eye' am always alert

Make faces with movable eyelids.

### ● You will need

Sheets of A4 card, crayons, felt-tipped pens, scissors, sticky tape, rubber bands

### ● Preparation

Place all the supplies in one area, spreading items within reach of the children.

### ● Handy hint

Ask two children to stand at one end of the room, one with his or her back turned to the other children, pretending to be asleep but able to see the second child. The second child holds a wake-up face and faces the group of children and the first child. The children then sneak up to the child with his or her back turned. As soon as the second child makes the craft face 'wake up', the first child can turn around and try to tag any children before they get back across the room. The first child tagged becomes the new sleeping child. Take a few turns letting different children be the wake-up signal.

### ● Step-by-step

1. Cut a large oval shape for a face out of card. Draw in the eyes, eyebrows, nose and mouth with felt-tipped pens. Using the scrap pieces of card, cut two mushroom-shaped pieces (football shapes with long stem), bigger than the eyes on the face.
2. Cut a small slot above each eye in the eyebrow. Slide the stem of each oval cut piece into the slot so that each oval covers an eye. Draw eyelashes on the bottom portion of each oval.

3. Carefully flip the face over and fold each stem over the end of a rubber band. Tape the stem to the rubber band without letting excess tape stick to the back of the face. Cut or pinch together excess tape.

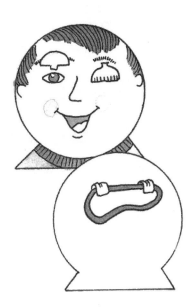

## Teaching point

Let the children practise holding the face up and pulling down on the rubber band to make the eyelids move. Read the Bible passage while they make the eyes open. Then ask:

• Why might God want us to watch for him?
• Why is it hard for us to wait for Jesus to return?

Explain that Jesus wants us to be excited about his return. Since we don't know when it will be, it is easy to think about other things in our life. Jesus wants us to live for him so that we will be ready for him to come. God wants us to watch for him now so that we will always be ready for him.

# Build up your neighbour

> ### Bible story
> Romans 15:2
>
> ### Bible point
> **God wants us to appreciate others.**

## Activity

### The great traits trophy

Make trophies to show appreciation for each other.

### ● You will need

Heavy duty aluminium foil, paper plates, paper cups in two sizes, split-pin fasteners, gel pens, glue sticks

### ● Preparation

Cut ten pieces of foil, each measuring 3cm x 20cm, for each child. Put the ten pieces on a paper plate for each child. Place the rest of the supplies within reach of the children.

### ● Handy hint

When the trophies are finished, have a simple award ceremony, handing out the trophies and sharing out loud some of what's written on each one.

### ● Step-by-step

1. Using a pen tip, poke a small hole in the centre of the bottom of a small cup and a larger cup. Place the bottoms of the two paper cups together and attach them with a split-pin fastener.

2. Ask the children to write their name on a plate and keep the foil pieces from covering it. Each child then leaves his or her plate and walks to someone else's plate. Everyone then uses a gel pen to write a single-word compliment gently on to one of the foil pieces on that person's plate. Ask everyone to write on the right-hand side of the foil. Leaving the foil piece at that person's plate, the children then move to the next plate to write a different compliment. When everyone has finished, make sure they each have ten pieces of foil. Ask a leader to add a compliment to any foil strips that are still blank.

3. Each child then glues each piece of their foil to the outside of the cups with the taller cup on top, displaying the compliments. Let each piece slightly overlap the next piece. Fold the excess foil into the top and bottom of the cups. Use fingers to smooth wrinkles and use fingernails to trace around the lip and bottom rim of the top cup to outline a trophy shape. Ask the children to write their name across the bottom of the trophy.

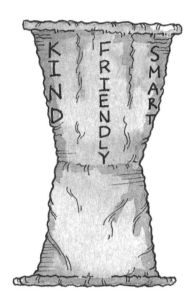

## Teaching point

Ask the children to line the trophies up together and then join you in a circle to hear the Bible verse. Read the verse and then ask:

- How does it feel to get compliments?
- How does it feel when we give a compliment?
- Why might God want us to show others that we appreciate them?
- What are some other ways to show people we appreciate them?

Explain that God has made everyone special and he wants us to appreciate what is special about each person. When we build our neighbour up with compliments, we are also building ourselves up with kindness and love. God is proud when we show others the good we see in them. God wants us to appreciate others.

# 1 Corinthians

## God brings the harvest

> **Bible story**
> 1 Corinthians 3:6–9
>
> **Bible point**
> **We plant but God makes things grow.**

## Activity

### Hanging planters

Make hanging planters.

### ● You will need

Lemonade bottles, card, sticky-back vinyl, string, hole punch, scissors, potting compost, grass seed, spoon, water, rulers

### ● Preparation

Create two work areas. Put the supplies for decorating the pots on a table. Cover a floor area with newspaper for planting the seeds.

### ● Handy hint

Keep the hanging planters in church and let the children give them a haircut each week. Make sure someone waters them during the week.

### ● Step-by-step

1. Cut 10cm off the bottom of a lemonade bottle. Keep the bottom to make the planter and throw away the top half of the bottle. Punch three holes equally spaced around the edge of the planter.
2. Cut a nose, mouth and eyes from card. Cut pieces of sticky-back vinyl slightly bigger than the face parts and use them to attach the face parts to the outside of your planter.
3. Cut three 30cm pieces of string. Fold each one in half and thread it through one of the three holes. Tie the six ends together to make a hanger.

4. Fill the planter half full with potting compost. Sprinkle the grass seeds over the soil and cover with another 2cm of soil. Carefully add just enough water to make it moist.

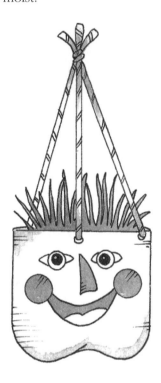

## Teaching point

When the children have finished their hanging planters, ask them to join you in a circle as you introduce or review the story. Then ask:

- What will help the seeds to grow?
- How will we be able to tell that our seeds have grown?
- How might we plant the good news about Jesus?
- What can we do to help the gospel grow?

Explain that we put seeds in the soil and watered them. We can place them in a window to get warm sunshine. But we can't make our plants grow. Only God can do that. We can tell people the things we know about God, but they have to respond to God so that he can help them grow.

# Jesus the master builder

> ### Bible story
> 1 Corinthians 3:9–15
>
> ### Bible point
> **The kind of foundation we build
> will be tested.**

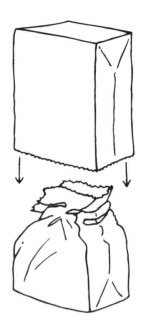

## Activity

### Bogus building blocks

Make building blocks as a reminder that Jesus is the only real foundation to build on.

● **You will need**

Paper bags, felt-tipped pens, crayons, newspaper, masking tape, large bin bag

● **Preparation**

Clear a large work area on the floor for the children to make their blocks.

● **Handy hint**

Ask the children to write 'Jesus the master builder' on one of their blocks to take home as a reminder. Put the rest of the blocks in a large bin bag and store them at church for future use.

● **Step-by-step**

1. Stuff a paper bag full of crumpled newspaper. Pull an empty bag over the full one and tape it around the bottom. Work the bag in your hands and flatten the sides to shape it to look like a block. Repeat until you have several blocks.
2. Use crayons and felt-tipped pens to make the blocks look like brick or stone.
3. Work with friends and use the blocks to build a walled area you can sit inside.

## Teaching point

When the children have finished building their structures, sit behind the walls with them as you introduce or review the story. Then ask:

- Does the material we used to make blocks make a strong wall? Why or why not?
- What kinds of things lay good foundations in our lives?
- How can we build our lives on Jesus?

Explain that the blocks look like bricks and stones but, if we tried to push the walls over, they wouldn't stand. They would be found out to be bogus or fake. The Bible tells us that Jesus is our firm and strong foundation. When we read our Bibles and pray, we are building our lives on truth and holiness. If we use any other kind of material to build our lives, we will find that sooner or later they fall apart.

# Our bodies are God's temple

> Bible story
> 1 Corinthians 6:20
>
> Bible point
> **We can praise God with our bodies.**

## Activity

### Shake, rattle and praise shakers

Make instruments from disposable bowls to praise God.

### ● You will need

Two polystyrene bowls per child, knitting wool, hole punch, dried beans, felt-tipped pens, stickers, sticky tape, darning needle

### ● Preparation

Punch around the rims of two bowls for each child. Make sure the holes line up for sewing. Put the rest of the craft supplies on a table.

### ● Handy hint

Let the children play their shakers as you teach them to sing this song to the tune of Jack and Jill.

*Jesus bought me with a price,*
*And I will give him honour!*
*I will praise the Lord my God.*
*I'll give him praise and honour!*

Make copies of this song and other easy songs for the children to take home and use with their shakers.

### ● Step-by-step

1. Thread a 20cm piece of wool through a darning needle. Tie a knot in the end. Poke the needle up through the centre inside one bowl and back down to make a loop to fit the hand. Tie the ends tightly.
2. Cut a 125cm piece of wool. Roll one end with tape. Start sewing the rims of the two bowls together. Pull the wool tightly as you go. When you get about three-quarters of the way round, put half a cup of dried beans in the bowls and sew the rest of the way.
3. Write 'Praise God' on the bottom of the shaker and decorate the rest of the shaker with stickers.

## Teaching point

Ask the children to bring their shakers to the circle as you introduce or review the story. Then ask:

- Why does the Bible say we belong to Jesus?
- What are some ways we can praise God with our bodies?

Explain that today we made an instrument that will help us use our hands and voices to praise God. God is pleased when we praise him because he made us, and our bodies are his temples.

# Race for the prize

Age guide: 5–7s

## Activity

### A prize-winning ribbon

Make gold ribbons as a reminder to race for the prize that God has to offer us.

● **You will need**

Yellow card, jam jar lids, gold ribbon, gold glitter, silver stars, pinking shears, craft glue, safety pin, tape, felt-tipped pens, clothes pegs

● **Preparation**

Set up one work area spread with newspaper to do the glittering. Put all the other craft supplies on a table. Cut a 10cm and a 5cm circle from yellow card for each child and pink the edges.

● **Handy hint**

Create an awards ceremony. Let the children come up one at a time and pin their ribbon on them. Remind them that this ribbon will eventually fall apart but the prize they receive for serving God will never perish.

● **Step-by-step**

1. Use craft glue to put the number 1 on the small circle and sprinkle it with glitter.
2. With a felt-tipped pen, write 'Run to win! 1 Corinthians 9:24' on the back of the large circle. Tape the safety pin to the top back.
3. Cut 35cm of gold ribbon. Fold the ribbon in half and cut a triangle notch in the ends. Glue the ribbon to the front centre of the large circle and glue the lid over the ribbon.
4. Glue the small circle to the centre of the lid and add stars. Use a couple of clothes pegs to hold the layers together while they dry.

## Teaching point

While the crafts are drying, gather the children in a circle to review or read the Bible story. Then ask:

• What kinds of races have we participated in?
• How do people prepare for a race?
• How can we win the race, to win the prize of eternal life?

Explain that we have made a ribbon that looks like the kind of prize we would get if we were to win a race. Paul tells us that it's important to run with all our might for eternal life, like the runner who runs hard to win a race. God wants us to race with all our might to know and love him more each day.

# Paul teaches about spiritual gifts

> Bible story
> 1 Corinthians 12:12–26
>
> Bible point
> **Everyone is important in the body of believers.**

## Activity

### Body puzzles

Make puzzles as a reminder that all the parts are important to make a complete body.

### ● You will need

Art foam or large polystyrene food trays (one per child), scissors, felt-tipped pens

### ● Preparation

Place all the materials on a work table. Prepare cardboard templates of a simple body shape for the children to trace.

### ● Handy hint

Write out a simple prayer, thanking God for making us part of his family. Let the children pass it around and each read a few words. Remind the children that each one of them is important to complete the prayer.

### ● Step-by-step

1. Trace a body shape on to a piece of art foam or food tray. Cut around the outside.
2. Use the felt-tipped pens to draw a face on the head and colour the rest of the outline to look like clothes. The children can make their person look like themselves if they wish.
3. Write 'We are one body' on the back of the body.
4. Draw lines on the back in pencil to make an interlocking jigsaw puzzle. Cut out the body to make the puzzle.

## Teaching point

Ask the children to bring the puzzle pieces with them as you introduce or review the story. Then ask:

- Who or what is the body of Christ?
- Why does each part look different?
- Which parts are the most important?

Explain that we need all the pieces of the puzzle to make a picture. If we lose one, the body will not look complete. Paul told us that all Christians make up the body of Christ. No one person is more important than another and we can't get along without one another. Everyone is important in the body of Christ.

# Paul describes true love

Age guide: 7–11s

---

> Bible story
> 1 Corinthians 13
>
> Bible point
> **We are nothing without love.**

## Activity

### Giant love cards

Make giant cards, showing our love for someone special.

### ● You will need

Sheets of A3 card (one per child), heart-shaped stamps, stickers, paper doilies, felt-tipped pens, glue sticks, sticky tape, scissors

### ● Preparation

Fold the card in half widthways to make a large opening card. Put the supplies on a table.

### ● Handy hint

Children also enjoy sponge-painting hearts or using heart-shaped biscuit cutters to stamp on to their cards for different effects. Let children try adding a three-dimensional touch to their cards by gluing on heart-shaped doilies or cutting the hearts out of heart-printed wrapping paper. Practise singing a song about God's love with the children. Arrange to share the song with the wider church family.

### ● Step-by-step

1. Decorate the front of a folder with the heart-shaped stamps, paper doilies, felt-tipped pens and stickers.
2. Write a message on the inside that will express your love for someone special.

## Teaching point

Ask the children to bring their cards to the circle area as you introduce or review the story. Then ask:

- What are some of the words we use to describe love?
- Who should we say 'I love you' to?
- What are some ways we can show love?

Explain that we have made cards to express our love. Paul says that the ability to show love is the most important gift to have. We can be clever, talented, helpful and generous, but we still need to show God's love to others. The Bible says that without love we are nothing. People will never know we love them unless we tell them or show them through our actions. Our giant love cards are one way we can show God's love to others.

# 2 Corinthians

## We are sealed

> **Bible story**
> 2 Corinthians 1:21–22
>
> **Bible point**
> **We belong to God.**

## Activity

Make initial stamps to put our stamp on things we own, just as God puts his seal of ownership on us.

### ● You will need

4cm letter stencils, thin sponges, empty cotton reels or plastic corks (one per child), scissors, low-temperature glue gun, scraps of card, felt-tipped pens, glue sticks, stickers, water-based paint, newspaper, polystyrene trays, water, paper towel, small plastic bags (optional)

### ● Preparation

Set all the project supplies out on one table except the paint. Cover another table with newspaper and put the paint and some polystyrene trays on it.

### ● Handy hint

Put the initial stamps in plastic bags for the children to take home.

### ● Step-by-step

1. Using a letter stencil, ask the children to trace their first initial on to a sponge.
2. Cut out the letter and glue it to the top of an empty cotton reel or a plastic cork with the glue gun (assist the children as necessary).
3. Write 'We belong to God' on a scrap of card cut to fit around the centre of the reel or cork. Glue it in place with a glue stick. Hold the paper in place and count to 25 while it dries. Decorate the rest of the reel or cork with felt-tipped pens or stickers.
4. Pour a small amount of paint into one end of a tray. Dip the stamp in the paint, wait a few seconds and then dab it on the other end of the tray. Print your initial on paper. The sponge can be cleaned with water and dried with a paper towel before taking home.

## Teaching point

When the children have finished stamping, dip the stamps in warm water and dab them on several layers of paper towel to clean them. Let the stamps dry while the children gather to hear or review the story. Then ask:

- How might God be able to own us?
- What has God done to show that we belong to him?
- How can our actions show that we belong to God?

Explain that we like to show that things belong to us. Now that we have made our stamp with our own initial on it, we will be able to mark the things we make. God made us and he owns us. He has put his seal of ownership on us. God gave us his Holy Spirit in our hearts as a guarantee that we belong to him. Take time to let the children praise God for making them and then close with a prayer, thanking God because we belong to him.

# We are a fragrance to others

> Bible story
> 2 Corinthians 2:14–17
>
> Bible point
> Spread the gospel like a sweet fragrance.

## Activity

### Potpourri pandas

Make a sweet-smelling potpourri bear.

● **You will need**

Per child: two clear plastic cups, six medium-sized black pompoms, a medium-sized polystyrene ball, a tiny brown pompom, scraps of red paper, two small movable eyes, a darning needle; for the group: potpourri, glue sticks, scissors, parcel tape

● **Preparation**

Set all the project supplies out on a table.

● **Handy hint**

Suggest to the children that they can give their panda to someone they want to tell about God's love. Each time the person smells the potpourri, they will be reminded of the sweet message the child shared with them.

● **Step-by-step**

1. Use the needle to poke holes all over the sides of the plastic cups. Fill one cup full of potpourri. Put glue around the rim of the second cup and put it on top of the first cup. Wrap a piece of packing tape around the outside of the cup for added security.
2. Glue the polystyrene ball to the top centre of the cups for a head. Glue two black pompoms on top of the ball for ears.
3. Glue on the movable eyes and the brown pompom for a nose. Add a small red mouth made from card.
4. Glue two black pompoms to the top cup and two to the bottom cup for paws.

## Teaching point

Let the bears dry while the children gather to hear or review the story. Then ask:

- What will happen if we put our panda in a cupboard?
- What are some ways we can spread the good news about Jesus?
- How might spreading the gospel be like the fragrance of perfume?

Explain that we are attracted to things that smell good, like our potpourri pandas. Helping a neighbour, cheering up a friend who is unhappy or unwell, or showing kindness are all ways that we can become attractive to others. When we have Jesus in our lives, people will see his goodness or sweetness in us. Spreading the gospel is like a sweet fragrance.

# A light out of darkness

Age guide: 7–11s

Bible story
2 Corinthians 4:4–6

Bible point
Let Jesus shine through us.

## Activity

### Pinhole pictures

Make pinhole pictures that will let the light shine through and reveal a picture.

● **You will need**

Black and red card, white paper, towel, paperclips, hole punch, glue, scissors, suction pad

● **Preparation**

Create two work areas. Put all the supplies except the towel on one table. Make a second work area on the floor, where you have laid the folded towel. Cut two 30cm x 2.5cm strips and two 23cm x 2.5cm strips from red card for each child.

● **Handy hint**

Darken the room as much as possible and let the children take turns to hold a torch behind their pictures to see the light pour through.

● **Step-by-step**

1. Leaving at least a 2.5cm border around the edge, write the words 'Jesus shines through us' on the white paper. At the bottom, draw a picture of something that symbolises light. It could be a sunburst, light bulbs or something else that shows light.
2. Lay the white paper on the sheet of black card and paperclip the edges. Place the papers on the folded towel.
3. Straighten a large paperclip. Use the pointed end to poke holes through both papers, outlining the words and the picture, then remove the white paper and throw it away.

4. Take the red strips and glue them to the edges of the picture to make a frame. Punch a hole in the top centre for hanging with a suction pad.

## Teaching point

Ask the children to bring their pictures as you introduce or review the story. Then ask:

• How can we make it easy to see the picture on our papers?
• Why is it hard for people to follow God sometimes?
• How can we be like a light showing people the way to God?

Explain that when we look at the black paper, all we see is darkness. But when we hold it up to a window, the light shines through. Paul said that God has given us a light in the darkness; that light is Jesus. When we are kind, loving and forgiving, his light will shine out of our lives. We need to let Jesus shine through us. Let the children sing 'This little light of mine'. Close by praying that God will help us to keep our light shining for him.

# A new creation

> **Bible story**
> 2 Corinthians 5:17
>
> **Bible point**
> With Jesus, we become a new person.

## Activity

### Delicate butterfly magnet

Make butterfly magnets as a reminder that we can be a new creation in Christ.

### ● You will need

For each child: two gold doilies, black pipe cleaners, two hair grips, two small beads, magnets, a black permanent marker, glue sticks

### ● Preparation

Put all the craft supplies out on a table.

### ● Handy hint

Encourage the children to take their butterflies home and put them on their refrigerator as a daily reminder of the new creation they are in Jesus.

### ● Step-by-step

1. Take a doily and gather it through its middle, so that you get the effect of wings fanning out on either side of the gathered centre. Do the same with the second doily. Lay one above the other, overlapping the wings.
2. Fold the pipe cleaner in half. Fold again but this time leave the open end slightly longer.
3. Slide the two sets of wings inside the doubled wire. Pull the open ends of wire through the loop of folded wire and press down to secure the wings.
4. Slide a bead on to each of the two hair grips. Slide the hair grips on to the butterfly's wings, near the body, for antennae. Use the marker to make black circles on the beads for eyes.
5. Glue the magnet to the back.

## Teaching point

Ask the children to bring their butterflies to the circle area and introduce or review the story. Then ask:

- How does a caterpillar change into a butterfly?
- What does the Bible say happens when someone becomes a Christian?
- How does God help us to change our attitudes or actions?

Explain that we are born into a world which can sometimes feel drab or dull, but when we become Christians our lives are changed into something beautiful. With God's love we become a new person. A butterfly is a dull old caterpillar before it changes into a beautiful butterfly. Close in prayer by thanking God for giving us the chance to become a beautiful person in him.

# Ambassadors for Christ

> Bible story
> 2 Corinthians 5:20
>
> Bible point
> **Speak out for Christ.**

## Activity

### Chatterbox puppets

Make puppets from cereal boxes as a reminder to speak out for Christ.

### ● You will need

Individual size cereal box (one per child), lightweight paper, card, knitting yarn, felt-tipped pens, two movable eyes, glue sticks

### ● Preparation

Cut the top flaps off the cereal boxes. Cover the sides and bottom with a lightweight, light coloured paper. (Glue the paper to the box.) Place the rest of the supplies out on a table.

### ● Handy hint

Arrange for the children to use their puppets in church to put on a short drama telling about Christ's love.

### ● Step-by-step

1. Glue the movable eyes to the front of the box, with the opening on the bottom.
2. Use the felt-tipped pens and card to add features to the face. Cut a dress front or bow tie from card and glue it at the bottom of the box
3. For a girl puppet, cut the yarn into 20cm strands. Glue across the top of the box lengthwise, and tie the ends for pigtails. For a boy puppet, cut shorter strands, approximately 10cm in length, and glue across the box top from front to back.
4. The children will put their fist up inside the box and move it back and forth to make the puppet move and talk.

## Teaching point

Ask the children to bring their puppets to the circle and then introduce or review the story. Tell the children that an ambassador is someone who represents a country. Then ask:

- What makes our puppets seem as if they are speaking?
- What kind of things might an ambassador talk about?
- How can we become an ambassador for Christ?

Explain that just as we can use our puppets to speak for us, God uses ambassadors to speak for him. They tell others about Christ's love. We can be ambassadors for Christ by speaking out for him.

# Be a cheerful giver

> Bible story
> 2 Corinthians 9:7–8
>
> Bible point
> God loves a cheerful giver.

## Activity

### Smiley coin-throwing game

Make coin-throwing games as a reminder that God loves a cheerful giver.

● **You will need**

Clear plastic cups, smiley stickers, yellow and red cardboard, felt-tipped pens, scissors

● **Preparation**

Cut several 4cm cardboard circles for the children to use as templates. Put all the project supplies out on a table.

● **Handy hint**

Look for a project within your church that the children could help with. Remind the children that God wants them to give their time and talents cheerfully as well as their money.

● **Step-by-step**

1. Use a template to trace ten circles on yellow cardboard and ten circles on red. Cut them out.
2. Draw a smile on one side of each circle and the number 5, 10, 15, 20 or 25 on the other. (The numbers will be the point values. Make sure the two sets of coins add up to equal values.)
3. Write 'God loves a cheerful giver' on the plastic cup. Decorate the outside of the cup with the smiley stickers. To play, set the cup on the floor between two players. Give each player a set of the coins. Have them take turns throwing a coin toward the cup. Add up the points on each colour of coins inside the cup. The player with the most points wins.

## Teaching point

Ask the children to gather together, and introduce or review the story. Then ask:

- How does it feel inside when we give something?
- What kind of attitude should we have when we give?
- Besides money, what else can we give cheerfully?

Explain that two things happen when we give. First of all, those who have a need are helped and, second, God is praised through our giving. The Bible says that when we give something, God will make sure we have everything we need, too. We must remember to give cheerfully because God loves a cheerful giver.

# Galatians

## Sons and daughters of God

Bible story
Galatians 3:26–29

Bible point
**Children who belong to God are sons and daughters of God.**

## Activity

### Folded photo frame friends

Make folded photo frames.

### ● You will need

Thick cardboard, clear plastic, sticky tape, glue sticks, felt-tipped pens, stickers, pinking shears, frame templates, rulers

### ● Preparation

Provide cardboard templates for making frames approximately 8cm x 10cm in size, with an opening of 5cm x 7cm. Place the supplies out on a table.

### ● Handy hint

Ask the children to bring three or four photographs of themselves. They can put one on the front page of their photo frame and exchange the others with friends.

### ● Step-by-step

1. Cut a piece of cardboard into a 15cm x 40cm strip. Concertina-fold it into four equal sections.
2. Use the templates to trace and cut four photo frames. Remove the centres and cut around the edges with pinking shears.
3. Cut four 6cm x 8cm pieces of clear plastic. Tape one to the back of each frame, covering the opening.
4. Smear glue on three sides of the frames, leaving the top open, and attach one to each page of the folded poster board. Use a marker to write 'We are all sons and daughters of God' on the first page.
5. Decorate around the frames with stickers and felt-tipped pens.

## Teaching point

Ask the children to bring their frames and gather together. Introduce or review the story. Then ask:

• How do we become children of God?
• How can our actions show that we are sons and daughters of God?

Explain that everyone is equal in God's eyes. When we have finished putting pictures in our photo frames, not all the people will look the same, but children who belong to God are sons and daughters of God.

# Love your neighbour

Age guide:
7–11s

Bible story
Galatians 5:13–15

Bible point
We should love others as much as we love ourselves.

## Activity

### Friendship beads

Make beads from wrapping paper and straws to create a bracelet for a friend.

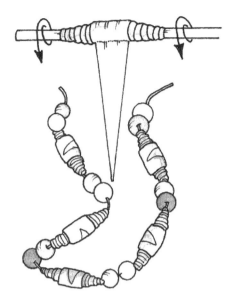

### ● You will need

Wrapping paper, plastic straws, glue sticks, 20cm shoelaces, beads, scissors

### ● Preparation

Cut long triangular strips from the wrapping paper that start at about 4cm wide and taper slowly to a point. Put all other supplies on a table.

### ● Handy hint

You can use magazine pages instead of wrapping paper to make the beads. Any colourful paper will work.

### ● Step-by-step

1. Lay a wrapping paper strip, colour side down, on the table. Use a glue stick to apply glue to the wide end. Lay a whole straw on the paper and start to roll it as tight and straight as possible. Apply more glue as you continue to roll to the end.
2. Cut away the straw on both sides of the paper. Repeat Steps 1 and 2 until you have nine friendship beads. (Each straw will make three beads.)
3. Thread an ordinary bead on to a shoelace, followed by a friendship bead. Repeat until the shoelace is full.
4. Tie the ends together and give the bracelet to someone special.

## Teaching point

Ask the children to bring their bracelets and gather together. Introduce or review the story. Then ask:

• Who are our neighbours?
• How can we serve one another with love?
• What does the Bible say will happen if we are hurtful toward others?

Explain that we have the freedom to serve one another by being kind, or to hurt one another by being selfish and mean. Today we have worked very hard making beads to create a beautiful bracelet. Giving our bracelets to someone special shows that we love them. We should love others as much as we love ourselves. Let children decide who they would like to give their bracelet to. Praise them for their decision and let them know that God is pleased with them for being kind and generous.

# Fruits of the Spirit

> Bible story
> Galatians 5:22–26
>
> Bible point
> **Let God produce good fruit in us.**

## Activity

### Fruitful pencil toppers

Make fruit-shaped pencil toppers as a reminder to let the good fruits grow in our lives.

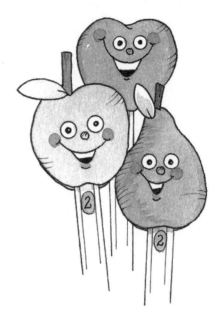

### ● You will need

Craft foam in red, yellow, purple, brown, green and pink; six small wobbly eyes per child; scissors; glue sticks; thin-line black marker; clothes pegs; pencils; cardboard

### ● Preparation

Make cardboard templates of an apple, a pear, a plum, a leaf and a stem. Put all the craft supplies out on a table.

### ● Handy hint

This project can also be made from card, which will cut cost and drying time. However, the toppers will not be as durable. If appropriate, the toppers could be used for fundraising.

### ● Step-by-step

1. Cut two apple shapes from red art foam, two pear shapes from yellow and two plums from purple. Cut two stems from brown foam and two leaves from green.
2. Put a line of glue around three sides of one apple, leaving the bottom open. Lay the stem on the top centre and put the other apple shape on top. Put a clothes peg on each side of the apple to hold it as it dries.
3. Glue the leaf on the top left side. Cut a small nose from pink art foam and add the movable eyes. Draw a mouth with the marker.
4. Repeat Steps 3 and 4 to make a pear and plum. NB: The plum doesn't have a stem and leaf.

## Teaching point

Ask the children to leave the toppers on the table to dry. Gather together and introduce or review the story. Then ask:

- How long does it take to grow fruit?
- How long does it take for us to learn to obey God?
- What are some good things we can grow in our lives?
- Why does God want us to be patient, joyful, and kind?

Explain that Paul compared the good things growing in our lives to fruit. When we see our foam fruits sitting on our pencils, we will be reminded to let love, joy, peace, patience, kindness, goodness, faithfulness, gentleness and self-control be seen in our lives. It is good to let God produce good fruit in us!

# Do good to all

Age guide: 5-7s

Bible story
Galatians 6:1–10

Bible point
**Let us do good to all.**

## Activity

### 'Do good' sun catcher

Make sun catchers as a reminder that we can brighten someone's day by doing good.

- **You will need**

Card, clear plastic, felt-tipped pens, hole punch, scissors, glue, suction pads or invisible thread

- **Preparation**

Make a 10cm x 16cm cardboard template for the children to use. Set the supplies out on a table.

- **Handy hint**

Supply suction pads and let the children decide if they want to brighten the church with their sun catchers or take them home as a reminder.

- **Step-by-step**

1. Fold a 23cm x 30cm sheet of card in half. Use the template to trace a rectangle in the centre of the card. Cut through both layers and remove the centre.
2. Cut a 12cm x 20cm rectangle from the clear plastic. Open the frame and smear glue around the edges. Lay the plastic sheet over the opening. Put a little more glue around the frame and close it. Press tightly.
3. Round the corners of the frame with scissors and punch a hole in the top centre.
4. Use the felt-tipped pens to write 'Let us do good to all (Galatians 6:10)' on the plastic.* Draw flowers and leaves on the sun catcher. Use the thread to hang the sun catcher in a sunny position, or a suction pad to hang on a window.

\* New International Version

## Teaching point

Ask the children to bring their sun catchers and gather in a circle. Introduce or review the story. Then ask:

- Why should we help someone with troubles or problems?
- Why shouldn't we get tired of doing good?
- Who should we be especially quick to help?

Explain that anything we do to help someone or to brighten their day is doing good for others. As these sun catchers brighten a window, they will remind us to do good. Let the children think of ways they could help or do good for someone they know. Make a list and then close in prayer, asking for God's help to do good.

# Ephesians

## Chosen by God

> Bible story
> Ephesians 1:3–6
>
> Bible point
> **God adopted us.**

## Activity

### God picked me!

Make plant decorators.

### ● You will need

Pink, purple, yellow and green fun foam; green garden canes; low-temperature glue gun; black felt-tipped pens; scissors; pencils; masking tape

### ● Preparation

Set up the supplies in one area and then set the glue gun in a separate working area.

### ● Handy hint

Safety is always the key when working with young children. Tape a piece of masking tape around one end of the cane so that the children can avoid injury until they get home to put their craft in a potted plant holder.

### ● Step-by-step

1. With a pencil, lightly draw the shape of a flower about the size of your hand on to the fun foam. Cut the flower out.
2. Draw the same shaped flower on to a different colour, but make it slightly smaller. Cut this out also.
3. Glue one end of the cane on to the larger flower. Place the smaller flower over the cane, so that the cane is sandwiched between the two flowers. Glue the edges of the two flowers together, making sure the cane is firmly in place.

4. Cut a circle of a different colour to be used for the centre of the flower. On the circle of the flower, draw a simple smily face and write the words 'God picked me!' Glue the circle on to the smaller sized flower. Cut leaves out of the green foam and glue them on to the cane.

## Teaching point

Because of the pointy garden canes, it's best to leave the flowers at the table for the group discussion. Ask the children to join you on the floor in a circle and introduce or review today's Bible verse. Then ask:

- If we could adopt someone into our families, who would it be? Why?
- Why might God want to adopt us into his family?

Explain that God didn't 'pick' us in the way that we would pick a flower or pick someone to be our friend. No, God chose us to be adopted into his heavenly family because we love Jesus. God has chosen us because we believe in his Son, Jesus. If Jesus lives in our hearts, we automatically become a part of his family. We are part of God's family!

# Sealed by the Spirit

Age guide: 7–11s

## Activity

### Dove paperweights

Make dove paperweights.

### ● You will need

Clean flat pebbles, pencils, white acrylic paint, small paintbrushes, black felt-tipped pens

### ● Preparation

Beforehand, draw a simple outline of a dove for the children to use as a reference when they make their own smaller version.

### ● Handy hint

Because this craft is so quick and easy to make, allow the children to make several to give to friends or place in strategic places around the church.

### ● Step-by-step

1. On the pebble, draw an outline of a dove.
2. Carefully colour the dove with white paint and allow to dry.
3. Use the felt-tipped pen to mark the dove's eye.

## Teaching point

When the children have finished their paperweights, ask them to join you and bring their crafts with them. Introduce or review the Bible verses. Then ask:

- How would it feel if someone close to us gave us £100, but came back the next day and took it away?
- How does it feel to know that God has given us his Holy Spirit and no one can take him away?

Explain that a dove is a symbol of peace, which is exactly what the Holy Spirit brings to us. By trusting in Christ as our Saviour, we have become God's own children. God promises us peace in our hearts and eternal life with him. No amount of money can buy this gift. Our paperweights remind us that God has given us his Holy Spirit. End this discussion with a prayer, thanking God for the gift of his Holy Spirit.

# Paul explains our relationship with Christ

Age guide: 7–11s

Bible story
Ephesians 2:8–9

Bible point
Salvation is not earned; it is a gift from God.

## Activity

### It's free!

Make gift boxes for a loved one.

### ● You will need

Plastic Binca canvas, decorative cord or knitting yarn, scissors, sticky tape, paper, pencils, glue sticks, beads (optional)

### ● Preparation

Beforehand, cut six 8cm x 8cm squares from the plastic canvas per child.

### ● Handy hint

If time allows, beads or additional string can be sewn or glued to the sides of the boxes to make them even more decorative. Encourage children to tell their parents that after all the slips of paper have been read and used, they may choose to put potpourri inside the box as a gift of fragrance that keeps on giving.

### ● Step-by-step

1. Cut a piece of cord or yarn about 30cm long. Tie a knot at one end and wrap a very small piece of tape around the other end to make a sharp point.
2. Take one piece of canvas and note this as being the base of the box. Lay another square of the canvas on top of the box base. This will be the first side. Skipping every other hole, stitch the two pieces together along one edge and tie a knot when you reach the end. When the side is finished, open the two pieces so that they lay flat next to each other.
3. Place a second piece of canvas on top of the box base and sew this to the second edge of the box

base. Open out and repeat twice more until there are four pieces of canvas sewn to the outer edge of the box base.
4. Bring all four sides up to form the shape of a box and sew the sides together using the same stitch as before.
5. Sew the sixth piece of canvas to one edge of the top of the box to make the lid. If desired, sew a decorative pattern around the other three edges of the lid and tie a bow to the top.
6. Decide who the gift is for and write on small pieces of paper the things you will do for that person as a gift of love.

## Teaching point

When the boxes are completed, ask the children to join you in a circle and introduce or review today's Bible verse. Then ask:

• How does it feel when we receive a gift for no reason at all?
• What are some things in life that are gifts that money can't ever buy?
• What does God's gift of grace mean?

Explain that if we bought a present for no reason at all, that would probably make us look pretty cool in the eyes of the person who received it. This is just what God has done for us. He has given us the gift of kindness and unconditional love, which means that we can be with him every day, and on into eternity. There's nothing we have done to earn his gift and no one can take it away from us.

# Forgiving others

Bible story
Ephesians 4:32

Bible point
Forgive others as God forgives us.

## Activity

### 'Son' catchers

Make beaded window decorations.

#### You will need

Craft lolly sticks, thin jewellery wire, clear beads, red beads, red paint, paintbrushes, low-temperature glue gun, ribbon, string

#### Preparation

For each child, cut nine strips of wire approximately 12cm long. It would be helpful if the children had individual trays to keep their work organised.

#### Handy hint

Some children may be capable of using string rather than wire. This would allow for the beads to hang more freely and not get bent up. Instead of bending the wire to secure it, you would have to use knots in the string.

#### Step-by-step

1. Paint two craft sticks red and lay them aside to dry.
2. Thread a clear bead on to a wire. Bend and twist the tip of the wire so that the bead won't fall off. Thread ten more clear beads on this wire so that there are eleven in total.
3. Firmly wrap one end of the beaded wire around a third craft stick. Do the same for the remaining eight wires, but follow the bead line-up below.
4. Second wire: eleven clear beads; third wire: seven clear beads, then one red bead, followed by three more clear beads; fourth wire: as third wire; fifth wire: eleven red beads; sixth wire: as third wire; seventh wire: as third wire; eighth and ninth wires: eleven clear beads on each.
5. Glue the painted craft sticks on to each side of the stick that has the beads dangling from it, covering up the wires. Add the words 'Forgive others'.

6. Tie a string around each end so that the craft can be hung in a window.

## Teaching point

Ask all the children to gather in a circle on the floor. Introduce or review today's Bible verse. Then ask:

* What are some kind and compassionate things we can do for others?
* What kind and compassionate things has God done for us?
* Knowing that God forgives us when we do things wrong, how can we be more forgiving towards others?

Explain that now the craft is finished, we can think of the patience it took to follow the directions so carefully. We can think of how gentle and tender we had to be as we beaded the fragile wires. We can think of how we had to forgive ourselves if we made a mistake and had to start again. Today's Bible verse tells us that we need those same qualities as we work and play with others. Our beaded crosses can remind us that Jesus gave his life for us. How much easier it is for us to forgive others!

# Living as children of light

> **Bible story**
> Ephesians 5:8–10
>
> **Bible point**
> Be children of light.

## Activity

### Shine on!

Make lanterns.

### ● You will need

Clean empty cans with the lids removed, leaving no jagged edges; 20-gauge wire; large nail; hammers; felt-tipped pens; tealight candles; towels; some large rocks

### ● Preparation

Beforehand, peel labels off the cans and fill the cans with water. Place them in the freezer so that the frozen water will make it easier to punch holes into the cans.

### ● Handy hint

If possible, ask the children to bring in a pair of gloves to do this project, as the cans will be extremely cold. Give adult supervision where needed and remind the children that they should always ask an adult for help when lighting a candle. The cans should be placed on a heatproof mat when the candle is lit

### ● Step-by-step

1. With the felt-tipped pen, draw the places on the can where you want to punch the holes. Be sure not to place the holes too close together, but allow for enough holes so that the light of a candle will really shine through.
2. Place the towel on the floor. Place the can between two large rocks to prevent from rolling away while you are working on it.
3. Place the nail on the spot where a hole is to be made and gently tap the hammer on the head of the nail until it punctures the can. The nail will easily go through the can because of the ice inside. Do this over the whole can.
4. Make a hole on each side of the can, close to the top, for the handle.

5. Wrap a piece of wire around a felt-tipped pen to make it curly. Place one end of the wire through each hole at the top and bend to make the handle. Empty out the ice and dry the can. Put a candle inside and enjoy!

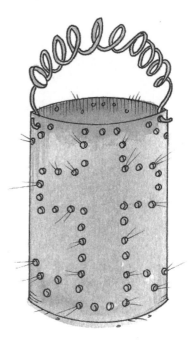

## Teaching point

When the children have finished their lanterns, ask them to join you in a circle on the floor. Introduce or review the Bible verse. Then ask:

- How does it feel when we are having a 'dark' day?
- What does it mean to live as children of light?
- What things make us a 'light to others'?

Explain that sometimes, when we are in a dark room all by ourselves, feelings such as fear, gloominess or even anger enter us. But when we turn the light on, suddenly that same room can feel warm, happy and inviting. God wants us to be light in the world. Even when things look gloomy and ugly, God wants us to turn to what pleases him and shine truth, goodness and righteousness when we are with people who don't know his love. As a lantern sheds light on a room, we need to remember to do the same wherever we are.

Close the discussion with a chain prayer in which everyone shares something they can do to be a light in the world.

# The armour of God

Bible story
Ephesians 6:10–17

Bible point
**Put on God's armour every day.**

## Activity

### Dress for success!

Make wardrobe door hangers as a reminder to dress in our 'spiritual clothes'.

### ● You will need

Thick card, poster paint, paintbrushes, photocopies of God's armour (see page 183), crayons or felt-tipped pens, fine-tipped permanent black marker, scissors, glue

### ● Preparation

Beforehand, cut the cardboard into rectangular pieces approximately 8–10cm wide and 25cm long. Cut a hole 6cm x 6cm on the top for the doorknob to fit through. This hole will be large enough to fit over any standard-sized doorknob without cutting or ripping the cardboard.

### ● Handy hint

Because of all the writing in this project, print out the words in Step 3.

### ● Step-by-step

1. Paint the doorknob hanger in one colour.
2. While waiting for the paint to dry, colour and cut out a copy of God's armour.
3. Glue the armour pictures in a vertical column below the hole for the doorknob, along the left side of the hanger. With the marker write in big letters, 'Dress for success!' On the back of the hanger write, 'Truth, justice, peace, faith, rescue, Holy Spirit'.

## Teaching point

When the children have finished, ask them to join you, bringing their hangers with them. Introduce or review the Bible story. Go through each piece of the armour and let the children pretend to put on each piece as you explain what it means. (For example, say, 'First of all, let's put on our belt of truth. This means we will always try to speak and seek God's truth in all we say or do.') Then ask:

• What does it mean to put on the armour of God?
• Why is it important that we do this?
• Think of ways in which wearing God's armour could help us at school or home.

Explain that when it's cold and raining outside, we put on a heavy jacket, boots, gloves and a hat to protect us. In the same way, we need God's armour to protect us from things such as bad feelings, or times when we are tempted to do wrong. When we put on God's armour, we will be prepared for anything. Invite the children to take turns prayerfully to share a situation in which they need to put on the armour of God. Start by sharing an example such as, 'Father, please help us to remember to put on our armour when we feel like being mean.'

# Armour of God template

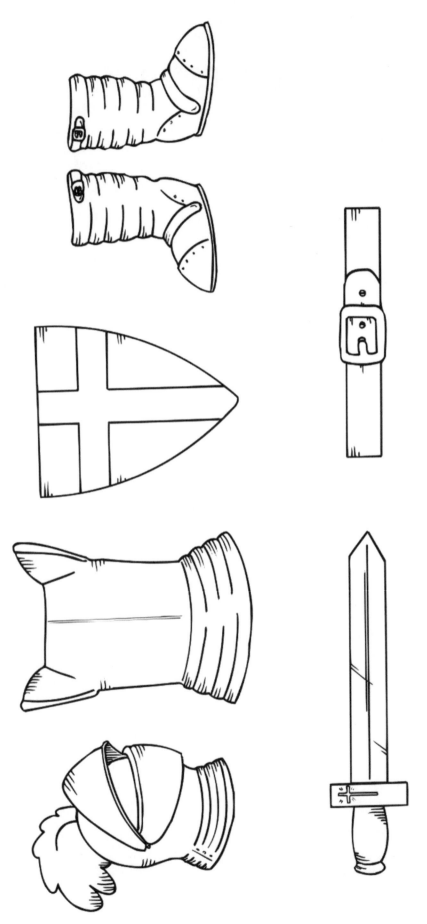

Reproduced with permission from *The Encyclopedia of Bible Crafts* published by BRF 2010 (978 1 84101 590 3) www.barnabasinschools.org.uk

# Philippians

## Helping others

> Bible story
> **Philippians 2:3–4**
>
> Bible point
> **God wants us to care about others.**

## Activity

### Flower power care gifts

Make flower power coupons to help us think of the needs of others.

#### • You will need

Flower power coupons (see page 185), paper, scissors, pipe cleaners, sticky tape, sheets of mini flower stickers or other stickers

#### • Preparation

Make photocopies of the flower power coupons (one set per child) and circle. Set up the rest of the supplies.

#### • Handy hint

For extra fun, give children empty yoghurt pots to make flowerpots. Let the children put some modelling dough in the bottom of the pot and stick their flower in it. If desired, they can decorate the pots with a mixture of several drops of acrylic paint stirred into white glue. This paint mixture will adhere to plastic.

#### • Step-by-step

1. Cut out the flower power coupons and stick them round the circle to look like petals.
2. Tape a pipe cleaner to the back of the flower for a stem.
3. Wrap another pipe cleaner once around the stem. Then bend the ends in to the middle and curl them around the stem to make leaves.
4. Tape a sheet of little stickers to the back of the flower.

Look out for the interests of others

## Teaching point

When the children have finished their flowers, ask them to join you and bring their creations with them. Introduce or review Philippians 2:3–4. Then ask:

* What does it mean to be selfish?
* Why should we think of others more than ourselves?
* How can we look out for the interests of others?

Explain that Jesus wants us to think of others as more important than ourselves because that's what he did. He didn't go around bragging that he was God, even though he created the universe. Instead, he served others quietly with love. One way we can be like Jesus is to look for ways to help others.

Invite the children to take their flower power coupons home and be on the lookout for ways to help others. When they see a way to help, they can write it on a coupon and give the coupon to that person. They should do the job straight away or tell the person that they can ask for it to be done another time. Each time the children give away a coupon, they can take one of the stickers off the back of their flower and put it inside the circle, where they removed a petal. When they have given all the petals away, they will still have a pretty flower to remind them to look out for the interests of others. God wants us to care about others.

# Flower power coupon template

Good for

Good for

Good for

Good for

Good for

Good for

Good for

Good for

Good for

Good for

Look out for the interests of others

# Talk to God about everything

> ### Bible story
> **Philippians 4:6–7**
>
> ### Bible point
> **Don't worry—pray!**

## Activity

### Prayer pockets

Make prayer pockets as a reminder to make our requests known to God.

### ● You will need

Pocket photo album pages, old magazines, scissors, fine-tipped felt pens, mini-stickers

### ● Preparation

Make a sample prayer pocket to show the children. If desired, tape it to the cover of a three-ring binder using coloured sticky tape around the edges and larger stickers in the corners. (Be careful not to tape the top pockets closed.) The children insert items into the pockets that represent their prayer requests.

### ● Handy hint

If your budget allows, purchase an inexpensive three-ring binder and a few sheets of lined notebook paper for each child. When children have made their prayer pockets, let them tape the pockets to the cover with sticky tape and stickers. Play quiet music in the background as they work and invite them each to write out a prayer to begin their prayer journal. Remind them to include a 'thank you' to God for hearing them. The children might want to share their prayers out loud with one another.

### ● Step-by-step

1. Find a few magazine pictures that represent things to pray about, and cut them out. For example, a picture of a child could represent asking God for a friend or to help a friend in need.
2. Insert the magazine pictures into the pockets. Don't fill every pocket.
3. Decorate the prayer pockets with small stickers and felt-tipped pens, but be sure to leave the centre of each pocket undecorated so that the prayer requests can be seen.

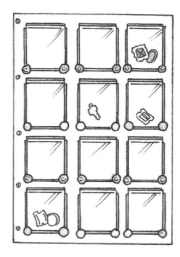

## Teaching point

When the children have finished making their prayer pockets, invite them to join you in the story area with their creations. Introduce or review Philippians 4:6 with the children. Then ask:

- What does this verse tell us to do?
- What are we not supposed to worry about?
- What things are we supposed to pray about?

Explain that God doesn't want us to worry about anything. He wants us to pray about everything. Ask a volunteer to read Philippians 4:6–7 aloud and then explain that when we pray about things, God gives us his peace. He wants us to know that he is with us and that he hears us. So remember, don't worry—pray!

Show children the prayer pocket you made. Explain briefly how the items represent things you're praying for. Invite children to use their prayer pockets at home and add photos and small items to represent their prayers. They can tape their prayer pockets to the cover of a binder or store it inside a binder, which can then become a prayer journal to write down their requests and record God's answers. Explain that when God answers their prayers, they can remove the items and replace them with others.

# Colossians

## Christit is the head of the Church

Bible story
Colossians 1:17–18

Bible point
Christ is the head of the Church.

## Activity

### Pop-up cross

Make cards with a pop-up cross inside as a reminder that Christ is the head of the Church.

### ● You will need

A sheet of card measuring 23cm x 30cm and a sheet of paper measuring 20cm x 28cm (per child), scissors, crayons or felt-tipped pens, glue, cross cut-outs, glitter

### ● Preparation

Make photocopies of the cross template for children to cut out. Prepare two work areas. One area will be for cutting and drawing and the other area will be for gluing and glittering.

### ● Handy hint

Make sure the children draw the church on the card before gluing the pop-up sheet inside.

### ● Step-by-step

1. Decorate a cross with glitter. Then set it aside to dry.
2. Fold the sheet of paper in half (like a card) and, from the fold, cut two 5cm slits 2.5cm apart.
3. Turn the slit inside out, creating a pop-up. Beneath the pop-up, write 'Christ is the head of the Church'.
4. Fold the card in half and draw a church on the outside. Make sure the fold is at the top.
5. Glue the paper (the one with the pop-up inside) inside the card. Then glue the cross on to the pop-up.

## Teaching point

When the children have finished their churches, ask them to join you. Introduce or review the Bible verses. Then ask:

- Who does the Bible say is the Church?
- How is Jesus important to the Church?

Explain that the Bible states that the body of believers—that's us—are the Church. Jesus is God's Son and he is the head of the Church. Our pop-up crosses can remind us that Christ is the head of the Church. Invite the children to think of something that makes church special to them. Then close in a prayer thanking God for the Church.

# Joined together in love

> ### Bible story
> Colossians 2:2
>
> ### Bible point
> Be encouraged and joined together in love.

## Activity

### Hanging hearts

Make hanging hearts as a reminder to be encouraged and joined together in love.

### ● You will need

Card, tissue paper, self-adhesive vinyl, hole punch, ribbon, scissors

### ● Preparation

Cut the card into rectangles measuring 15cm x 22cm. Cut the tissue paper into 2.5cm squares. Cut vinyl into six 43cm squares. In a work area, place the card, tissue paper and vinyl into separate piles. Then place the scissors, hole punch and ribbon in another area so that the children can work in assembly-line fashion to complete the craft.

### ● Handy hint

Ask the children to leave their hanging hearts for you to display in the church. Using sticky tape, hang them in a sunny window or from an arch or ceiling.

### ● Step-by-step

1. Fold the card in half. Cut out a heart shape and then another heart inside it to make an outline of a heart.
2. Fold the vinyl in half, creating a crease, and then unfold. Peel the backing off half of the vinyl and lay the heart outline on top of it. Fill in the heart with tissue paper squares.
3. Peel the backing off the rest of the vinyl and fold over the heart. Trim any excess vinyl. Then punch a hole into the top and add a ribbon.

## Teaching point

When the children have finished their hanging hearts, invite them to join you. Introduce or review the Bible verse. Then ask:

- What does it mean to be encouraged?
- What does it mean to be joined together?
- How can we be encouraged and joined together in love?

Explain that the apostle Paul wrote a letter to the Colossians, telling them that his purpose was for them to be encouraged and joined together in love. This way, they would fully understand God, because God is love. Our hanging hearts can remind us to be encouraged, which is to be inspired or confident in our hearts. They also can remind us to be joined together in love. Invite the children to share a way that they can be joined with others in love. Close by asking God to join everyone together in his love.

# Godly families

Bible story
Colossians 3:18–21

Bible point
**God wants us to do our part in the family.**

## Activity

### Fun in the family

Make paper doll family chains to show that everyone has a part in making a happy family.

### ● You will need

Paper, scissors, felt-tipped pens, old magazines, glue sticks, heart stickers, paper doll template (see page 190), sticky tape

### ● Preparation

Make photocopies of the template on page 190, at least one per child. An A4 piece of paper will yield four family figures. Make copies on larger paper for children with larger families.

### ● Handy hint

Some children may want to add extended family members to their chain, such as a grandparent or aunt or uncle. If they do, ask them during the discussion time to describe that person's part in the family. If a child's family is larger than the number of people on the template, let them fold and cut out more than one template and tape them together.

NB: Be sensitive to the children in the group who come from single-parent families and acknowledge them in a general way in the discussion. Say something like, 'Some families have only one parent, which means that that parent has two jobs—that of mum and dad. So they deserve a double amount of respect and love!'

### ● Step-by-step

1. Fold the template on the dotted lines and cut out the figure. Make sure you don't cut through the dotted line on the arms.

2. Ask the children to cut out faces from a magazine to represent the members of their family and glue them on to the figures.
3. Draw and colour clothing on the figures with felt-tipped pens. In the magazines, find accessory items that go with the family, such as hats, shoes, sports equipment or pets, and glue them on to the figures.

## Teaching point

When the children have finished their family chains, ask them to join you with the chains in the story area. Invite the children briefly to introduce their family to the person sitting next to them. Then explain that everyone in the family has a part to play in making it a happy one. Read the Bible verses out loud to the children. Then ask:

- What is each person's role in the family?
- Why is it important for us to obey our parents or the people who look after us?
- Why are families happiest when everyone plays their part?

Explain that God's plan is for families to be happy. That doesn't mean there won't be fights or problems—no family is perfect—but if we each do our job, our family will be stronger because of it. Ask the children to hold up their family chains and notice that all the people are all connected. No one stands alone. That's to show that God says each family member is important. Let's ask God to help us do our part to make our family strong.

Give out heart stickers and let the children put one sticker over each spot on the chains where the hands link together. Take turns to say, 'Dear God, help me to play my part in my family.' Then explain that even if someone in our family doesn't live according to God's rules, God still wants us to do our part. That's his job for us, no matter what anyone else does in our family. When we obey our parents, we bring God's love to our family. God wants us to play our part in the family.

# Paper doll template

FOLD

- - - - - - - - - - - - - - - - - - - - - - - - - - - - - - - - - - - - - - - - - - -

FOLD

- - - - - - - - - - - - - - - - - - - - - - - - - - - - - - - - - - - - - - - - - - -

DON'T CUT

DON'T CUT

FOLD

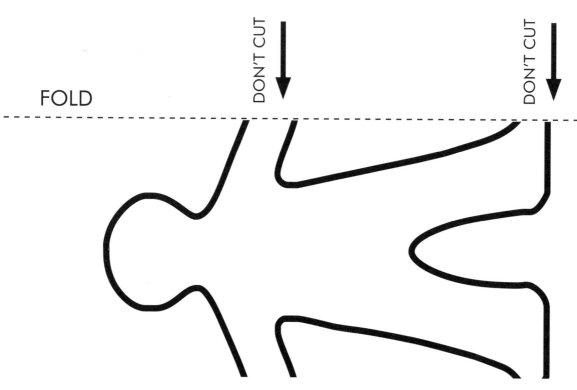

# Never give up praying

> **Bible story**
> Colossians 4:2–4
>
> **Bible point**
> God wants us to pray.

## Activity

### Prayer plaques

Make prayer plaques as a reminder to pray for others around the world.

### ● You will need

A globe or world atlas, cardboard or heavy duty paper plates (one per child), glue, yarn or cord, aluminium foil, miscellaneous 'sculpting' materials, water, paintbrushes

### ● Preparation

Gather one or more of the following items for children to add to their plaques besides the knitting yarn: paperclips, nails, buttons, beads, extra pieces of cardboard to cut shapes out of, screws and so on. Prepare a mixture of two parts glue to one part water.

### ● Handy hint

To speed up the drying of the glued items before applying the foil, blow-dry the plaques with a hairdryer on a low heat setting. The children can help with this under close supervision.

Some children might want to choose a city or even a certain area of their town to pray for. Encourage them to do so, telling them that people everywhere need prayer.

### ● Step-by-step

1. Look at the globe or world atlas and choose a country or continent to pray for.
2. Using the glue, write the name of the country or continent in big letters on the cardboard or paper plate. If you wish, draw the outline of the country with the name inside it.
3. Lay pieces of yarn or cord on top of the glue to create raised letters and glue some of the other sculpting objects around to decorate the plaque. For example, cut the shape of the country out of a piece of cardboard, or form its shape using beads,

paperclips or other objects, or make a border or other design with the objects.
4. When the country name and design are finished, let the plaque dry for a few minutes, then brush the glue and water mixture over the entire surface.
5. Lay a sheet of aluminium foil on top of the objects. Gently press and mould it around the yarn and other objects on the cardboard, wrapping the edges of the foil over the sides of the cardboard.

## Teaching point

When the children have finished their prayer plaques, ask them to join you in the story area. If possible, let the children read from their own Bibles as you read the verses out loud. After reading the verses, if necessary, explain that to devote ourselves to something means to give our time, strength and energy to it. Then ask:

- What does it mean to be watchful?
- Why should we be thankful when we pray?
- What do verses 3 and 4 tell us to pray for?

Explain to the children that one way to be watchful is to listen to news on TV or read a newspaper and then pray about those situations. Remind the children to pray for missionaries and ministers, as well as those who don't know Jesus. In these verses, Paul is asking the people to pray for him as he talks to others about Jesus. That's what we're going to do with our prayer plaques. We're going to pray for the people in other countries who are teaching people about Jesus. When we take our plaques home, we can put them somewhere to remind us to pray. Let the children take turns sharing about the country they chose, then lead the others in praying for that country.

# 1 Thessalonians

## Living for God

Bible story
1 Thessalonians 5:19–24

Bible point
**Don't put out the Holy Spirit's fire.**

## Activity

### Fire fighters

Make fire extinguishers as a reminder not to put out the Holy Spirit's fire.

### ● You will need

Empty lemonade bottles (without tops), red tissue paper, glue, index cards, white streamers, black felt-tipped pens, black card, scissors, tape and several plastic spray bottle nozzles

### ● Preparation

Arrange the tables to provide ample room for the craft assembly. If supplies are limited, set up workstations for the children to work together as a team.

### ● Handy hint

Encourage the children to think of some things that weaken our faith. Examples might include doubt, fear, wrong friendships or pride. Ask them to write their ideas down on the white streamer inside the fire extinguisher. Display the projects as a reminder of things to avoid.

### ● Step-by-step

1. Roll a large square of red tissue paper around an empty lemonade bottle. Tape the paper in place and mould the edges around the top and bottom of the bottle.
2. Insert a white streamer into the bottle, leaving a tail at the bottle opening.
3. Fold a piece of black card in half. Use a plastic spray nozzle to trace a nozzle shape on to the card. Cut

out both pieces. Glue the card nozzle at the top of the bottle.
4. To make a handle, cut a 20cm strip of black card and glue the edges to the side of the bottle. Write the Bible point on an index card. Glue the card on to the extinguisher and allow to dry.

## Teaching point

Introduce or review the verses from 1 Thessalonians. Then ask:

- Why is it important to live for God?
- What things pull us away from God?
- How can we stay excited about God?

Explain that Paul was encouraging the Christians in Thessalonica to become strong in their faith. The believers faced many struggles and problems. By obeying God, the Christians were able to recognise things that were wrong and stay away from them. Just as a fire extinguisher puts out flames, so the wrong things we say, think and do weaken our fire for God. God wants us to spend time reading our Bibles and getting to know him so that we don't put out his Holy Spirit's fire.

# 2 Thessalonians

**Age guide: 5–7s**

## Standing firm for God

Bible story
2 Thessalonians 2:15–17

Bible point
**Stand firm for God.**

## Activity

### Bold believer

Create statues as a reminder to stand firm for God.

### ● You will need

Large jam jar lids, wooden dolly pegs, fabric scraps, hot glue gun, scissors, glue, black and yellow or brown felt-tipped pens, card, pipe cleaners

### ● Preparation

Beforehand, using a hot glue gun, firmly attach a dolly peg to the centre of each lid (one per child). The pegs should be standing upright.

### ● Handy hint

Encourage the children to display their figures at home as a reminder to be bold for God.

### ● Step-by-step

1. Using a black felt-tipped pen, draw a face on the head of the dolly peg. Use the other felt-tipped pens to create hair.
2. Twist a pipe cleaner around the top half of the figure's body to create arms. Cut out fabric scraps to make clothes and glue them on to the figure.
3. Use card to make a Bible. Glue the Bible to the figure's hand. Let the statue dry.

## Teaching point

Introduce or review the verses from 2 Thessalonians. Then ask:

- How can we stand firm for Christ at school or home?
- What things make us lose our boldness for God?
- How does God help us to be bold?

Explain that in the Bible passage, Paul is encouraging Christians to stand firm for God. Many church members had become lazy and disobedient. Others wanted to turn away from living in God's way because of trials and troubles. Paul's message is to stand firm for Christ. When we face troubles, we mustn't waver in our faith. We must ask God to make us bold believers and stand firm for God.

# 1 Timothy

## Encourage and pray for others

Bible story
1 Timothy 2:1–4

Bible point
**We can encourage and pray for our leaders.**

## Teaching point

Introduce or review the themes of 1 Timothy 2:1–4. Then ask:

- Why should we pray for and encourage our leaders?
- How else can we support our leaders?
- How did Paul's letters help Timothy?

Explain that Paul's letters of encouragement were very important to Timothy as he struggled with leading a church. By writing and praying for our leaders, we can encourage them to continue doing their best. We can encourage and pray for leaders. Close in prayer, asking God to help us to encourage others.

## Activity

### Classy cards

Make cards to encourage and tell community leaders that we are praying for them.

### ● You will need

Sheets of A4 card, inkpads, ribbons, coloured pens, craft scissors, hole punch, postage stamps (optional)

### ● Preparation

If possible, invite a church member who enjoys making cards as a hobby to demonstrate various techniques. Select a few community leaders to send the cards to. Ideas might include a mayor, minister or teacher. Create a few cards to display to help generate ideas.

### ● Handy hint

To save postage costs, collect the cards and deliver them by hand. Commit a portion of your session time each week to continue praying for the community and its leaders.

### ● Step-by-step

1. Fold a sheet of card in half. Use the remaining supplies to decorate the outside and inside perimeter of the card. Use the craft scissors to make unique borders around the card.
2. Write an encouraging note to the recipient and sign your name.
3. Take a moment to pray for the person you are sending the card to.

# Young people can serve God

> Bible story
> **1 Timothy 4:12–13**
>
> Bible point
> **We can serve God.**

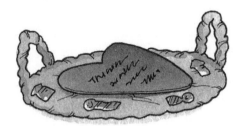

## Activity

### At his service

Make and decorate silver platters.

### ● You will need

Sheets of heavyweight A4 card, plastic lids, aluminium foil, red card, assorted Christian magazines, scissors, glue gun and glue sticks

### ● Preparation

Beforehand, cut the centres out of the plastic lids and cut them in half. Each C-shaped piece will serve as a handle for the tray. Use a hot glue gun to attach the 'handles' to the sides of the card trays. They should be standing upright and look like a rainbow on each end of the tray (see illustration). When the glue has dried, the trays will be ready to decorate.

### ● Handy hint

Ask the children to think of ideas for how they can serve the church and its members—for example, singing in the choir, helping to look after the church grounds or tidying the church after a service.

### ● Step-by-step

1. Cover the base of the tray with aluminium foil. Use the scissors to cut long strips of foil and wrap them around the tray handles. Be sure to cover any exposed area.
2. Use the card to make a large red heart. Cut it out and write the Bible point on the heart. Glue this to the centre of the tray.
3. Search through the magazines and cut out pictures of young people serving God, or pictures of ways children can serve him. Glue these on to the tray. Dry and display.

## Teaching point

Introduce or review the theme of 1 Timothy 4:12–13. Then ask:

- Has anyone ever looked down on us because of our age? When?
- What advice did Paul give Timothy about this?
- How can we use our talents for God?

Explain that Timothy was a young minister in the church at Ephesus. He became upset when others looked down on him because of his age. Paul's letter reminded Timothy that age is not an obstacle to serving God. When we look at our silver platters, we can think about serving God. Remind the children that even young people can serve God and be effective for him.

# 2 Timothy

## Be bold for God

Bible story
2 Timothy 2:3–4

Bible point
Be a soldier for Christ.

## Activity

### Spoon soldier

Make wooden spoon soldiers, as a reminder to become 'good soldiers' for Jesus Christ.

- ### You will need

Wooden spoons, black felt-tipped pens, scissors, uniform template (see page 197), glue

- ### Preparation

Make photocopies of the uniform template (one per child). Set out the supplies.

- ### Handy hint

If time permits, children can enhance the soldiers' uniforms by adding buttons or fabric scraps.

- ### Step-by-step

1. Draw a face on the head of the spoon. Leave room at the top of the spoon to attach a hat.
2. Colour the uniform and cut it out. Glue it on to the spoon handle.
3. Using card, make a hat for the soldier. Glue it in place and dry.

## Teaching point

While the soldiers are drying, introduce or review 2 Timothy 2:3–4. Then ask:

- Why is it hard to be a soldier?
- Why does God want us to be bold?
- How can we be brave for God?

Explain that a soldier must be courageous and strong. Paul told Timothy to be a soldier for Jesus and to accept the hardships that come along with being Jesus' follower. When we feel afraid or alone, we need to remember that God is with us. Just like Timothy, we have been given a spirit of power. We need to remember to be bold in our faith and stand strong.

# Uniform template

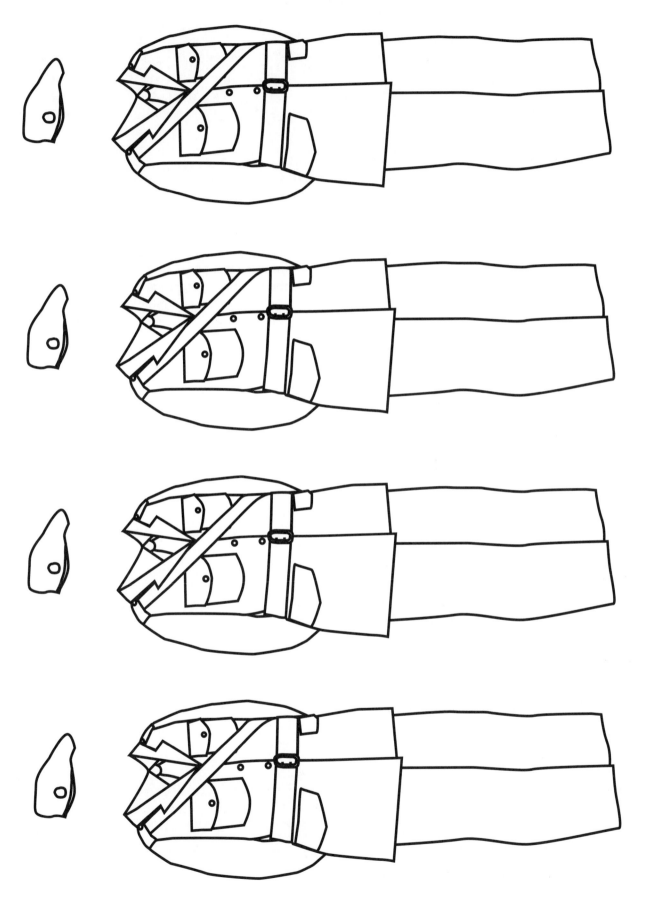

Reproduced with permission from *The Encyclopedia of Bible Crafts* published by BRF 2010 (978 1 84101 590 3) **www.barnabasinschools.org.uk**

# Paul encourages Timothy to lead

Age guide: 6–10s

Bible story
2 Timothy 3:10—4:8

Bible point
**Lead others to Jesus.**

## Activity

### Flaming torch

Make flaming torches as a reminder of Paul passing the torch of leadership to Timothy.

#### ● You will need

Empty paper towel rolls; stapler; A4 card in red, yellow, orange and black; glue; index cards; felt-tipped pens; sticky tape

#### ● Preparation

Beforehand, sort the card into piles containing one sheet of each colour. Each child will need one of these piles. Make a group torch, as an example and also to be used each week (see below).

#### ● Handy hint

Adapt this craft for older children by cutting plastic tubing into 30cm pieces and letting them stuff one end with ribbons. The children can then paint and decorate the tubing with stickers.

Pass a leadership torch around the group. Select someone for a special assignment, such as reading the Bible passage. When the child has fulfilled the task, give him or her the group torch to pass to another child. Retain the torch and allow a different child to serve each week.

#### ● Step-by-step

1. Wrap a piece of black card around the empty roll and secure it with tape.
2. Write the Bible point on an index card and glue it to the roll.
3. Cut flames from the remaining card. Insert the flames into the roll and glue in place. Allow to dry.

## Teaching point

Introduce or review the verses from 2 Timothy. Then ask:

- Why did Paul write this letter to Timothy?
- Who do we turn to for advice or encouragement?
- How can we lead people to Christ?

Explain that passing a torch often symbolises a change of runner. Paul is writing his last words of advice to Timothy as Paul prepares to die in a Roman prison. Timothy is now becoming a leader for the Christian faith. Paul encourages Timothy to use his abilities for God. We can also lead others to Christ by giving our time and talents. God wants us to lead others to Jesus.

# Titus

Age guide: 7–11s

## We are heirs to eternal life

> Bible story
> Titus 3:4–8
>
> Bible point
> **We are God's heirs.**

## Activity

### Heavenly heirs

Make posters listing all the blessings God gives to his heirs.

### ● You will need

Decorative paper, calligraphy pens, gold seals, craft foam, scrap paper, pencils, glue

### ● Preparation

Set out the craft supplies.

### ● Handy hint

Encourage the children to display their posters at home and to share them with their families.

### ● Step-by-step

1. Share ideas about what gifts God gives his children. Make a list on scrap paper and then include the ideas in the posters.
2. Use the decorative paper, calligraphy pens and gold seals to write and decorate the posters.
3. Frame the posters on craft foam with glue. Dry and display.

## Teaching point

Introduce or review the theme and verses from Titus. Then ask:

- What are some things God has given us?
- How can we accept God's gifts?

Explain that when we accept Christ into our hearts, we become God's adopted children and receive every blessing he has prepared for us. We are God's heirs. The greatest gift he gives us is eternal life. In this Bible story, Paul is writing a letter to Titus, a leader of the church in Crete. Paul reminds Titus that God's gifts are free and cannot be earnt. When we look at our posters, we can remember to thank God for being a loving Father and for giving us all his good gifts.

# Philemon

## Philemon's kindness refreshes others

> Bible story
> Philemon 1:4–7
>
> Bible point
> Kindness refreshes the hearts of others.

## Activity

### Heart refresher

Make heart-shaped potpourri sachets as a reminder of how kindness refreshes the hearts of others.

● **You will need**

Binca canvas, glue, scissors, potpourri, hole punch, ribbons

● **Preparation**

Bring in some large heart-shaped biscuit cutters for the children to trace around. If none are available, create a few cardboard hearts for the children instead.

● **Handy hint**

Encourage the children to give their heart sachet to someone who they may have difficulty showing kindness to. Examples might include a bully, an unlikely friend, or someone who has treated them unfairly. Remember that Paul encouraged Philemon to go beyond forgiveness and extend kindness to someone who had wronged him.

● **Step-by-step**

1. Use the cutters to trace two heart shapes on a piece of canvas. Cut out the hearts, then use the hole punch to make a hole at the top of each heart.
2. Insert a small handful of potpourri between the two hearts. Place glue around the edges of both hearts and press them firmly together.
3. String a ribbon through the holes and tie. Present the heart as a gift of kindness.

## Teaching point

Introduce or review the theme of Philemon. Then ask:

- Why should we show kindness to others?
- How does a kind deed refresh our hearts?
- When is it most difficult to be kind? Why?

Explain that Philemon had a reputation for a sincere kindness and genuine love of others. Paul wrote this letter to ask Philemon to extend his kindness to Onesimus, his runaway slave. Paul encouraged Philemon to think of Onesimus more like a brother rather than a slave. We can refresh the hearts of others by extending kindness to them.

# Hebrews

## God's word keeps us anchored

Bible story
**Hebrews 2:1**

Bible point
**Be anchored in God's word.**

## Activity

### Anchored to faith

Make anchor bookmarks for a Bible.

### ● You will need
Card, fine-tipped felt pens, glue sticks, scissors, 2.5cm wide ribbon, glitter glue pens or stickers

### ● Preparation
Cut the card into 2.5cm squares (one per child). Place supplies together in one work area.

### ● Handy hint
Show the children the many different cross symbols that have been used in the church throughout history. (For example, see *A-cross the World* by Martyn Payne and Betty Pedley, Barnabas, 2005.) Show the children the cross symbol that looks like an anchor. Ask them how they would explain this symbol of the cross to a friend.

### ● Step-by-step
1. Draw and decorate an anchor on the card square, using the template shown. Glue the card to the top of the ribbon.
2. Fold and cut the ends of the ribbon to form a 'V' shape and two points.
3. Write the Bible point on the bookmark. Use the bookmark to mark a favourite Bible verse or your place when reading the Bible.

## Teaching point

Bring children together to read the Bible passage and then ask:

* How does an anchor remind us not to drift away from God?
* How can we stay anchored to God's word?
* What are ways to become better listeners to God's word?

Explain that we listen for God's word so that we can stay anchored to God and grow stronger in our faith. Knowing why we must listen carefully helps us learn to become better listeners to God's word. God's word keeps us safely anchored to him.

# We are God's house

> Bible story
> Hebrews 3:1–6
>
> Bible point
> **We are God's house.**

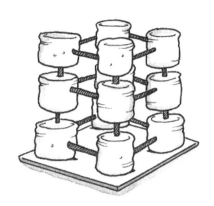

## Activity

### Home, sweet home

Build houses and then connect them together to create a town.

● **You will need**

Mini marshmallows, cocktail sticks, paper plates

● **Preparation**

Place several marshmallows and cocktail sticks on each plate. Put one plate in front of each child at a table

● **Handy hint**

If you don't want to use marshmallows, give each child a small piece of clay and instruct them to break off pieces of clay and roll them into balls. Use the clay balls to connect the cocktail sticks into houses. Alternatively, if you want to use marshmallows but not cocktail sticks, replace the latter with dry spaghetti.

● **Step-by-step**

1. Place a marshmallow on each end of the first and second cocktail stick and place them on the plate, parallel to each other. Insert two sticks into the marshmallows opposite each other to form a square base.
2. Placing sticks into marshmallows for stability, build a three dimensional 'house' upward from the square base on the plate
3. Slide the plate close to someone else's and use a few cocktail sticks and marshmallows to join the houses into one. Collect up any extra sticks and marshmallows.

## Teaching point

Place the children's artwork aside and gather the children in a separate area. Read the Bible verses, and then ask:

- Why does God call us his house?
- What kind of a house can we be for God?
- What does it mean to be brave and hope in God?

Explain that we are God's house. God made us and lives inside us. He deserves all the credit for making us. God can use us if we are brave and hopeful.

# Nothing can hide from God

Age guide:
6–10s

> Bible story
> **Hebrews 4:12–13**
>
> Bible point
> **God knows us inside and out.**

## Activity

### See-through ID

Describing our attributes.

### ● You will need

Paper plates (two per child), split-pin fasteners, paper towels, vegetable oil, newspaper, felt-tipped pens, sticky tape, a bowl of soapy water and a hand towel

### ● Preparation

Place newspaper down in one work area with the oil, fasteners and half the paper plates. Put the felt-tipped pens and other paper plates in a second work area.

### ● Handy hint

Put tape on the back of each plate and hang each plate on the wall. Have the children cut out card bodies and tape them below each plate 'head' so that you have a portrait of each child on the wall.

### ● Step-by-step

1. Ask the children to use the felt-tipped pens to draw their faces, then write several words describing themselves all over a paper plate. Then ask them to write their name on the back.
2. Using paper towels, carefully wipe vegetable oil all over the other plate until the plate becomes translucent. Make sure the plate is completely dry by wiping any excess oil off the front and back of the plate with paper towels. Use a split-pin fastener to connect the two plates in the centre, putting the plate with the vegetable oil on top.

## Teaching point

Let the children help to clear away the paper towels and newspaper and then wash their hands before joining you in a circle. Read the Bible passage and then ask:

- In what ways does this craft remind us that God knows us inside and out?
- How does it feel to know that nothing is hidden from God?

Explain that God knows everything about us—even the things we might try to hide. He knows what we need and how we feel. God understands us even when we don't understand ourselves. He knows us well enough to help us choose to do what's right and to live the best way we can. God knows us inside and out, and God loves us!

# Be determined to run the race

Age guide: 6–10s

> ## Bible story
> Hebrews 12:1–3
>
> ## Bible point
> Be a faithful hero for God.

## Activity

### Surrounded by heroes of faith

Make chequered flags as a reminder that biblical people of faith are cheering us on.

### ● You will need

White satin-style fabric, black acrylic paint, shallow bowls, paper plates, sponges cut into 2.5cm squares, sticky tape, coloured fine-tipped felt pens, newspaper, paper towels

### ● Preparation

Cut the white fabric into rectangles measuring 12cm x 23cm. Cover the workspace with newspapers and then set out shallow bowls of black paint.

### ● Handy hint

Ask someone in your church to sew the edges of the squares so that they don't fray. Have several relay races, transporting index cards with Bible verses on them across the room. Let children take turns waving their chequered flags at the end of each relay race. Time everyone to see how fast they can spread God's word and then let them work together to beat their own record time.

### ● Step-by-step

1. If your fabric edges haven't been sewn, take a piece of fabric and fold a piece of tape over the edge of the fabric lengthwise, so that the fabric will not fray. Repeat the process around all the other edges.
2. Starting with the top right corner of the shiny side of the fabric, stamp black squares in a row, leaving a white square space between each black square. Lift the sponge straight up when the square has been

made so that it won't smear. Make black squares on the fabric in the second row, alternating with a white square underneath the first black square. Continue stamping black squares spaced with white squares until the chequered flag is filled between the tape edges.

3. While the flag is drying, roll a single narrow sheet of newspaper as tightly as possible from bottom to top to make a flagpole. Pull the newspaper from inside the roll and twist to make the flagpole taller. Tape the edge of the newspaper so that it won't unroll.
4. When the flag is dry, give help if needed to write names of biblical heroes and the child's own name in some of the white squares. Wrap the left-hand edge of the flag around the thicker end of the newspaper pole and use tape to stick the fabric to the back of the flag, vertically down the pole.

## Teaching point

Ask the children to set the flags aside to dry while you are reading the Bible passage. Then ask:

- What are some things that are hard for us to do?
- How do people encourage us in those things?
- What are some things that make it hard to serve God?
- Who encourages us to keep following God?

Explain that we are servants of God, just like the Bible heroes we read about. When things get hard, we can persevere with God's help. He helped people in Bible times and he helps us today. We are encouraged to do God's work and run the race of faith, knowing that other servants of God want us to do our best for God, too. We can be faithful heroes for God just as the Bible heroes persevered. Invite the children to say why they chose particular biblical heroes and name a hero of faith that they know today—from the church, or their family and friends.

# James

## Think before you speak

Bible story
James 1:19–20

Bible point
**God wants us to think before we speak.**

## Activity

### My lips are sealed

Make lip-shaped straw toppers.

#### ● You will need
Pink or red fun foam cut into 8cm x 10cm pieces, lips template (see illustration), scissors, straws, pens, heavyweight card, juice and beakers

#### ● Preparation
Trace the lip template on to several pieces of heavyweight card for the children to trace. Prepare a work area where each child will have ample room to trace the lips and then cut them out.

#### ● Handy hint
Pour juice into beakers and let the children drink using their decorated straws.

#### ● Step-by-step
1. Trace the lips template on to a piece of fun foam and then cut the lips out.
2. Fold the lips in half and make two small slits with scissors to form a mouth.
3. Write 'Think before you speak' on the lips. Slide the lips over a straw and tape them to the straw from underneath.

## Teaching point

When the children have finished their straw toppers, ask them to join you. Introduce or review the Bible verses. Then ask:

- What happens when we speak before we think?
- How does it feel when we hurt someone's feelings?
- How can we remember to think before we speak?

Explain that the Bible says that God wants us to watch what we say. It's easy to lose our temper and say things that we don't really mean. God wants us to use self-control to listen more and talk less. When we use our straws, we can look at the lips and remember to think before we speak.

# Act out your faith

> **Bible story**
> James 2:14–17
>
> **Bible point**
> Our actions show our faith in God.

## Activity

### Living faith murals

Make living murals depicting actions of faith.

#### • You will need

A sheet of card measuring 50cm x 70cm for every two children, felt-tipped pens, scissors

#### • Preparation

Clear a large area on the floor for children to work. Set the card, felt-tipped pens and scissors in the centre of the area. Ask the children to form groups of two or three. Before beginning the project, help the children think of actions that show they want to please God. For example, being kind to pets, sharing with others or helping a parent or teacher with a task all demonstrate a desire to please God.

#### • Handy hint

Encourage the children's creativity to use their bodies in the murals in surprising ways. For example, arms don't always have to be arms—they could be the leaves of a flower, the legs of an animal or the hands on a clock. Faces can be flowers or animals, as well as people, and so on. If necessary, help the children to choose scenes that use a variety of sizes and placement of openings.

#### • Step-by-step

1.  On the card, draw a scene that shows a way we can act out our faith. Make the drawing large. Cut out holes for hands, feet or face to show through. For example, the drawing could depict two people facing each other with face and hand holes, and the action could be giving or sharing a toy. Alternatively, the drawing might be a child and a pet with face

holes for each and hand holes for the child. The action would then be stroking and taking care of the pet.
2.  Complete the drawing and colour in.
3.  Show the children how to put their hands, feet or faces through the holes and practise faith action with their partners.

## Teaching point

When the children have finished making their murals, gather them together with the murals. Introduce or review the Bible verses with the children. Then ask:

*   What does God want us to do with our faith?
*   What are some ways we should act if we say we believe in God?

Explain that our actions are often greater examples to others than our words alone. We may say that we are Christians but we need to act accordingly. If we say we love God but, for example, we are unkind to others, the Bible says that our faith is dead. If we say we believe in God, then we should act as if we do. We must prove we are alive with our actions. Invite the children to act out their living mural actions for one another. Let the other children guess what the faithful actions are. When each pair has had a turn to show their living mural, invite the children to share a way that they will act out their faith this week.

# 1 Peter

Age guide: 5–7s

## He cares for you

Bible story
1 Peter 5:7

Bible point
Take your concerns to Jesus.

My Worry Tree

## Activity

### Worry tree poster

Make posters to hang, on which to hang our concerns.

### ● You will need
Sheets of blue or white card measuring 30cm x 45cm, pieces of brown and green card measuring 23cm x 30cm, scissors, crayons, glue, five paperclips per child.

### ● Preparation
Put all the supplies on a table. Have a couple of sample trees cut out in case some children would like to trace a tree instead of drawing freehand.

### ● Handy hint
Create a large tree for everyone to use. Let the children add prayer requests, worries or joys to the tree each week. When worries are prayed about, they can be turned over on the tree. Prayer requests that are met may also be turned over.

### ● Step-by-step
1. Draw a large tree on brown card, making sure it has at least five big branches. Cut out the tree and glue to the larger piece of card.
2. Cut out five large leaves of any shape. Write or draw pictures of things that cause concern on the leaves.
3. Twist open five paperclips. Hook the paperclips through the leaves. Then attach the leaves to the branches of the tree by pushing the paperclip through the poster. Write 'Take your concerns to Jesus' on the poster.

## Teaching point

When the trees are completed, read 1 Peter 5:7. Then ask:

- What kinds of things do we worry about?
- What does the Bible tell us to do with our worries and anxieties?
- How would we feel if we had no worries?

Explain that God wants to see us happy. He cares for us so much that he wants us to take all our anxieties to him so that he can help us. We can give our worries to God when we pray. Invite the children to look at their worry trees and think about one worry that they have. Invite them to ask God silently to take that worry away. Show the children how to turn the leaf around so that the worry is hidden. Let the children continue praying in this way until all leaves are turned around.

Each time we feel worried, we can know that God will always be with us to help us. When we have any worries, we can add them to our trees and ask God to help us to take our worries away. We can remember to take our worries to Jesus.

# 2 Peter

## How do Christians grow?

> Bible story
> 2 Peter 1:3–9
>
> Bible point
> **God gives us everything we need.**

## Activity

### Recipe for Christian growth

Make fruit kebabs.

### ● You will need

Wooden skewers, marshmallows, cut fruit (such as apples, bananas, pineapple, grapes, strawberries, melon and blueberries), paper plates, serviettes or paper towels, bowls of soapy water and hand towels

### ● Preparation

Put all the ingredients and supplies on a table. Remind children to wash their hands before beginning this snack craft.

### ● Handy hint

Be aware of food allergies and provide alternative ingredients where necessary.

### ● Step-by-step

1. Put a marshmallow on one end of a skewer.
2. Add different pieces of fruit in any order after the marshmallow.

## Teaching point

When the children have made their kebabs, read the Bible passage. Then ask:

- Why does God tell us a recipe in the Bible to help us grow?
- How is our kebab like the recipe to make Christians grow?
- If we had all these ingredients in us, what is something that God would be happy to see us do?

Explain that God gives us everything we need to help us grow into strong Christians. We just have to know what he wants. Invite the children to get into pairs, work through the list in the passage and share examples of how we might live out each word. Each time they share an example, they can eat a piece of fruit from their kebab. Tell them not to eat the marshmallow yet. When the children have finished sharing their examples of living in God's way, ask them to share the name of one person to whom they want to show God's love. Invite everyone to eat their marshmallows together. As they do so, invite them to thank God for giving us everything we need to grow as Christians.

# 1 John

## God forgives us

Bible story
1 John 1:9

Bible point
**Jesus always forgives us when we say we're sorry.**

## Activity

### Puddle prints

Make puddle prints.

### ● You will need

Washable table or surface, shaving foam, red poster paint, sheets of A4 paper (one per child), paper towels, painting aprons, pencils, a washing-up bowl of warm soapy water

### ● Preparation

Set out the supplies. Put a bowl of warm soapy water in the centre of the table so that children can reach it. Place the roll of paper towels next to it.

### ● Handy hint

To save time, organise your helpers and supplies so that as many children as possible can do the activity at one sitting. Shaving foam expands more than you think. A golf-ball sized squirt is more than enough for each child. If you give children too much, it'll make cleaning up more difficult.

### ● Step-by-step

1. Give each child a painting apron. Squirt some shaving foam on the table in front of the child and let him or her spread it out with their fingers.
2. Squirt two drops of red paint on to the foam. Let the child mix it with his or her fingers and spread it out to about the size of a piece of A4 paper.
3. Let the child draw a design, such as a cross or a heart, in the centre of the paint. Then wash and dry their hands.
4. Give the child a piece of A4 paper and let them write their name on the back. Tell them to press the paper gently over the design, then lift the paper carefully by the corner and peel it away from the table. Set the paper aside to dry.
5. Scrape up the shaving foam and throw it into a lined waste bin. Quickly clean the work area with water and paper towels, ready for the next person.

## Teaching point

As the prints are drying, gather children in the story area. Ask a volunteer to read 1 John 1:9. Then ask:

• What does it mean to confess our sins?
• How do we feel when someone forgives us?

Explain that Jesus tells us that he'll forgive us when we confess our sins. When we do something wrong, if we tell someone what we have done, we can then say we are sorry. The puddle prints started with a little white puddle. The puddles are like our hearts. Then paint was squirted on. The paint is like the things we do wrong. Then we mixed up the paint and the foam. Sometimes we get mixed up and do wrong things. When we cleaned the table, it was like when Jesus forgives us and makes us clean again. The prints we made remind us that Jesus always forgives us when we say we're sorry.

# 2 John

## Love one another

> ### Bible story
> 2 John 5–6
>
> ### Bible point
> **God wants us to love one another.**

## Activity

### Stick with love

Make friendship stickers with a hidden message to encourage others.

● **You will need**

Old magazines, scissors, greaseproof paper, PVA glue, white vinegar, small paper cups, measuring spoons, paintbrushes, resealable plastic bags or envelopes

● **Preparation**

To speed up the process, you may want to cut out a supply of magazine letters and words ahead of time. Mix two tablespoons of white glue with one tablespoon of white vinegar in a container and seal it with a lid until the session, then pour it into small paper cups just before the children begin. This will be enough glue for about ten children. Cut greaseproof squares as a drying surface for the stickers.

● **Handy hint**

Allow the children to make extra stickers for themselves. They can make stickers out of their own designs if they wish. If the children are interested, write down the recipe for them so that they can make stickers at home.

● **Step-by-step**

1. Let the children think of someone they want to encourage or show God's love to. Then ask them to cut out three or four small magazine pictures that they think that person would like. Also cut out letters or words from headlines that spell out a simple message for that person such as, 'The best' or 'Friends'.
2. Spread the back of each picture, word or letter lightly with the glue.
3. Put the pictures on greaseproof paper to dry, sticky side up.

## Teaching point

While the stickers are drying, gather the children in the story area. Ask for volunteers to help read 2 John 5–6. Then ask:

- What are these verses telling us to do?
- What do you think it means to do what God tells us?
- What are some ways we can show love to others?

Explain that God wants us to love one another. There are lots of ways to show people God's love. We could invite someone to play with us, say kind things when someone is sad or lonely, or give little gifts. Today we can decide who we want to give our stickers to. It should be someone who needs to be encouraged or to know that Jesus loves him or her. When we give that person the stickers, we can explain that there's a special hidden message for him or her in the bag. Let some of the children share who they would like to give their stickers to. Hand out resealable plastic bags to the children. Make sure the stickers are dry before putting them inside the bags. Remind the children to stick with love.

# 3 John

Age guide: 6–10s

## Imitate what is good

Bible story
3 John 11

Bible point
God is happy when we copy what is good.

## Activity

### Copy cat

Paint and print designs as a reminder to imitate what is good.

### ● You will need
Sheets of A4 paper, felt-tipped pens, a few colours of poster paint, paintbrushes, bowls of soapy water and paper towels

### ● Preparation
Set the art supplies on a table in the work area.

### ● Handy hint
Hold up some of the children's paintings and point out that pressing the paper together made a copy or 'imitation' of their original design. Praise all the children for their work. Tell them their pictures are to remind them to imitate everything that is good—to be copy cats and imitators of Jesus!

### ● Step-by-step
1. Fold the paper in half so that it opens like a book. Ask the children to work with a partner and think of good things they have seen people do, that they think they could do also. It could be someone they know or something they have read about or seen on TV or in a film. Then write a short list on the front of the paper, listing the good things they want to imitate. Add decorations around the list.

2. Open up the paper and quickly paint a simple design or picture on the right-hand side of the fold.
3. Before the paint dries, fold the paper back down over the design and gently press the paper.
4. Slowly open the paper to see what has happened to the design. It's been copied—an imitation! Set it aside to dry.

## Teaching point

While the paintings are drying, gather everyone in the story area. Ask:

• Is it good or bad to be a copy or to imitate someone? Why?

Ask for a volunteer to read 3 John 11 out loud. Then ask:

• When would it be good to copy or imitate others?
• What does God wants us to learn from this verse?

Explain that Jesus is love and everything he does is good. He wants us to be like him, so he loves it when we do good things too. John wrote this verse to encourage us to do good things. So when we see someone doing something that we know is right and good, we can copy them. It makes God happy to see us being that kind of copycat! God is happy when we imitate what is good.

# Jude

Age guide: 6–10s

## Always remember your faith

Bible story
**Jude 17–23**

Bible point
**Knowing what we believe will help us to stay strong.**

## Activity

### Faith fans

Make fans as a reminder of each part of our faith.

● **You will need**

Fan template (see page 213), sheets of medium-weight A4 card, scissors, knitting yarn, hole punch, felt-tipped pens

● **Preparation**

Photocopy the fan template on to the card. Cut the yarn into 15cm lengths. Give each child a piece of the card, scissors and felt-tipped pens.

● **Handy hint**

As a group, come up with belief statements that apply to faith in Jesus. For example, 'I believe that Jesus is the Son of God.' On a big piece of paper, write them out so the children can put them on their fans.

● **Step-by-step**

1. Cut out the pieces of the fan and decorate one side of the fan pieces with the felt-tipped pens.
2. On the other side of the fan pieces, write things you believe about Jesus—for example, 'I believe that Jesus died on the cross for me'.
3. Punch a hole at the narrow end of each fan piece. String each fan piece on to the yarn and tie it loosely.

4. Punch a hole in the centre of each fan piece. String each fan piece on to the yarn and tie it loosely so that the fan can open just enough for the fan pieces still to overlap.

## Teaching point

- Review the letter of Jude. Ask a few volunteers to read verses 17–23. Then ask:

- What things does Jude warn us about?
- Why is it important to remember what we believe?
- When are the times we might forget about being a Christian?

Explain that Jude warns us to keep our faith strong, to guard against the evil that's in the world. Our fans remind us of the things God wants us to remember wherever we go. When we are having a tough time, our fans can remind us of the wonderful things God does for us. We can use our fans to explain about Jesus to our friends. Fans also keep us cool, and it's cool to be strong. God wants us to stay strong in our faith. Knowing what we believe will help us to stay strong.

# Fan template

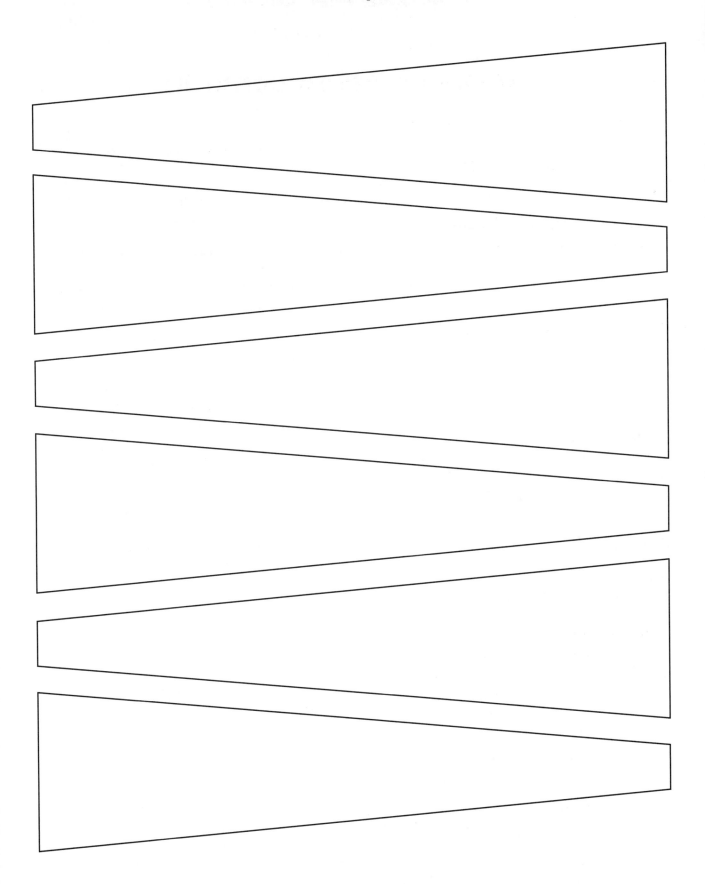

Reproduced with permission from *The Encyclopedia of Bible Crafts* published by BRF 2010 (978 1 84101 590 3) www.barnabasinschools.org.uk

# Revelation

Age guide: 5–7s

## Jesus wants to come in

> Bible story
> Revelation 3:20
>
> Bible point
> **Jesus wants to be our best friend.**

## Activity

### Knock, knock!

Make and eat snacks to learn that Jesus wants to be our best friend.

### ● You will need

Paper plates, malted milk biscuits (two per child), ready-made fondant icing, tubes of writing icing, plastic spoons, cake decorations, serviettes, a bowl of soapy water, paper towels

### ● Preparation

Set the snack items in the work area and direct children to wash their hands.

### ● Handy hint

Beware of food allergies and have an alternative square or rectangular biscuit for those with mild allergies. Have extra biscuits in the story area to use up extra icing.

### ● Step-by-step

1. Spread a spoonful of icing in the centre of a paper plate. It should be about the size of two biscuits laid side by side.
2. Use a tube of writing icing to draw a heart in the centre, or use cake decorations carefully sprinkled in a heart shape.
3. Gently, place two biscuits next to each other on top of the icing to make a set of double doors. Make little doorknobs and a window or two with a dot of icing. Don't eat yet!

## Teaching point

Let the children carry their biscuit doors and a serviette to the story area. Read Revelation 3:20 and then ask:

- When a friend knocks on the door of our house, what do we do?
- What are some things we do with our friends when we invite them to our house?

Explain that this verse from Revelation tells us that Jesus wants to be our friend. Jesus says, 'Listen! I am standing and knocking at your door.' Let's knock gently on the little biscuit doors we have made. Jesus then says, 'If you hear my voice and open the door, I will come in and we will eat together.' That means Jesus wants to come into our lives. Let's open our doors to show Jesus that he's invited. Show the children how to open their biscuit doors, like double doors, to reveal the icing heart. When we invite Jesus to be our friend, he comes right in. Of course he can't really eat with us, but he wants to be close to us, just like when a friend comes over for lunch to eat and play. Let's eat our snacks now and thank Jesus for wanting to be our friend.

# Heaven waits for us

> **Bible story**
> Revelation 21:1—22:6
>
> **Bible point**
> Jesus has prepared a place for us to be with him in heaven.

## Activity

### All that glitters

Make heavenly collages.

### ● You will need

Sheets of A4 card, glue, scissors, glitter glue, silver and gold star stickers, a variety of collage items (such as gold and silver foil wrapping paper, coloured tissue paper, bits of shiny ribbon, rickrack, laces, shiny craft beads or stick-on jewels)

### ● Preparation

Beforehand, read the Bible passage and decide which verses you want to read to the children. You may wish to use a children's Bible. Be prepared to read the verses before children make the craft and again as they work. Then set all the craft items in the work area except the star stickers.

### ● Handy hint

Consider playing worship music in the background as you read the Bible verses and the children work. You may want to give the children stick-on jewels or shiny craft beads to glue to their collages to represent the jewels mentioned in the Bible passage.

### ● Step-by-step

1. Invite the children to close their eyes while the passage is being read. Ask them to try to imagine what heaven might look like.
2. Reread some of the verses about heaven while the children glue collage items to a piece of card to make a design that represents the way they imagine heaven to be.
3. Together, chat about what heaven might be like.

## Teaching point

As the children are putting the finishing touches on their heavenly collages, bring out the star stickers. Explain that no one knows exactly what heaven looks like. We can only use our imagination when we read about it in the Bible, but we know it will be a beautiful and happy place. Ask a volunteer to read Revelation 21:4 again. Then ask:

- What four things will not be in heaven?
- How will it feel to be in a place like that?

Explain that we have a lot to look forward to in heaven. We can praise God for making a beautiful place for us. Invite the children to praise God, for example, by saying, 'God, you are so good!' or 'Jesus, thank you that you promise us heaven'. Then give everyone some gold and silver stars to add to their collage. When we look at our collages, we can remember to praise Jesus because he has made it possible for us to be with him in heaven.

# Age guide index

The crafts in this book have a suggested age guide. Please note that this is for guidance only and suitability for each craft is dependent on ability as well as age. Also, leaders may wish to tailor the crafts to suit their particular group of children. The age guides are as follows.

5–7s
6–10s
7–11s

## 5–7s

## 6–10s

## 7–11s

# Bible index

# Messy Church

## Fresh ideas for building a Christ-centred community

## Lucy Moore

*Messy Church* is bursting with easy-to-do ideas to draw people of all ages together and help them to experience what it means to be part of a Christian community outside of Sunday worship.

At its heart, *Messy Church* aims to create the opportunity for parents, carers and children to enjoy expressing their creativity, sit down together to eat a meal, experience worship and have fun within a church context.

The book sets out the theory and practice of *Messy Church* and offers 15 themed programme ideas to get you started, each including:

- Bible references and background information
- Suggestions for ten easy-to-do creative art and craft activities
- Easy-to-prepare everyday recipes
- Family-friendly worship outlines.

For more information, visit www.messychurch.org.uk

*ISBN 978 1 84101 503 3    £8.99*
*Available from your local Christian bookshop or, in case of difficulty, direct from BRF using the order form opposite.*

## ORDERFORM

| REF | TITLE | | PRICE | QTY | TOTAL |
|-----|-------|---|-------|-----|-------|
| 503 3 | Messy Church | | £8.99 | | |

| POSTAGE AND PACKING CHARGES | | | | | Postage and packing | |
|------|----|------|---------|---------|---|---|
| Order value | UK | Europe | Surface | Air Mail | Donation | |
| £7.00 & under | £1.25 | £3.00 | £3.50 | £5.50 | **TOTAL** | |
| £7.10–£30.00 | £2.25 | £5.50 | £6.50 | £10.00 | | |
| Over £30.00 | FREE | prices on request | | | | |

Name _____ Account Number _____

Address _____

_____ Postcode _____

Telephone Number_____

Email _____

**Payment by:** ❑ Cheque ❑ Mastercard ❑ Visa ❑ Postal Order ❑ Maestro

Card no [ ][ ][ ][ ] [ ][ ][ ][ ] [ ][ ][ ][ ] [ ][ ][ ][ ] [ ][ ][ ]

Valid from [ ][ ][ ][ ]   Expires [ ][ ][ ][ ]   Issue no. [ ][ ][ ]

Security code* [ ][ ][ ]   *Last 3 digits on the reverse of the card.
ESSENTIAL IN ORDER TO PROCESS YOUR ORDER   Shaded boxes for Maestro use only

Signature _____ Date _____

*All orders must be accompanied by the appropriate payment.*

**Please send your completed order form to:**
BRF, 15 The Chambers, Vineyard, Abingdon OX14 3FE
Tel. 01865 319700 / Fax. 01865 319701  Email: enquiries@brf.org.uk

❑ Please send me further information about BRF publications.

Available from your local Christian bookshop.                BRF is a Registered Charity